Praise for *How to Self-Publish Your Book*

"Highly recommended"

"[C]overs in detail every major step for would-be writers to follow on their path to publishing . . . provides helpful tips for the novice to avoid being taken advantage of by the many publishing services out there . . . with self-publishing an increasingly common option for writers today, it would be hard to imagine a more useful and easy-to-follow guide than this comprehensive volume. Highly recommended to everyone hoping to self-publish a book that won't look self-published."

—Library Journal (starred review)

"Accessible, and thorough"

"Realistic, accessible, and thorough . . . Yager's advice on everything from margin size and elements of a cover design to a sensible approach to social media and press coverage is useful and clearly laid out . . . [a] solid choice for authors who have written a book and are ready for the next step."

—Booklist

"Invaluable"

"Leveraging an extensive career in traditional and self-publishing, Yager (*When Friendship Hurts*) offers a comprehensive guide to the latter field, with separate sections on writing one's book, publishing it, and marketing it . . . [*How to Self-Publish Your Book*] will prove invaluable to anyone seeking to self-publish in a professional manner."

—Publishers Weekly

"Unreservedly recommended"

"How to Self-Publish Your Book by Jan Yager is a complete road map
to becoming a successfully self-published author . . . this is one of the
most comprehensive, practical, and 'user-friendly' how-to instructional guides
available today on the subject of self-publishing . . . if you only have the time
or budget for one 'how to' book on the subject, then you would be well served
as an aspiring but unknown author seeking publication to give *How to
Self-Publish Your Book* a careful reading . . . unreservedly recommended."

—Midwest Book Review

"Helpful"

"The most comprehensive book ever on self-publishing—
and the most helpful."

—Irwin Zucker

Founder - Book Publicists of Southern California

"Comprehensive"

"I enthusiastically recommend *How to Self-Publish Your Book.*
It covers all the bases from writing and getting the content ready
for publication to publishing it in various formats. It goes on to
describe promoting your self-published book, including selling
foreign rights. This comprehensive guide is a gift to every book
author who is considering self-publishing."

—Brian Jud

*Executive Director of the Association of Publishers for Special Sales
and author of* **How to Make Real Money Selling Books**

HOW TO SELF
PUBLISH
YOUR BOOK

A COMPLETE GUIDE
TO WRITING, EDITING,
MARKETING & SELLING
YOUR OWN BOOK

DR. JAN YAGER

SQUAREONE
WRITERS GUIDES

COVER DESIGNER: Jeannie Rosado
IN-HOUSE EDITOR: Michael Weatherhead
TYPESETTER: Gary A. Rosenberg

Square One Publishers
115 Herricks Road
Garden City Park, New York 11040
(516) 535–2010 • www.squareonepublishers.com

Publisher's Cataloging-in-Publication Data

Names: Yager, Jan, 1948- author.
Title: How to self-publish your book / Jan Yager.
Description: Garden City Park, NY : Square One Publishers, [2019] | Series:
  Square One Writers Guides | Includes bibliographical references and
  index.
Identifiers: LCCN 2018045394 (print) | LCCN 2018053704 (ebook) | ISBN
  9780757054655 (e-book) | ISBN 9780757004650 (pbk. : alk. paper)
Subjects: LCSH: Self-publishing—United States.
Classification: LCC Z285.5 (ebook) | LCC Z285.5 .Y34 2019 (print) | DDC
  070.5/930973—dc23
LC record available at https://lccn.loc.gov/2018045394

Printed in the United States of America

10   9   8   7   6   5   4   3   2

CONTENTS

Conclusion, 223

For all the writers who are inspired
to put their words into print.
May this work be a helpful tool
on your journey to publication.

$\mathcal{A}$CKNOWLEDGMENTS

I would like to thank the many editors, publicists, book marketers, and others in the field with whom I have worked over the years, whose help and feedback have been invaluable to me. These people include Nancy Creshkoff, Mary Claycomb, Brian Southam, Norman Franklin, Phillipa Brewster, Patricia Cristol, Howard Epstein, James Chambers, David Wildasin, Terry Nathan, Steve Dunlop, the late Jan Nathan, Brian Jud, Tad Crawford, Mark Gompertz, Darcie Rowen, M. J. Rose, Judie Hottenson, Susan Richman, Irwin Zucker, Chuck Monroe, Laurie Cotumaccio, Jill Lublin, Janette Lynn, Janet Fritsch, Liz Kelly, Susannah Greenberg, Drew Gerber, John Goodman, Dan Janal, Jennifer Vanderslice, Richard Quinney, Joanne McCall, Shida Carr, Christine Bronstein, Jane Ubell-Meyer, Holly Cosby, Jeff Yager, Fred Yager, Eileen Hoffman, Don Gabor, Scott Yager, Lindsay Yager, Linda Swindling, Jim Cox, and many others.

Thanks also go to the producers and bookers who were responsible for landing me radio and TV interviews, as well as the countless reviewers and reporters who reviewed or wrote about one or more of my books or the books published by my company, Hannacroix Creek Books, Inc. Even though you're not being named individually, know that I am very grateful for your interest in the titles I have either written, published, or represented.

I would also like to thank the foreign rights co-agents and foreign publishers with whom I have worked, including Henry Shin, Sue Yang, the late Evelyn Lee, Yinghong, Wendy King, Lily Chen, Dr. Luc Kwanten, Vincent Lin, Erica Zhou, Duran Kim, Doris Wang, Adriana Navarro, Ib and Bebbe Lauritzen, Susanne Sinclair, Wendy Wu, Akash Shah, Fr. Joby, Fr. Joe, Elisa Diniz, the late R. H. Sharma, Flavia Sala, Simona Kessler, Andrea Focsaneanu, Rex Finch, Pimol of Tuttle Mori Agency (Thailand), Novo Seculo,

Cristina Purchio, Oyvind Asbjornsen, Lars Asbjornsen, Editora Gente, Sabine Schultz, TEA-I Tascabili Degli Editori Associati, Hinkler Books, Knjiga Komerc, Fritt Forlag, Fangzhou Yang, Annie Wang, Winnie Yu, Flemming Moldrup, Self-Improvement Publishing, House of Guides, Jaico Publishing House, Editora Pensamento-Cultriz, Editorial Trillas, Laura Ignacio Olalde, Sungwoo Publishing, Tawanson Publishing, Mehta Publishing House, Beijing YunLei Culture Communication, U.S. Commercial Service, Jarir Bookstore, Sunil Mehta, Harper Collins India, Pearson India, Johnson Chacko, SSP, Commercial Press, Preeti Sao, Nallini and Olivannan at Emerald Publishers, and so many others.

I also want to thank everyone who responded to my various HARO (Help a Reporter Out) queries, as well as the additional authors and publishing people I interviewed, including George Slowik Jr., Carl Pritzkat, Cevin Bryerman, Jon Malinovski, Richard Quinney, Stu Silver, Loree Lough, Simon T. Bailey, Dave Kocotos, Kilbourn Gordon III, John Vanek, Rhonda Rees, Clay Kahler, Dan Blanchard, Tosha Mills, Kerry Wekelo, Christine Luken, W. Adranatte, Phyllis Zimbler Miller, Bill Hirsch, Jennifer Hancock, Jennifer Reich, Lauren Beale, Nancy Friedman, Hyapatia Lee, Lauren Cecora, Anthony R. Howard, Catherine Dougherty, Kelly Hayes-Raitt, Issa Asad, Nancy Friedman, William J. Hirsch, Devorah Fox, Roni Lambrecht, Stacy Newton, Rev. Sherri Heller, Janet M. Perry, Shaylynn Hayes, M. L. Ruscsak, Shel Horowitz, Milena Perepyolkina, Nandita, Bernadette L. Harris, Roberto R. Hernandez, Linda Ruescher, Naresh Vissa, Jennifer Bright Reich, Lauren Beale, Christopher J. Lynch, Mandy Brown, James W. Lewis, June Greig, Susan Whited, Yvette Carmon, Rev. Stephanie Clarke, Larry Jorgensen, Robert Barrows, Nanette Miner, Carol Gee, Racheline Maltese, Alan N. Canton, Managing Partner, NewMedia Create, Shannon Howard, William Seavey, Carla Jenkins, Rebecca Klemm, Don Allison, Caleb Backe, Stacy Newton, David R. Ellingson, Leslie Jacobs, Kelly Meister-Yetter, Avi Ehrlich, J. C. Beichner, J. Hope, Thomas M. Cirignano, Scott Deuty, and Bruce Blizard.

I would also like to express my gratitude to those who have helped my small press over the years with their superb proofreading, e-book conversion, or design skills, including Peggy Stautberg, Allyson Foster, Amit Dey, Nancy Batra, Dave Cole, Daniel Middleton, Darlene Swanson, and Stephanee Killen.

Last, but not least, I would like to thank my team at Square One Publishers, publisher of *How to Self-Publish Your Book:* Rudy Shur, founder and CEO; Michael Weatherhead, my editor; and Anthony Pomes, marketing manager.

PREFACE

At a certain point in my career, although I had previously published books through traditional publishers—including major houses such as Scribner, Prentice-Hall, Doubleday, and Wiley—I knew I wanted more control over the finished product, as well as a larger share of revenue. So, I founded my own publishing company, Hannacroix Creek Books, Inc. Fortunately, my experiences as both a published author and an employee of two well-known publishing companies, Macmillan and Grove Press, had prepared me for all the work that was to come, because when you're a self-publisher, you have not only more control over your finished book, but also all the responsibility of producing, marketing, promoting, and selling it.

The encouraging news is that today, more than ever before, self-publishing is not just an option of last resort for getting published but a viable and respectable method of doing so. No longer does self-publishing automatically imply that you couldn't sell your material to a commercial publisher.

Once I had made up my mind to self-publish, I discovered Dan Poynter's *Self-Publishing Manual*, which was of enormous value to me in my quest. (Poynter, who sadly passed away in 2015, was considered a self-publishing guru, having mentored countless authors and self-publishers along the way.) Another self-publishing guide I found especially helpful in those early days was *The Complete Guide to Self-Publishing* by Tom and Marilyn Ross, two other self-publishing pioneers. My goal in writing *How to Self-Publish Your Book* was to create a book that would be as helpful to you in your journey as the aforementioned texts were to me in mine.

A NOTE ON GENDER

In order to avoid awkward phrasing within sentences while acknowledging both genders, the publisher has chosen to alternate between the use of male and female pronouns according to chapter. When referring to someone in the third person, odd-numbered chapters will use female pronouns, while even-numbered chapters will use male pronouns.

$\mathcal{I}$NTRODUCTION

We live in a do-it-yourself, or "DIY," world thanks, in part, to advances in technology, communications, and social media, all of which are contributing to one of the fastest-growing global DIY industries: self-publishing. The total number of ISBNs (which are required for book sales in bookstores and online) issued to self-published books in one year has surpassed 1 million. This number continues to grow year after year. Today, self-publishing has gone global, taking off in China, Sweden, Norway, Japan, Brazil, South Korea, Taiwan, India, the United Kingdom, Australia, and a number of other countries.

The phenomenon of self-publishing, however, is not a new one. Up until the early nineteenth century, many novelists had to publish their own books, as most printers were focused on printing only religious texts. Notable self-published books of that time include Benjamin Franklin's *Poor Richard's Almanack* and William Blake's *Songs of Innocence and Songs of Experience.* In terms of more recent books, *The Joy of Cooking* began as a self-published title in 1931 and has since sold millions of copies. In 1966, singer-songwriter Rod McKuen self-published a book of poetry called *Stanyan Street and Other Sorrows,* the first of his many best-selling books. Finally, *The Martian* started out as a self-published novel by Andrew Weir in 2011 and was then adapted into a highly successful feature film in 2015.

Hundreds of thousands of books are self-published every year by authors whose names you may or may not recognize. Some sell fewer than 100 copies, while others sell tens of thousands of copies or more. Reasons for self-publishing vary, and making money is not always on the list. There are many other motivations, such as having control over the final product as well as the speed with which you can bring your book to market, having the freedom to tackle any subject in your writing, no matter how controversial, and simply wanting to satisfy your curiosity about the process of doing it yourself.

One of the missions of *How to Self-Publish Your Book* is to provide you with enough information about self-publishing to make it less likely for you to be taken advantage of by those who might prey on unsuspecting authors. An author desperate to publish might be susceptible to unscrupulous vendors. For example, I have heard of individuals who paid thousands of dollars to have their manuscripts proofread only to discover countless typos that should have been caught and corrected. I have also heard one horror story of an author who thought he was going to be a self-publisher but instead got involved with a so-called vanity publisher. He ended up spending lots of money and getting only a few pennies for any of the books that were sold, and then he had to buy back the rights to his book so he could start from scratch and actually self-publish his work properly.

As a self-publisher, if someone promises to make your book a bestseller for a certain price, you should run, not walk, in the opposite direction. No one can guarantee a bestseller. *How to Self-Publish Your Book* reveals what you should expect to encounter in the world of self-publishing, including the normal range of fees that you may need to pay for services, thereby decreasing the likelihood that you will be scammed. Fortunately, most people available to help you make your self-published book a reality are reliable and legitimate. With the growth of self-publishing service providers, if you would prefer to delegate some of the tasks that go into self-publishing to these professionals, and you are able to afford it, you no longer have to do everything yourself. But it is still useful to understand all aspects of self-publishing.

The good news is that self-publishing is now more acceptable to the mainstream than it has ever been. Your self-published book definitely has a chance of getting reviewed, publicized, and sold through bookstores as well as other sales outlets. Simply put, a self-published book is now more likely to be judged on its own merits.

CHAPTER 1

Writing Your Book

---

*Most writers will confess that they write because they
have to write, not necessarily because they want to write.*
—DIANA RAAB, *WRITING FOR BLISS*

Over the last decade, the business of *self-publishing* has grown by leaps and bounds. It is estimated that over 1 million new self-published titles are produced each year. If you are a writer but consider yourself too independently minded to work with a publisher, then self-publishing may be the way to get your book into print without making a slew of compromises.

The first step on the road to self-publishing is to ask yourself why you're writing a book instead of an article or blog, and why you think the world needs your book. Your answers will help keep you motivated as you go from being an author to a self-publisher. While there is no wrong answer to the question of why you are writing a book, it is important that you feel a need for the book you're writing, as finishing a book takes a lot of hard work and fortitude, and publishing a book takes even more. In fact, you may look back and realize that the writing of your book was the easiest part of the entire enterprise.

Writing a book and becoming an author can be life-changing experiences, and can allow you to have an effect on thousands, even millions, of people. The process of writing a book, however, can be rather complicated. Even for a seasoned writer, coming up with the right book idea can be a challenge. Wanting to write a great book is a noble goal. It is commendable to aim for greatness, but you will also want to avoid deliberately mimicking well-known books in your attempt to achieve it. You must write your own best book.

As an aspiring self-publisher, one of the biggest mistakes you can make is to be too hard on yourself and to set unrealistic standards of success. The other is not to set high enough standards of success. Every author wants to "hit the ground running" and have a critical and commercial success with her first self-published book. But the reality is that writing books is a skill mastered through practice, as is the case with most skills in life. You must resist the temptation to publish the first draft of your novel or nonfiction work, which more than likely has not been edited, proofread, or as thoroughly researched as you know it should be. You want your book, even your very first self-published book, to be the best book you are able to write at this point in your writing career. It might not win any awards or get all the accolades that your second, third, or fourth book might receive, but then again, it just might.

WHAT IS YOUR MOTIVATION?

What's really motivating you to get your book into print? Every writer who is seeking to get her work published is also being driven by some sort of motivation. Some of the most common ones include gaining respected literary status, advancing image, generating income, contributing to a particular field, and even changing society. Of course, a writer may be motivated by a combination of these ideas, but there is often one that leads the pack.

Some writers believe that getting a book published by anything other than a high-profile company doesn't count. In 1996, my primary reason for self-publishing my book *Friendshifts* was that getting my book published had become more important to me than having a major publishing company produce it. By that time, I had already had other works published by Scribner's, Doubleday, Wiley, Prentice-Hall, and Grove Press. But this book was a bit more academic than the mainstream publishers were used to, since it was an outgrowth of my sociology doctoral dissertation on friendship. Ironically, academic publishers found it too commercial, so I founded my own publishing company, Hannacroix Creek Books, Inc., and released it myself.

Being quite familiar with the world of book publishing, I figured it would be a piece of cake to publish just one book on my own. I was wrong. Back then, without the technology that is available today to do *print-on-demand books, e-books,* or *audiobooks,* I started off doing offset printing, or what is also called a *short run.* I even hired a consultant to teach me PageMaker, the design software I used to typeset the Microsoft Word document. It was a laborious process, and thankfully my original printer was very patient with me, teaching me a lot along the way.

The good news is that the book did very well critically and commercially. I even sent myself on a cross-country author tour for *Friendshifts,* in addition to being interviewed on *The View, The Oprah Winfrey Show,* and the *Today Show.* The success of that book led to a deal with Simon & Schuster for my next book on friendship, *When Friendship Hurts,* which also ended up doing well. Simon & Schuster sent me on a four-city tour for *When Friendship Hurts.* Soon after being included in a *New York Times* feature article on the subject, I was interviewed on *Good Morning America.*

At the end of the day, my motivation for writing both books was the same: to help people see friendship in a new way and to help them with their friendship challenges. It was irrelevant to me—and, fortunately, inconsequential to the media and my readers—who published these books. I simply wished to get my message across.

> Although self-publishing involves a lot of effort, it is an excellent option for a writer who has an entrepreneurial spirit and wants to take on the challenge of being both an author and a publisher.

THE IMPORTANCE OF HAVING A GOAL

You may say that your goal is to publish your book, and you wouldn't be wrong in saying so, since that's pretty much the goal of every writer who is in the process of writing a book or aspiring to write one. Nevertheless, I think you should have a stronger motivation. If you do, you'll be more likely to stick with your book and its publication, especially when you are tempted, as almost all writers are, to abandon your project because it is becoming more work than you had anticipated.

Writing and self-publishing a book are not for the faint of heart. You need to keep yourself driven to finish your book. Commercial publishers provide motivation by giving you a deadline and, in most cases, an *advance,* which you will have to pay back if you fail to finish and deliver your book. As a self-publisher, you will need to get your motivation in some other way, as you may not know your book's future profitability.

When I was starting out, there was a joke in the book industry: If you want to make a small fortune in book publishing, start with a big one. It is crucial that you know why you want to be published, if only because the previously referenced epigram is funny but often true. You may have something to say that is significant—something that will help make a difference, address a specific cause, share a discovery of some sort, or convey a new point of view on a particular subject. It may be helpful for you to clarify your reason for writing and publishing your book. Your reason may be:

- I am writing this book to encourage people to change their behavior.

- I am writing this book to share my expertise in a certain field.

- I am writing this book to increase my credibility in a certain field.

- I am writing this novel because I have an interesting story to tell.

- I am writing this memoir because I want to share my life's story.

- I am writing this biography because I wish to share someone else's life's story.

- I am writing this children's book to inspire or educate children in the same way children's books have inspired or educated me.

- I am writing a middle grade or young adult (YA) novel or nonfiction book to entertain or educate preteens and teens.

"I want to help people," wrote Connecticut-based organizer Leslie Jacobs, who self-published *Survival in the Unemployment Line.* Based on his extensive years as a physician, Dr. Kilbourn Gordon wrote and self-published *Med School 101 for Patients* because he saw a need to provide patients with a step-by-step handbook on how to get the most out of their office visits. His goal is reflected in the subtitle of this book: *A Patient's Guide to Creating an Exceptional Doctor's Visit.*

For some, it is a relatively quick process from idea to finished manuscript—a range of months rather than years. For others, the journey may be considerably longer. For example, take New Hampshire-based writer Catherine Dougherty. On the subject of her first book, she said, "I've always wanted to be a published author and the book idea just came to me and wouldn't leave me. My first book, *In Polyester Pajamas*, took me seven years to complete. I published this book after turning fifty. After the first book, I learned to take each chapter as a story in itself. It helped me from getting overwhelmed and kept me moving forward. My next three books took less than one year each to be written and published."

If you do not see your goal in the previous list, think about what it is and then write it down. Articulating your motivation and then reading it whenever you lose faith in yourself or run out of patience with the writing process should help you keep going until you finish your work and release it to the public.

It is worth noting that research has shown money to be a poor motivator. In their online *Forbes* article "Money Is Not the Best Motivator," Jon R. Katzenbach and Zia Kahn, coauthors of *Leading Outside the Lines*, highlight the results of their extensive research into motivation, in which they studied Navy Seals, Green Berets, and Marines, as well as hundreds more in dozens of companies. Reflecting on their findings as well as on the work of executive coach David Rock and neuroscientist Jeffry Schwartz, they state that wanting to elevate one's status and take pride in one's work is a better motivator than money.

This is good news for self-publishers. Not only is the likelihood of making money from your book uncertain, but self-publishing it is going to cost you money. Keep this in mind as you go on this writing and self-publishing adventure.

The likelihood of making money from your self-published book is uncertain, so when you are searching for the drive to finish your work, don't use the potential of turning a profit as a motivator. You need to be driven by something more.

WHAT CONSTITUTES GOOD WRITING?

How to Self-Publish Your Book is not a substitute for a writing course or a book on the subject of good writing. The process of writing is just too big of a subject to cover in one chapter. Nevertheless, I have

Good writing means
rewriting, not overwriting.
Be mindful of this fact
when you are working
on your manuscript.

been writing books since the age of ten, and have been a published author since the age of twenty-six. I also have experience teaching nonfiction writing at the college level, including two courses at Penn State many years ago, and, more recently, courses that include an intensive writing component at two different colleges. I have learned a thing or two along the way about what constitutes outstanding writing, what constitutes writing that is merely good enough, and what constitutes writing that simply fails to meet minimum standards.

Rewriting

The most rewarding aspect of teaching writing courses is being able to witness firsthand the power of rewriting. For most of my students, the rewriting experience is a new and unique one. My current course requires that students do at least three drafts of their writing assignments: a first draft that is read by a tutor at the writing center or by a classmate, a second draft that is handed in to me for review and comments, and a third and final draft, which involves incorporating any suggested changes into the text. It becomes quickly apparent to each student that this method works a lot better than turning in a first draft, which may have been finished just hours before it was due.

Although good writing often means rewriting, be careful not to overwrite or inadvertently abandon the best parts of previous drafts, of course. Most writers, even seasoned ones, rarely get it right on the first try, but don't throw out your good writing along with your writing that is not as good simply because of proximity. Some of your first thoughts may actually be your best thoughts.

Finally, while feedback may be useful, always remember that your book is *your* book. It is your name that will be on it once it has been published, so make sure you are comfortable with your book in light of any changes you might have made as a result of input from others. The first reader you need to please is yourself.

Writing Nonfiction

When it comes to the category of nonfiction, the strength of your writing has a lot to do with the strength of your research. Take as much time as you need to do all the research your particular book requires. In addition, whether your nonfiction book takes a narrow or broad focus on a subject, contribute something new to the topic. Nonfiction works need to be interesting and fresh. Your topic can be an old one, of course, but you should say something different about it, or look at familiar concepts from a different perspective. Overall, seek to inform but also engage your readers.

Avoid making the mistake of thinking there is no room in the marketplace for your book because there are already many other books on your topic. In the 1970s, numerous books on the subject of rape were published. Rape victims' rights were becoming a lot more of a concern than ever before, thanks in large part to the women's movement and the establishment of women's centers to deal with such sensitive issues as rape and sexual assault. In 1975, Susan Brownmiller's *Against Our Will* was published despite there being many competing books on the issue. More comprehensive than these other books, and written in a style that seemed to impress both critics and the public, Brownmiller's book became a bestseller.

Writing Fiction

When writing fiction, how you say something is just as important as what you say. Even in your first book, you should have your own style of writing. It may evolve, of course, over time, but it should always be present. Rather than consciously worry about developing your own style, though, just write and keep writing. Your style will come.

Also, do not discount the power of a book's first line. Think of some of the great first lines in fiction. Perhaps the most well known is "It was the best of times, it was the worst of times" from Charles Dickens' *A Tale of Two Cities*. The first sentence of Jane Austen's *Emma* also comes to mind: "Emma Woodhouse, handsome, clever, and rich, with a comfortable home and happy disposition, seemed to unite some of the best blessings of existence; and had lived nearly twenty-one years in the world with very little to distress or vex her." While you should take care in writing every sentence in your book, you should give its first line special attention.

Finally, consider your characters. Do you like spending time with your characters? If your answer is yes, then there is a good chance your readers will like spending time with them as well. Great characters have less to do with whether they are "good" or "bad" people, and more to do with whether they are memorable, distinctive, and somehow ring true despite being fictional.

Writing a Children's Book

Most children's books have messages, but if you are writing a children's book, try to avoid sounding preachy. Of course, your children's book should be geared to a particular age group, so you might find it helpful to check out other books that have been written for your target audience and see what they look like and how they read.

Since you are self-publishing, you will be able to choose an illustrator for your book. Even if you love an illustrator's work, make sure your text works independently of illustrations, as you might find certain markets for your book, especially international ones, that would prefer to redo the illustrations to fit their needs.

Seriously consider the advantages and disadvantages of writing a children's book in rhyme versus prose. There are some fabulous rhyming children's books, including Dr. Seuss classics such as *The Cat in the Hat* and *Green Eggs and Ham*, but rhyming books may be more challenging to translate into other languages. Finally, before you finalize your book, read it to a few of your potential readers, if possible. If you have children at home, read it to them and their friends. If you have a local library that does children's events, you could even ask to read from your book in progress to get reader reactions and possibly even some suggestions.

Improving Your Writing

You may improve your writing by taking a course on writing. You may even be able to find one that focuses on the *genre*, or artistic classification, of your book. It could be an in-person course at a college or university, or even one offered by your community at a local high school. If you cannot find an in-person course, you could take an online writing course instead. You could also form a writing group of other authors who are at your level of proficiency. Members could offer feedback and advice on one another's work.

You could try to get a job as an editorial assistant or, if your skills are more advanced, as an editor at a book publishing company, newspaper, magazine, or online publication, where your job would be to write and edit copy all day long. Finally, you should read more in general, including books, magazines, newspapers, and online publications. A few books on writing should also be on your reading list.

One of the most enjoyable ways to become a better writer is to read. Reading exposes you to different writing styles and voices. Read attentively, with an eye for writing, and you will learn many "tricks" of the trade.

Books on Writing

As I am sure you are aware, there are countless books on writing. So many, in fact, that it may seem a daunting task to choose one over another. Besides my own book *Effective Business and Nonfiction Writing*, I have added a number of classic works on writing to the Resources (see page 231), each of which provides the aspiring writer with helpful information and suggestions.

WHAT MAKES A BOOK GREAT?

You want to write a great book. It is certainly a noble goal. I actually have a section of my bookcase reserved for classic books—nonfiction titles such as *The One Minute Manager, Final Gifts,* and *Men Are From Mars, Women Are from Venus;* fiction titles such as Dostoyevsky's *Crime and Punishment* and F. Scott Fitzgerald's *The Great Gatsby;* and children's books such as Margaret Wise Brown's *Goodnight Moon* and Dr. Seuss's *The Cat in the Hat.*

What do all these great books have in common? Each one has a memorable title, a strong point of view, and something about it that is interesting and unique. Each one is a good read, as they say. Whether it's a runaway bestseller, a slow but consistent seller with numerous translations (indicating that the book has a global reach), or a title that is gaining traction through solid word-of-mouth recommendations, a great book is a great book.

It is terrific to aim high. But you must also determine whether you are creating a standard for yourself that might make it hard for you to finish the book you are working on in a reasonable amount of time. Yes, it is wonderful to work hard and aspire to greatness, but you also want to be realistic and allow yourself to complete your book. You won't have anything to publish if you never finish what you've started. By allowing yourself to write your "best book," you may avoid getting bogged down by your own unrealistic expectations.

WRITING YOUR BEST BOOK

As you navigate the process of writing your book, be careful not to set standards for yourself that are either too high or not high enough.

If I had to pick the two biggest mistakes an aspiring self-publisher can make—the ones that can sabotage an author's goal of self-publishing entirely—I would choose these scenarios:

- She sets an unrealistic standard of success for herself, giving herself the goal of writing another *Gone with the Wind*, *Harry Potter and the Sorcerer's Stone*, or *How to Win Friends and Influence People* on her first try.

- She sets a standard of success that is not high enough.

It's natural for an author to want to enjoy critical and commercial success with her first book. The reality, however, is that the practice of writing books, like almost every other skill in life, is mastered over time by writing. You will improve by doing it. But setting a literary standard that is simply too high to reach at the moment can be paralyzing to a beginner author. It can put an end to a writing career before it has even begun. This does not mean, of course, that you should allow yourself to publish a novel with which you are truly unhappy, or a nonfiction work that has not been researched carefully enough. You want your book, even your very first self-published book, to be your best book, which is to say the best book you are able to write at this point in your writing career.

Here is where it gets a bit tricky for aspiring self-publishers. Even if you know in your heart of hearts that you must let go of your book because it is the best book you are able to write, it nevertheless should not appear as though it has been self-published. Here is where your standards of success must be high. Your book must look just as professionally complete and well designed as the books published by major publishing houses. No book should have typos, of course, but they happen. Since your book is going to be self-published, however, you cannot afford to have even one. Unfortunately, self-publishing may still carry a stigma, and, as a result, self-publishers may not get the same amount of slack afforded a major publisher. When a major publisher's book contains an error, it is often overlooked as a small matter that slipped through the cracks. Conversely, if your book were to have a typo, read as though it needed a better editor, or look as though it missed the proofreading stage, it could easily be dismissed as amateurish and not reviewed, taken seriously, or even fully read. You cannot give a reader an excuse to trivialize your book.

So, if you plan to self-publish, the first rule for writing your best book has nothing to do with its genre or subject matter, or even your writing style. The first rule is that you set practical standards of work and appearance for your book that are high enough to result in a book that looks just as "real" or "professional" as any book put out by major publishers. The first acclaim you should wish to hear is praise for how great your book looks.

The highest compliment a potential reader or member of the media could say when she gets a copy of your book, after learning it is a self-published work, would be to exclaim, "I never would have guessed this is a self-published book!"

As you embark upon the journey of writing your best book, it is important to distinguish between literary standards and publication standards. When literary standards are unreasonably high, they can seriously hinder your progress and ultimate success. When publication standards are not high enough, however, you may unknowingly sabotage your own work and ensure that your book never gets the readership it may deserve.

The question is: How do you know when your manuscript is good enough for you to move ahead in the next stage of the self-publishing process?

When Is Your Book Good Enough?

For those writers who are such perfectionists that they just keep rewriting or doing so much additional research that they never seem to let go of their books, the concept of a book being "good enough" is an important one to learn. When a book is good enough, this does not mean it is inferior or slipshod. It just means that you have reached the point at which you know you must let go of your work and allow yourself to go to the next step: publication. Oftentimes, a fresh set of eyes is required for you to find out if your book is good enough for publication. Yes, you could keep writing and rewriting until your book seems good enough to you and you alone, but reworking your material too much can backfire, putting you too close to your work, unable to truly see it for what it is. If you are able to pass it along to an editor or even just a friend, you might get some worthwhile feedback that will get you to the next phase in publication.

Second Book Syndrome

Be careful to avoid what could be called "second book syndrome," which is the faulty notion that you do not have to put all relevant ideas into your first book because there will probably be follow-up books. It is only because the first book in a proposed series is so excellent that there exist any sequels. If you hold back great ideas while writing your first book, reassuring yourself that you are saving these exciting scenes, descriptions, or characters for a subsequent book, your first book might not end up as wonderful as it needs to be. In falling victim to second book syndrome, you might also be undermining the chance that your story will have an audience for a second book.

Category-Specific and Genre-Specific Considerations

Before you finish your manuscript, you might want to consider if what you are writing conforms to the expectations associated with your book's category. If you are writing a nonfiction book, you need to be sure you have done enough research to offer a fresh and accurate view of whatever topic you are writing about. If you are working in the fiction category, your book needs to be well written and fresh. Characters should be memorable and distinctive. The plot must be novel enough that readers do not feel like they have read your book before.

In terms of genre-specific considerations, for example, if you are writing a memoir, you will want to add narrative flow or structure to your story and explore your life in as detailed and self-critical a way as possible to ensure your book contains some meaning for your reader.

> Anytime you sit down to write a manuscript, consider the category and genre in which you are working. If you are writing a nonfiction book, your research should be thorough and up to date. If you are writing a work of fiction, your characters should be memorable and distinctive.

EXAMPLES OF NONFICTION GENRES	
Autobiography & Biography	Humor
Business & Economics	Pets
Crafts & Hobbies	Self-Help
History	True Crime

EXAMPLES OF FICTION GENRES	
Fairy Tales & Folklore	Romance
Fantasy	Science Fiction (Sci-Fi)
Historical Novel	Thriller
Mystery & Detective	Young Adult (YA)

There are so many genres, of course, that it would take an entire book to list them all. To get a clearer idea of your genre, consult the Book Industry Study Group's website, which hosts an updated list of genre classifications known as the "Complete BISAC Subject Headings List." (See page 244 of the Resources.) Another key piece of advice I can give you about any genre-specific considerations for your book is this: Go to your local library or bookstore and look over samples of the genre in which you have chosen to write. See what is expected in this genre. In relation to children's books, for example: How many pages is a typical picture book aimed for four-year-olds? You will see that most children's books of this sort are twenty-four to thirty-six pages in length. Are you writing a nonfiction self-help book? You will see that most books in this genre are six inches by nine inches in size and use a certain style and size of font. You will also notice that nonfiction books tend to be between two hundred and three hundred pages—not too short but not too long.

So, once you know your genre, find a book in this genre's section of your library or bookstore and, without copying this book, use it as a model for your work and share it with the person who is going to design the cover of your book, as well as with the person who is going to design your book's interior, should you decide to hire such designers.

CONCLUSION

I hope you are charged up and raring to go on your self-publishing journey. Articulating your reasons for writing your book as specifically as possible should keep you motivated to write and rewrite until you have finished. Writing a book can be a very challenging undertaking, whether it's your first or your tenth book, but it is not the only challenging part of the publishing process. After you've written your book, you still have to publish it and then find readers and buyers. Of course, by the time you find yourself asking people to read your words—and to pay for the privilege of doing so—you'd better have made sure those words are worth their time and money.

CHAPTER 2

$\mathcal{S}$EQUENCING YOUR MANUSCRIPT

There are books of which the backs and
covers are by far the best parts.
—CHARLES DICKENS, *OLIVER TWIST*

Many authors who decide to self-publish their works are bewildered when they start to turn their manuscripts into proper books. As someone who is new to self-publishing, you may not have noticed the numerous details involved in turning all those words into a finished product. Since you have decided to become a self-publisher, you should want your book to look like it belongs alongside the titles released by major publishing houses. In other words, it should include all the essential elements a professionally published book contains.

When a buyer at a bookstore looks at a book, he can immediately tell if it does not conform to the rules of commercially published titles. If your book has no title page or the title page also contains the copyright notice; if your book's table of contents is entitled "Table of Contents" instead of just "Contents"; or if the pages of front matter are numbered in Arabic numbers (e.g., 1, 2, 3) instead of Roman numerals (e.g., i, ii, iii); then your book contains obvious "tells," which let discerning readers know the book is the work of an amateur. By following the simple guidelines set forth in this chapter, you will end up with a book that includes the right sections and sequences these sections in the right order. This chapter is designed to guide you through the process of creating a professional-looking book that passes any buyer's or reader's scrutiny.

The anatomy of a book is made up of three main parts: *front matter*, also known as *preliminaries* or *prematter*; *body matter*, also called *body text*; and *back matter*, also known as *end matter*. As a self-publisher, you need to make sure that each of these parts has been included appropriately in your book before you consider it as finished and release it. If you fail to do so, your book won't look like a book that has been published by one of the major commercial houses.

While certain elements of a book are mandatory, some are optional. The inclusion of certain sections may also depend upon the category of your book. For example, back matter of a nonfiction title typically features sections such as a bibliography and an index, while back matter of a fiction title does not. This chapter will teach you what to include, where to include it, and when it's up to you.

FRONT MATTER

Front matter, sometimes called preliminaries or prematter, consists of the opening sections of your book. In both nonfiction and fiction titles, front matter reserves one or two pages for the book's title and author, and one for copyright information. Both fiction and nonfiction front matter may incorporate optional sections, but certain optional elements are more commonly found in one category of book than another.

For example, both nonfiction and fiction titles may include a foreword, preface, or introduction, but these sections are much more typical of nonfiction books. And while a fiction book such as a novel may have a table of contents (although it would be an extremely rare occurrence), this element is required of a nonfiction work. Finally, certain optional sections are used in only one category. A prologue, for instance, would appear only in a work of fiction. Once you are aware of the necessary components of front matter and have considered which optional sections would be of benefit to your book, you are on your way to having a comprehensive and professional-looking publication.

Half-Title Page (Optional)

A *half-title page* is simply a page that features the title of a book without inclusion of its subtitle, author's name, or publisher's logo. If you choose to include a half-title page, it should be the first page of your book, which is a right-hand page, also known as a *recto*. Some publishers do not include this page and go right to the title page. Sometimes a page of advance praise takes the place of a half-title page. Never include both a half-title page and a page of advance praise (discussed below). You can use one or the other.

Most of the sample pages in this book are intended to serve as formatting guides, not as legible text. No magnifying glass is required because the actual text will be different for every book.

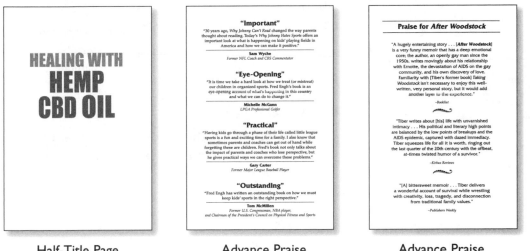

Half-Title Page
Sample

Advance Praise
Sample

Advance Praise
Sample

Advance Praise (Optional)

A page dedicated to *advance praise* for your book is worth considering if you have any valuable quotations from other authors or critics. This page often begins with the words "Praise for" followed by your book's title. The space below the title of your book should then be filled with positive comments about your book made by other writers or excerpts from good reviews by critics. This page should begin on a right-hand page, spilling over to the back of the page (the left-hand page, or *verso*) if you have a large number of quotations. As mentioned above, you can include either a page of advance praise or a half-title page—not both. (See sample on next page.)

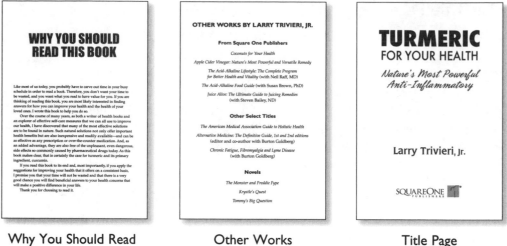

Why You Should Read
This Book Sample

Other Works
Sample

Title Page
Sample

Other Works (Optional)

When an author has published other books, sometimes they are listed on the back (verso) of the half-title page under the heading *Other Works.* If you have not published any other title, obviously other works would not be added.

Why You Should Read This Book (Nonfiction, Optional)

In a nonfiction book, you may wish to add one page dedicated to promotional copy that tells the reader why it is important to read your book, briefly details the information it offers, and explains what the reader may gain by reading it. Beginning with the heading *Why You Should Read This Book*, this page may appear in place of a half-title page or follow it.

Title Page

If you decide to include a half-title page, the *title page* should be the first right-hand page that follows (or, if applicable, the first right-hand page after *Why You Should Read This Book*). In many books, however, the very first page is the title page. On this page should appear the title of the book. Below the title should be the subtitle, if any, followed by the number of the edition in the case of a revised version. The name of the author should also be listed on this page, either below or above the book's title.

The name of the publishing company should also appear on the title page, and below this name should be noted the city and state in which the book was published. This information is typically centered at the bottom of the page.

Copyright Page

The *copyright page* should appear on the back of the title page. You may begin your copyright page by listing the names of the applicable individuals responsible for putting the book together as follows:

- Cover Designer:

- Interior Designer:

- Editor:

- Typesetter:

Beneath these names should appear the name of the publisher, publisher's address, publisher's phone number, and publisher's website. This contact information should be followed by *Library of Congress Cataloging-in-Publication data (CIP data)* or a *Library of Congress Control Number (LCCN)*.

CIP Data or LCCN

If this is the first book you are publishing on your own, you will not be eligible to receive the Cataloging-in-Publication data normally provided by the Library of Congress because to qualify for this free program, you must have already published three different authors besides yourself. You will, however, be eligible to receive what is known as a Library of Congress Control Number (LCCN). To get an LCCN for your book, you will need to submit an application to participate in the program through the website of the Library of

Congress, which may be done at https://www.loc.gov/publish/ pcn/newaccount.html. Once you have an account, you will be granted access to the form necessary to request an LCCN.

ISBN

US publishers must purchase their ISBNs from R. R. Bowker LLC. In Canada, however, ISBNs are provided free of charge by the federal government to Canadian-based publishers.

Whether for CIP data or an LCCN, the application will ask for the *International Standard Book Number*, or *ISBN*, of your title. An ISBN is a thirteen-digit number that acts as a unique identifier of a book for booksellers, libraries, book wholesalers, and book distributors. Essentially, you will need one if you wish to sell your book to these entities. International Standard Book Numbers are specific to their countries of issuance, and in the United States, they are exclusively provided by a company called R. R. Bowker LLC.

To acquire an ISBN for your book, visit the Bowker identifier services website at www.myidentifiers.com and consult the drop-down menu marked "ISBN," which should present you with options for purchasing one or more ISBNs. Use of an ISBN is limited to the exact edition of the book for which it has been acquired. For example, a hardcover version of a book requires a different ISBN than its paperback edition. Moreover, if you were to add material or make substantial changes to a book and release it as a second edition, a new ISBN would be needed. A reprint without major changes, however, would not necessitate a new ISBN.

It is important to reiterate that each ISBN is a unique identifier. Under no circumstances should you assign a particular ISBN twice. Even if you have assigned an ISBN to a title that you then decide not to publish, you must "retire" that ISBN number. It cannot be used in association with a book that you publish, or with any other book for that matter. It is therefore very important to keep track of the ISBNs you have assigned to books or formats of a title.

While an ISBN is generally not required by e-book retailers (they typically use their own systems of tracking titles), a dedicated ISBN for the e-book format of your book is needed if you would like your e-book sales figures sent to industry sales reporting agencies. Keep in mind, though, that the major e-publishers provide their own up-to-the-minute sales reports to their authors. Granted, if you have distributed your book nonexclusively to all major e-retailers, it may be a hassle to check your sales figures on each website. In this case, you may wish to use a service that collates all your sales data for you in one place, and this type of service may ask that you attach a dedicated ISBN to your e-book to facilitate tracking.

If you receive Library of Congress Cataloging-in-Publication data, it will include the ISBN number in the block of information. If your book is in printed and electronic formats, the CIP data may note both ISBNs (e.g., ISBN xxx-x-xxxx-xxxx-x [paperback], ISBN xxx-x-xxxx-xxxx-x [e-book]). Besides ISBN and LCCN information, the CIP data block will include the author's name, title of the book, description of the book, and the subject or subjects of the book. If you have only an LCCN, you may add your ISBN information below it.

Copyright Holder

Below the CIP data or LCCN should appear the name of the copyright holder. This information should be noted by using the term "copyright" followed by the copyright symbol, the year of copyright, and the name of the copyright holder, which is usually the author (e.g., Copyright © 2019 by Jan Yager).

The information and advice contained in this book are based upon the research and the personal and professional experiences of the authors. They are not intended as a substitute for consulting with a health care professional. The publisher and author are not responsible for any adverse effects or consequences resulting from the use of any of the suggestions, preparations, or procedures discussed in this book. All matters pertaining to your physical health should be supervised by a health care professional. If it is a sign of wisdom, not cowardice, to seek a second or third opinion.

EDITOR: Erica Shur
COVER DESIGNER: Jeannie Rosado
TYPESETTER: Gary A. Rosenberg (InDesign)

Square One Publishers
115 Herricks Road
Garden City Park, NY 11040
(516) 535-2010 • (877) 900-BOOK
www.squareonepublishers.com

Library of Congress Cataloging-in-Publication Data
Names: Mindell, Earl, author.
Title: Healing with hemp CBD oil : a simple guide to using powerful and proven health benefits of CBD / Earl Mindell, RPh, PhD.
Description: Garden City Park, NY : Square One Publishers, [2018] | Includes bibliographical references and index.
Identifiers: LCCN 2017042197 (print) | LCCN 2017039200 (ebook) | ISBN 9780757004551 (paperback) | ISBN 9780757054556
Subjects: LCSH: Cannabis—Therapeutic use. | Hemp seed oil—Therapeutic use. | Hemp—Therapeutic use.
Classification: LCC RM666.C266 M56 2017 (ebook) | LCC RM666.C266 (print) | DDC 615.7/827—dc23
LC record available at HYPERLINK "https://lccn.loc.gov/2017042197" https://lccn.loc.gov/2017042197

Copyright © 2018 by Earl Mindell

All rights reserved. No part of this publication may be reproduced, scanned, uploaded, stored in a retrieval system, or transmitted, in any form or by any means, electronic, mechanical, photocopying, recording, or otherwise, without the prior written permission of the publisher.

Printed in the United States of America

10 9 8 7 6 5 4 3 2 1

This book is a work of fiction. Names, characters, places, and incidents either are products of the author's imagination or are used fictitiously. Any resemblance to actual events or locales or persons, living or dead, is entirely coincidental.

Copyright © 201/ by James A. Misko.

All rights reserved, including the right of reproduction in whole or in part in any form. No part of this book may be reproduced, stored in a retrieval system, or transmitted by any means, electronic, mechanical, photocopying, recording, or otherwise, without written permission from the author.

For information regarding special discounts for bulk purchases, please contact Square One Publishers at 877-900-2665.

Cover and interior design by Frame25 Productions
Cover photo by Honza Krej c/o Shutterstock.com
Tamarack, Oregon map created by Thomas Eley/Mapping Solutions

Library of Congress Cataloging-In-Publiucation Data
Names: Misko, James A., author.
Title: The path of the wind / by James A. Misko.
Description: Garden City Park, NY : Square One Publishers, 2017.
Identifiers: LCCN 2016053938 (print) | LCCN 2016055582 (ebook) | ISBN 9780757004445 (pbk.) | ISBN 9780757054440
Subjects: LCSH: Teachers—Fiction.
Classification: LCC PS3613.I8447 P38 2017 (print) | LCC PS3613.I8447 (ebook) | DDC 813/.6—dc23
LC record available at https://lccn.loc.gov/2016053938

ISBN 978-0-7570-0444-5

Manufactured in the United States of America

10 9 8 7 6 5 4 3 2 1

Two Sample Copyright Pages

All Rights Reserved

Below the name of the copyright holder, the following statement is usually printed, advising readers that the book cannot be copied or shared without written permission of the copyright holder. Sample wording is as follows:

> All rights reserved. No part of this publication may be reproduced, scanned, uploaded, stored in a retrieval system, or transmitted, in any form or by any means, electronic, mechanical, photocopying, recording, or otherwise, without the prior written permission of the publisher.

After this statement you may also note the country in which the book was printed. For example, you may include the phrase "Printed in the United States of America."

Copyrighting Your Book

According to the U.S. Copyright Office, "Copyright exists automatically in an original work of authorship once it is fixed in a tangible medium." In other words, as soon as you write your book, you become its rightful copyright owner and may claim yourself as such to anyone who attempts to use this work without your permission.

Should you ever wish to settle a copyright dispute in a court of law, however, you will first need to register the work in question at the U.S. Copyright Office, which states, "Although registering a work is not mandatory, for works of U.S. origin, registration (or refusal) is necessary to enforce the exclusive rights of copyright through litigation."

Registering a work costs between $35 and $55 for one book, but you will find it money well spent if any serious legal problems arise in connection with the rights to your material.

After you submit an application to register your copyright along with a copy of the material being registered and the associated registration fee, you should receive notification of copyright registration by mail in approximately twelve to eighteen months, though the date on the copyright notice will be the date on which you submitted your application. You can get started at https://www.copyright.gov/registration.

Printer's Key

If you will be printing a certain number of copies of your book, also known as a *print run*, rather than relying solely on print-on-demand services, it is customary to indicate the print run by using a *printer's key*. The printer's key of a first edition is typically listed as:

1 2 3 4 5 6 7 8 9 10

or

10 9 8 7 6 5 4 3 2 1

With each subsequent printing a number is removed to illustrate the print run. In other words, the second print run of a book would not have the "1" included in its printer's key.

Disclaimer (Optional)

You may want to include a *disclaimer* at the top of the copyright page. A disclaimer is an official statement absolving the publisher of any legal responsibility for the contents of the book. For instance, a work of fiction typically includes a disclaimer such as:

> This is a work of fiction. Names, characters, places, and incidents either are the product of the author's imagination or are used fictitiously, and any resemblance to an actual person, living or dead, business, companies, events, or locales is entirely coincidental.

In a nonfiction self-help or health-related title, you should include a disclaimer such as:

> The information and advice contained in this book are based upon the research and the personal and professional experiences of the author. They are not intended as a substitute for consulting with a healthcare professional. The publisher and author are not responsible for any adverse effects or consequences resulting from the use of any of the suggestions, preparations, or procedures discussed in this book. All matters

pertaining to your physical health should be supervised by a healthcare professional. It is a sign of wisdom, not cowardice, to seek a second or third opinion.

Contents Page (Optional in Fiction Only)

The *contents page* should always be headed simply as "Contents," never as "Table of Contents," and is usually found only in nonfiction books. (Works of fiction often go straight to the first chapter at this point.) In order for this page to appear professionally formatted, do not include the word "chapter" next to each chapter number. Doing so would be a "tell." In other words, it would give away the fact that the book has been self-published. You need only list the number and title of each chapter, followed by the number of the page on which the chapter begins.

Contents
Page
Samples

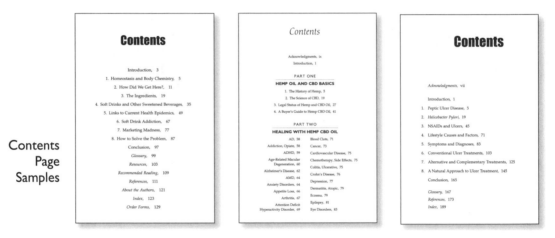

Dedication Page (Optional)

Both fiction and nonfiction books often have a *dedication page*. This page follows the contents page or the copyright page if there is no contents page. It should fall on a right-hand page, with the verso usually left blank.

A dedication may be as simple as "For Joan, always," the way novelist Elmore Leonard dedicated his novel *Stick,* or as detailed as the dedication to Kelly Corrigan's *The Middle Place,* "Most everything I do these days is dedicated to Edward and the girls, but this book is for Phoebe, who wouldn't let it go."

Dedication
Sample

Acknowledgments
Sample

Foreword
Sample

Acknowledgments (Optional)

Acknowledgments may appear in the front matter or back matter of a book. In nonfiction, the acknowledgments section is typically set before the preface. In fiction, the acknowledgments often appear at the end of the book.

The acknowledgments are the part of a book in which the people involved in its creation and completion are recognized and thanked, such as the people who acted as inspirations for the book, the individuals who were interviewed for the work, or those who read the manuscript and offered helpful suggestions and advice on how to turn it into a successful finished text. It may feature professional associates, such as agents or editors. It may also list loved ones or anyone who has advanced the author's career along the way.

The acknowledgments section gives you an opportunity to thank everyone who contributed to the creation of your book. The people you include can range from experts who provided up-to-date information on a pertinent subject to family members who offered encouragement and emotional support throughout the writing process.

Foreword (Optional)

A book may also have a *foreword*, which is an introduction that has been written by a third party whose reputation will lend credibility to the book. (Please note the spelling of the word "foreword." Misspelling this section as "forward" is a giant red flag of poor writing and proofreading, and another possible "tell" of a self-publisher.)

Preface Sample

Introduction Sample

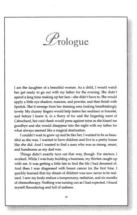

Prologue Sample

Preface (Optional)

Written by the author, a *preface* outlines the story behind or inspiration for the writing of a book. For example, in the preface to my book *Victims*, which is based on several years of extensive research into victims of violent crimes and property crimes, I reveal that my motivation to study crime victims and pursue a master's degree in criminal justice was sparked by my older brother's senseless mugging and subsequent death from the wounds inflicted on him by the gang that had robbed him.

Introduction (Optional)

An author of nonfiction may use an *introduction* to provide an overview of the topic of his book and put the new book into a broader context of contemporary or historical trends. A nonfiction author may also use an introduction to highlight what readers will learn in each chapter as a way of motivating them to read the entire book after they have quickly skimmed the front matter and are trying to decide whether or not to dedicate more time to the subject.

Works of fiction do not normally feature introductions, although there are exceptions. For example, if a novel has been translated, it may include an introduction written by the translator or a scholar who comments on the translation or author. Occasionally, an introduction to a novel will seek to cast the book in a certain literary or historical light.

Prologue (Fiction, Optional)

A novel might start with a *prologue*, which appears just before the first chapter. The main objective of a prologue is to provide a background to the upcoming story. It may present the reader with some knowledge of certain characters, time period, or setting. For example, before launching into the play's opening scene, Shakespeare uses the prologue to *Romeo and Juliet* to set up the notion of two adversarial families and the two star-crossed lovers whose deaths brought the conflict to an end.

Quotations

In some cases, a chapter title may be followed by a short quotation of a single line to four sentences in length that bears some relevance to the chapter or book. For consistency's sake, if using quotations, try to find one for every chapter. A quotation should be followed by the name of the individual or source being quoted. Please remember that when quoting copyrighted material, permission must be obtained to use the quotation unless the source is no longer under copyright protection.

Chapter Opener with
Quote Sample

BODY MATTER

The *body matter* of a book refers to its chapters. Whether your work is nonfiction or fiction, the first page of your first chapter should always begin on a right-hand page. If it starts on a left-hand page, you would have allowed another "tell" that your book has been, in all likelihood, self-published. It is also important to know the differences between nonfiction and fiction chapter headings, mistakes in which can also be "tells" to a keen reader.

Nonfiction Chapter Headings

In nonfiction books, chapter headings should include the chapter number and title. For example, the first chapter would be called "Chapter One," "Chapter 1," "One," or "1," which would be followed by the title of the chapter. Try to keep chapter titles reasonably concise. Each one should be no more than three lines when typeset. Avoid using a subtitle line to clarify a chapter title. The title should be clear enough on its own to identify what the reader will find in the chapter.

Chapter Opener
Sample

Fiction Chapter Headings

In fiction, the format of chapter headings is left to the author's discretion much more than it is in nonfiction. Although years ago, the chapters in works of fiction were marked by both numbers and

Chapter Opener
Sample

titles, most contemporary fiction simply uses numbered chapters to divide the story into sections. But there is plenty of opportunity to be creative. If you choose to use chapter titles, make sure that they contribute to your work in a meaningful way.

BACK MATTER

Back matter, or *end matter*, comprises any section that is meant to bring closure to the main text, offer additional clarification of subjects mentioned in the book, or suggest related works. Depending on the category of the book, back matter may include sections such as a conclusion, afterword, epilogue, glossary, or resources, among others.

Conclusion (Nonfiction, Optional)

A *conclusion* should summarize in a few pages the information laid out in the main text of a nonfiction title. It is a means of helping the reader mentally digest, so to speak, what he has just taken in.

Epilogue (Fiction, Optional)

In a work of fiction, sometimes an author will write an *epilogue*, which acts as the final chapter of a book and often serves to tie up loose ends regarding the fates of its characters. It may take place at a point in time long after the end of the main plot and perhaps even set up the possibility of a sequel. Sometimes it is used to include a closing scene that is worthwhile but only peripherally related to the main characters.

Afterword (Optional)

An author uses an *afterword* to explain what drove him to write his book, or to tell the story of how the idea for his book developed, making it similar in structure and content to a preface. To avoid redundancy, generally an author would not include both an afterword and a preface in a book. On occasion, someone other than the author may write an afterword to add a cultural or historical perspective.

Appendices

Appendices are used to add supplementary information or supporting data that the reader may find relevant, but which would impede the flow of the main text were it to be placed there. Nonfiction works contain appendices much more frequently than do fiction books, and they mainly consist of the glossary, bibliography, and references, but could include charts, tables, figures, letters, or other informative materials. Some genres of fiction are better suited to the inclusion of appendices than others. A historical novel, for example, could include a bibliography or references, while children's literature has been known to use glossaries for terms with which young readers may be unfamiliar.

Glossary (Optional)

A book should include a *glossary* to explain any terms that appear in the text and might be new or unfamiliar to its readers. Nonfiction books that contain numerous technical terms often include glossaries. As mentioned, while fiction titles do not often use glossaries, a children's book will sometimes add one to help young readers improve their vocabularies.

In nonfiction works, the glossary generally includes terms used within the book that are newly introduced, specialized, or uncommon.

Resources (Nonfiction, Optional)

The *resources* generally refer to a list of businesses or organizations that are associated in some way with a book's subject matter. Each entry should include the name, address or website, contact information, and a brief description of the resource.

Recommended Reading (Nonfiction, Optional)

As its heading suggests, recommended reading is a list of other works that might broaden a reader's understanding of a particular nonfiction book or complement its subject matter.

References or Bibliography (Nonfiction)

Proper citations add credibility to your nonfiction book and support your arguments. Citations also give readers the opportunity to further explore the subject of your work.

Citations are used to give credit to the sources utilized by an author in the writing of his book. A citation generally includes the name of the referenced work, its author, and its publication information. Although a *bibliography* and *references* are each used to cite pertinent works, they actually perform slightly different functions. An author may employ one or both, depending on his need. (If using both, the bibliography should appear immediately after the references.) References credit only those sources that have been used to support a point or argument directly. A bibliography is a list of every text consulted by an author in the writing of his book, which may include works directly referenced as well as any other material used for the purpose of research.

Entries in a bibliography are typically listed alphabetically. References may be arranged alphabetically but are frequently formatted numerically, as seen in footnotes and endnotes, which use corresponding superscript numbers to indicate when supporting material has been used in a text. These numbers are placed at the end of their associated statements. Footnotes, however, are not relevant to this discussion of back matter, as they appear at the bottom of pages in body matter. Endnotes, however, point readers to sources noted at the back of a book and tend to be a tidier choice if there are copious instances of supporting references.

In addition to alphabetizing entries in a bibliography, some authors like to list works by category (alphabetizing within each category), making it easier for readers to find works on specific topics highlighted in a book. Some authors create annotated bibliographies, which include a brief summary of each entry. Any one of these bibliographical formats is acceptable. The most important rule is to be consistent.

When it comes to typing citations, an author must choose to follow a particular citation style, which dictates the information required in a citation and the order in which this information should appear. The choice of citation style is often based on the type of book being produced. Texts on education, psychology, and sciences generally use APA (American Psychological Association) citation style.

Texts on topics found in the humanities typically use MLA (Modern Language Association) style. Books on history, business, or fine arts tend to use Chicago style. (Turabian style is a slightly modified version of Chicago style that is used in high school or college papers, theses, or dissertations.) Once an author decides on which style to follow, he should cite each source according to the style rules for its type. The following list illustrates the rules for different kinds of referenced material according to the major citation styles, along with examples.

APA (AMERICAN PSYCHOLOGICAL ASSOCIATION)

BOOK

Author's last name, first initial. (Year of publication). *Title of work.* Publisher City, State: Publisher.

Example:

Yager, J. (1997). *Friendshifts.* Stamford, CT: Hannacroix Creek Books, Inc.

JOURNAL

Author's last name, first initial. (Year of publication). Title of article. *Title of Journal, volume* (issue), page range.

Example:

Rosado, J. (2010). Nietzsche and the flogging of a horse in Turin. *Perspectives on Philosophy,* 88(6), 271–289.

NEWSPAPER

Author's last name, first initial. (Year, Month Date of Publication). Title of article. *Title of Newspaper,* page range.

Example:

Palin, T. (1985, March 28). Reunited and it feels so good. *Gimli Press,* p. C5.

MAGAZINE

Author's last name, first initial. (Year, Month Date of Publication). Title of article. *Title of Magazine, volume* (issue), page range.

Example:

Jarkels, P. (2010, July 23–30). Holiday spirit: Witnessing the power of wishing others well. *People and Places Worldwide*, 150(7), 37–39.

WEBSITE

Author's last name, first initial. (Year, Month Date of Publication). Title of webpage/article. Retrieved from URL.

Example:

Foley, D. (2016, October 1). Even a little bit of exercise can go a long way. Retrieved from http://exercisedaily.com/even-a-little-bit-of-exercise-can-go-a-long-way-1526798495.

MLA (MODERN LANGUAGE ASSOCIATION)

BOOK

Author's last name, first name. *Title of work*. Publisher, Year of Publication, page range.

Example:

Yager, Jan. *Friendshifts*. Hannacroix Creek Books, Inc., 1997, 64–65.

JOURNAL

Author's last name, first name. "Title of article." *Title of Journal*, volume, issue, Month Year of Publication, page range.

Example:

Rosado, Jeannie. "Nietzsche and the Flogging of a Horse in Turin." *Perspectives on Philosophy*, vol. 88, no. 6, Oct. 2010, pp. 271–289.

NEWSPAPER

"Title of the article." *Title of Newspaper,* Date Month Year of Publication, edition (if applicable), page range.

Example:

Palin, Teddy. "Reunited and It Feels So Good." *Gimli Press*, 28 March 1985, late ed., p. C5.

MAGAZINE

Author's last name, first name. "Title of the article." *Title of Magazine,* volume (if applicable), issue (if applicable), Date Month Year of Publication, page range.

Example:

Jarkels, Paul. "Holiday Spirit: Witnessing the Power of Wishing Others Well." *People and Places Worldwide,* vol. 150, no. 7, 23–30 July 2010, pp. 37–39.

WEBSITE

Author's last name, first name. "Title of the Article or Individual Page." *Title of website,* Name of Publisher, Date Month Year of Publication, URL.

Example:

Foley, Derek. "Even a Little Bit of Exercise Can Go a Long Way." *Exercise Daily,* Muscles Media, 1 Oct. 2016, http://exercisedaily.com/even-a-little -bit-of-exercise-can-go-a-long-way-1526798495.

CHICAGO (CHICAGO MANUAL OF STYLE)

BOOK

Author's last name, first name. *Title of Work.* Publisher's City and State: Publisher, Year of Publication.

Example:

Yager, Jan. *Friendshifts.* Stamford, CT: Hannacroix Creek Books, Inc., 1997.

JOURNAL

Author's last name, first name. "Title of article." *Title of Journal* volume, issue (Year of Publication). page range.

Example:

Rosado, Jeannie. "Nietzsche and the Flogging of a Horse in Turin." *Perspectives on Philosophy* 88, no. 6 (2010). 271–289.

NEWSPAPER

Author's last name, first name. "Article Title." *Title of Newspaper,* Month Date, Year of Publication.

Example:

Palin, Teddy. "Reunited and It Feels So Good." *Gimli Press,* March 28, 1985.

MAGAZINE

Author's last name, first name. "Article Title." *Title of Magazine,* Month Date, Year of Publication.

Example:

Jarkels, Paul. "Holiday Spirit: Witnessing the Power of Wishing Others Well." *People and Places Worldwide,* July 23–30, 2010.

WEBSITE

Last name, First name. "Article Title." Title of Website. Month Date, Year of Publication. Modified Month Date, Year (if applicable). URL (accessed Month date, Year).

Example:

Foley, Derek. "Even a Little Bit of Exercise Can Go a Long Way." Exercise Daily. Oct. 1, 2016. http://exercisedaily.com/even-a-little-bit-of-exercise-can-go-a-long-way-1526798495 (accessed Jan. 3, 2017).

When it comes to self-publishing, one of the fastest and easiest ways to create a high-quality product is to find a book you admire for its professionalism and emulate it. There is no need to reinvent the wheel. If you plan to include citations in a nonfiction book, choose a nonfiction title that is in your subcategory (e.g., a business book or self-help title), see which citation style it follows, and then use its citations as a guide as you prepare your own.

About the Author (Optional)

A book may dedicate a page after the citations to relevant biographical information regarding its author (entitled "About the Author").

The literacy website www.easybib.com provides examples of MLA, APA, and Chicago style entries and can also format your citations automatically.

It typically includes the educational background, credentials, work history, and other published works of the author. Often a shorter version of this biography will appear on the back cover (or on the back flap of the dust jacket if it is a hardcover book).

In works of fiction, the author biography is usually quite brief, mentioning the author's name, place of birth, current place of residence, and noteworthy previous releases. The biographies of nonfiction authors, however, tend to be much longer—sometimes even as long as two pages. This is because a nonfiction author's biography is essentially meant to convince readers of the merits of his book by touting his authority in a particular subject. It is a sales tactic.

Occasionally author biographies are accompanied by headshots of the authors, but this is typically reserved for dust jackets.

Index (Nonfiction, Optional)

An *index* is an alphabetical list of important words, terms, or concepts mentioned in a book and the corresponding pages on which each of them is discussed. Readers usually appreciate an index in a nonfiction book. Libraries sometimes make it a requirement for purchasing a book. An index can be challenging to create and may require the help of a professional *indexer*. This is an additional expense for which, unfortunately, too few self-publishers budget, much to their disappointment when the academic, library, or average reader response to their nonfiction book is, "Where is the index?"

Nevertheless, an index is optional, so you should decide whether you have the time and money to include a good index in your nonfiction book. If you decide to write your own index, be sure to consult the index of a professionally published book as a guide.

CONCLUSION

Have you ever looked inside a book and noticed that something seemed a bit off? Maybe the publishing company's information was on an inappropriate page, or the copyright information appeared at the end of the book. When a book has been improperly sequenced, you may not be able to determine exactly why that book looks unprofessional, but it will look like the work of an amateur all the same. Errors in sequencing can be huge "tells" that a book is self-published. Thankfully, by simply following the standard rules of sequencing that a majority of the book industry follows, you should be able to get your text to look like the bestsellers you see on the shelves. Now that you know these rules, it is time to learn how to turn your finished manuscript into a published book.

CHAPTER 3

$\mathcal{G}$ETTING YOUR MANUSCRIPT READY FOR PUBLICATION

---

*A well-composed book is a magic carpet
on which we are wafted to a world that
we cannot enter in any other way.*
—CAROLINE GORDON, AUTHOR AND CRITIC

The day has finally arrived. Whether it has taken you years, months, or just a few weeks to complete your manuscript, you have now decided that it is officially finished. There is a point at which every writer must say, "Enough. It is done." You are ready for the next phase in this process, which involves getting your book edited, proofread, and perhaps even reviewed by your peers. The value of good editing and proofreading cannot be stressed enough. It is a critical and necessary step to ensure that your publication presents itself professionally.

FINALIZING YOUR COPY

In the publishing houses of years past, you may have found a number of different editorial professionals working to finalize a manuscript, including the following individuals:

- **Developmental editor, or substantive editor.** Individual who works with a writer to help develop or flesh out the themes of a fictional story or the information provided in a nonfiction work.

- **Copy editor, or line editor.** Individual who corrects grammatical errors in a manuscript and ensures consistency of style and format.

- **Proofreader.** Individual who reviews the preliminary version of a typeset book (also called a *galley*) for typos, page balance, and layout.

- **Indexer.** Individual who creates an alphabetical listing of words, terms, or concepts and the corresponding pages on which these words, terms, or concepts appear in a book.

In contrast, many of the publishing houses of today task only one or two individuals to perform a number of these responsibilities. These individuals may be in-house employees or freelancers. As a writer, the more you understand the various talents necessary to finalize your manuscript, the better prepared you will be to figure out what your work may need and who you may need to hire to do this work.

Editing

An editor is not a proofreader but rather provides more substantive feedback. She manages the contents of a book and how it reads. In nonfiction, an editor deals with whether a book is well organized and covers its topic thoroughly. She will make sure there are no unanswered questions that may leave readers frustrated. She will also make sure that the terms in a manuscript conform to its *style sheet*. (See "Style Sheet" on page 43.) Moreover, she will confirm that all of the expected elements of a nonfiction book are present, including the title page, copyright page (including ISBN number and LCCN), table of contents, citations, index, and author biography.

In fiction, an editor will look for a variety of issues, from continuity (if a car is red in the beginning of a chapter, is it still red later on in the novel?) to whether a book's storyline is clear, its characters distinctive, and its dialogue believable. In children's literature, an editor might verify that a book's wording and illustrations are appropriate for its targeted age group.

To save time, you might have an editor review the final draft of your book while some or all the chapters are with others for peer review.

Peer Review

Peer review is different from sharing some or all your final manuscript with others to get advance praise. Getting feedback from other authors or experts is a step you might want to take if you are concerned about your book's reception. Sending one or all chapters out for peer review will slow down the process of publishing your book, but you might find it a worthwhile endeavor.

When I was working on my first self-published book, I was so determined that its quality would meet the standards set by my previous books, which had been produced by major publishing houses, that I sent a portion of the manuscript out for peer review by various psychologists and sociologists. After I had considered their constructive comments and made a few changes to the text, I went back to a number of these individuals to ask if I could send my entire manuscript to them for possible advance praise. Having already read one or two chapters, they were eager to read the entire book.

Having your final manuscript reviewed by knowledgeable peers may add time to your publishing schedule, but it may also identify faults you hadn't noticed and help you avoid criticism upon publication.

Proofreading

Proofreading is an important part of the publishing process and something for which you are responsible as a self-publisher. Once an editor's changes have been accepted and incorporated, it is time to turn your finalized manuscript over to your proofreader.

You will want to hire a perfectionist as your proofreader. An excellent proofreader should catch every typographical or spelling error. Of course, no one is perfect, so you should review your proofreader's job yourself and even consider having a second or third pair of eyes take a look at the final proofread manuscript. The point is that you will need at least one proofreader to review, or "proof," your

When it comes to proofreading, using a spell-check program isn't sufficient. You need a human touch, or, more precisely, a human eye. A good proofreader will catch errors a computer will miss, particularly in regard to grammar.

book. You might think that using a spell-check program in software such as Microsoft Word would be sufficient, but you would be incorrect. A trained proofreader with a careful eye for typos, spelling, and grammatical errors will find things a software program will miss. Most spell-check programs have blind spots, such as being unable to check words typed in all caps, recognize certain proper nouns, or adequately point out grammatical errors. You need a proofreader who can catch all these problems. Just one typo or textual error can cause a reader to question the professionalism of a book. Just one mistake can signal "amateur self-publisher" to anyone, especially critics and others in the media.

The cost of hiring a proofreader can range from as low as $1 per page to as high as $2.50 or more per page, depending upon the location of the proofreader, the complexity of the material, how quickly you need your manuscript proofread, if this project may lead to repeat business, the length of your manuscript, and other factors. Although most proofreaders charge by the page, some may charge by the hour, and others may be open to accepting a flat fee.

Here are tasks that a proofreader is expected to handle:

- Catching and correcting any typos.

- Catching and correcting any spelling errors. (Hopefully there will be few of these if you have used an editor, who should have already addressed them.)

- Double-checking the consistency of a manuscript by consulting the style sheet. (See "Style Sheet" on page 43.)

- Catching grammatical errors an editor might have missed.

- Fact-checking when asked to do so.

These days, proofreaders typically work on electronic documents directly, using Microsoft Word's "track changes" feature to make any changes. Authors then have an opportunity to accept or reject each change. (Each person working on a document should use a different color font when making any changes or suggestions, which should allow the author to see the origin of any recommendation clearly.)

> ## *Style Sheet*
>
> As you write your manuscript, compose a document that will help you achieve consistency of style throughout. This is called a *style sheet*, and should include the spelling of technical terms (e.g., "angiogenesis"); the chosen spelling of words that may be spelled in different ways (e.g., "travelling" rather than "traveling"); whether to capitalize a word or not; and any other style decisions made during the processes of writing and editing your manuscript. Keep it handy and refer to it any time you have forgotten your book's stylistic rules.

If a proofreader does not have Microsoft Word or prefers to proofread the old-fashioned way, using a hard copy, recommended changes might end up easier to discern, but then someone must go to the master document and make corrections.

A proofreader is the last pair of eyes on a manuscript before it goes to the interior book designer. Although some designers are willing to work with an edited manuscript rather than a finalized version to create sample pages, it is best to have a proofread version ready or very close to ready at this point.

Although minor changes may be made to a proofread text, in most cases, you should think of your proofread manuscript as being set in stone. You may still review your proofread manuscript and address any questions about facts, spelling, or any other technical or creative issues, but your proofreader is usually the last person to read your book cover to cover before it is presented to the public.

Working with Freelancers

An editor and a proofreader serve different functions, but both are necessary players in the manuscript-to-finished-book process. Unfortunately, too many self-publishers think they can act as their own editors and proofreaders, or edit their own manuscripts and hire just proofreaders, or hire editors and then do their own proofreading. They may save some money in editing or proofing their own work,

Before you hire a freelance editor, be sure to determine the type of editorial role she will play. Will she focus on the overall view of your book, handle sentence structure and grammar, or deal with all editorial aspects of your work? All these elements will need to be addressed, so you should find out whether you will have to hire more than one freelancer to finalize your manuscript.

but it will be difficult for them to recognize any resultant sacrifice in quality until their book is in print and it is too late to do anything about it.

If you were publishing your book with a traditional publisher, the acquisitions editor (who read your manuscript and then offered you a contract to publish your book) would assign your manuscript to an in-house or freelance copy editor. As a self-publisher, however, you are responsible for finding an editor, provided you have made the (right) decision not to edit your manuscript yourself.

Freelance editors are usually paid by the page or by the project. When looking for an editor, it is important to distinguish between the functions of a *developmental editor*, who looks at the "big picture" of a manuscript, and those of a *copy editor*, who is more concerned with grammar and sentence structure. Both these editorial roles are useful, so if you can afford to hire a separate editor to handle each one, you might want to do so. Otherwise, be sure to hire an editor who can manage the two tasks well.

If you're writing a nonfiction book, a certain amount of expertise in a particular subject may be of value in an editor. In this case, you might want to hire an editor who has some knowledge in your book's field of interest. If you are concerned only with whether your nonfiction book is understandable to the average reader, you might simply hire a skilled editor rather than someone who is also considered a "subject matter expert," or SME, and alert her of this concern.

Whether you call the person who will take your finished manuscript and craft it into its finalized version a copy editor, book editor, developmental editor, or some other title, this is the individual who is supposed to make sure your book reads as well as it can, removing unnecessary text, rearranging paragraphs, and questioning whether more information might be needed. In the end, a good editor is invaluable in determining whether your manuscript will succeed as a novel, nonfiction work, cookbook, or whatever type of book you may be writing.

Norwegian-based author Heidi Eljarbø describes her process of hiring an editor as follows:

So you finish writing your novel. You write "The End," and that overwhelming feeling of accomplishment sets in. You celebrate and become excited about getting your book out there, until a little voice whispers a four-letter word in your ear: EDIT.

By many called the dreaded edits. I feel differently about it. Editing is great. It polishes your story and makes it shine.

One of the most important things before publishing is to have someone truly competent go through your book in detail. I sent the first chapter to three different professional editors and asked them for a free sample edit. When I received the samples back, it was easy to choose. The three editors worked very differently. The first had a know-it-all attitude. I felt right away that I would have problems going through my manuscript with him. The second had misunderstood his editing job and changed my chapter into an unrecognizable story with words I would never have used. The third picked up on every mistake and noticed if I missed a beat or the storyline had too many bumps. She politely suggested changes to sentences that were incomprehensible to the reader and explained why.

At this point, I did not worry if the third editor cost a dollar or two more than the others.

The most important thing was that she could help my manuscript become even better. Luckily, she charged a fair price, almost half of what the first editor asked. A happy win-win situation for me.

I have learned to love editing. I learn so much and get excited about the progress and improved manuscript. It's an investment that makes me feel safer when the time comes to present my book to the world.

When looking for an editor, you might find someone has worked at a publishing company or simply holds a bachelor of arts degree with a major in English literature. Developmental editors are editors who should have a track record of crafting books that go on to critical and, hopefully, commercial success. Developmental editors are especially helpful to self-publishers of nonfiction who do not see themselves as authors per se, but rather as experts with information

Before hiring a freelance editor, it's a good idea to ask her to perform a free sample edit of a portion of your manuscript. This will enable you to determine if she has the skills needed to do the job and if the two of you will be able to work together productively.

to share, or to self-publishers of fiction who feel they have stories to tell but need a second pair of eyes to ensure they avoid sounding redundant or inconsistent in their writings.

A copy editor will likely read your manuscript not once but usually three times: Once to get an overview of the book; a second time to look at each and every paragraph, sentence, and word and note any errors, inconsistencies, or grammatical or structural problems; and, after these issues have been fixed, a third time to ensure the changes have been made properly.

Some proofreaders will include editing as part of their proofreading cost, but, as noted, be careful about using one person for these two functions. You might save money in the short run, but in the long run you might regret that you did not have an additional pair of eyes to give you feedback before finalizing your manuscript.

Especially in regard to nonfiction books, if you need to clear permissions for any sources you have quoted, you may want to do so after your editor and you agree on the final version of your manuscript but before you give it to your proofreader. If someone you thought would grant permission for the use of a quotation decides to change her mind, make extensive changes to the quotation, or request too steep of a fee to reprint the material, you may choose not to include the quoted text and have to make a few changes to your book. A proofreader should review the final version of your book, so it is best to have such editorial matters sorted out in advance of having it proofread.

CLEARING ANY NECESSARY PERMISSIONS

You may need to get permission to use printed material, charts, tables, photographs, or illustrations that are not your own, particularly if you are writing a nonfiction book. On occasion, this can be a time-consuming task, so make sure you allocate enough time to complete it.

Publishers usually use standard release letters to secure permissions, which are drawn up by company lawyers. As a self-publisher, if you would like to reprint material that was created by someone other than yourself, you may draft a simple release letter for the

Permission Letter with Release Form

(Current Date)

Ms. Schneidler

_____ Street

_____, NY 10000

Dear Ms. _____,

I am in the process of preparing my forthcoming book tentatively entitled _____, to be published by [name of your company] [or "to be self-published"]. May I have permission to reprint the attached [material, photo, recipe, graphic, etc.]? Naturally, you will be credited as the [author, creator, photographer, etc.] of the [material, photo, recipe, graphic, etc.].

Please provide the desired credit line:

_____

_____

For your convenience, a release form is provided below. Please print this letter, sign the form below, and return it to me at your earliest convenience.

Thank you for your attention to this matter. I look forward to hearing from you.

Sincerely,

Author's name

Address

Phone contact

Email address

I (We) grant permission for the use requested above.

Name _____   Date _____

creator of this material to sign. It should include a copy of the requested material and may allow the original author to edit it for publication as she sees fit. You may, however, wish to add language that states the source will be waiving her right to see the final quotation or graphic, which may be edited for grammar or length.

If you think this condition might upset the source of the requested material, you could either wait to get permission until the format of the usage has been finalized or show it to the source twice—once to get preliminary approval and a second time to get final approval after any edits have been made.

An example of a permission letter with release form is provided on page 47.

GETTING ENDORSEMENTS

Blurbs, or advance praise, as these quotations are known, can foster early positive attention for your book. For my first self-published book, *Friendshifts,* I used Stephen Covey's blockbuster title *The 7 Habits of Highly Effective People* as a model. If Covey's book included more than fifteen blurbs, so should mine. I asked Dr. James Shuart, the president of my alma mater, Hofstra University, for a blurb and he gladly provided an enthusiastic statement. I also asked psychologists, sociologists, and popular authors and was granted many more words of advance praise.

Now, to save time, I aim for no more than half a dozen advance quotations. It is a time-consuming task to get them, and today, people are more pressed for time than ever before. Nevertheless, if you feel you need a lot of advance praise, that's fine. Keep in mind that you can always put additional advance praise in your marketing materials at a later date.

Be aware that if you want to get six advance quotations, you might have to ask twice or even three times as many people, as not everyone will have time to write an endorsement. The other benefit of asking for more quotations than you plan on using is that you just might get them all, giving yourself options from which to choose. If you get an amazing blurb from someone who is especially recognizable, either as a celebrity or someone associated with your topic or genre, you might even put that quotation on the front cover of your book. Remember that whatever goes on the front cover will be visible not only to people shopping at brick-and-mortar bookstores but also to people browsing online retailers, which typically display the covers of the books they sell.

Still, advance praise is totally optional, so do not fret if you do not have the time or the inclination to seek out endorsements. I like advance praise and have never been shy about asking people to read and endorse one of my books. I figure someone could always say no, and occasionally someone has said no. I try to approach individuals who I think will say yes, and I work hard on crafting a compelling email to make my request, hoping to increase the likelihood that they will agree to help me.

Here is my advice for getting endorsements for your book:

- Be persistent. Remember that an endorsement is usually more important to you than it is to the person giving it to you, especially if it is coming from a high-profile business person or celebrity.

- Make a list that includes extra people in case some of those you contact simply cannot do it. By the time you get to the endorsement stage, you are usually moving along quickly to publication and time is of the essence. If you have many people to contact, when one of them says no, you can simply go to the next one on the list without slowing down to figure out what you should do or worrying about getting left empty-handed.

- If you already have one or more blurbs, you can share them with any new sources of advance praise so that they might avoid duplication. This will also show them the types of comments you're hoping for.

- If possible, get the mailing address of each of your sources so you can send a complimentary copy of your book to each person. It's a way of saying thank you and spreading the word about your book.

Although endorsements can bring attention to your book, don't worry if you cannot seem to get any, or if you simply don't want to dedicate the time it takes to seek them out. They are optional.

BECOMING A BUSINESS

Once you have decided to self-publish your book, you are no longer just an author; you must also become a business. First, of course, you must name your business. The name of your publishing company should be something other than your name (or pen name). For example, I named my publishing company Hannacroix Creek Books after a creek that ran behind my husband's childhood home. Once you have chosen the name of your company, perform an online search to be sure it isn't already in use by another publisher.

Next, determine which type of business entity you would like your company to be. If you have an attorney, consult with her on this matter. If you do not have an attorney, consider discussing this issue with a literary lawyer on a flat-fee basis, or at least do some research on the benefits of creating a corporation, limited liability company (LLC), or some other form of business entity for your self-publishing venture. Websites such as www.incorporate.com and www.legalzoom.com contain information on the differences between business entities and can register your company as the entity of your choice for a fee.

You can always register your company as a "Doing Business As," or DBA, instead of a proper business entity. (Ask your municipal clerk's office how to do so.) If you choose to use a DBA, all business

Books in Print (BIP)

Maintained by R.R. Bowker LLC, Books in Print (www.booksin-print.com) is a bibliographic database with information on over 20 million titles. It is a valuable resource for potential buyers, including retailers, consumers, and libraries around the world. BIP lists in-print, forthcoming, and out-of-print titles. To add your book to this database, you may create a free account and enter the required data. If you must change your book's publication date or price, make sure you make these amendments in the master listing of Books in Print so the data associated with your title is up to date and accurate.

income will be linked to your personal social security number, or SSN, instead of an employer identification number, or EIN, which is issued by the Internal Revenue Service (IRS). Although the use of a DBA is a perfectly reasonable option, registering your company as a separate business entity offers certain legal protections that you would not have otherwise.

Talk to a lawyer or an accountant to find out the pros or cons of each of these approaches to starting your company.

AVOIDING SCAMMERS

Self-publishers are an eager group. Each self-publisher is typically driven by a passion for a cause or a creative story. This enthusiasm may also leave self-publishers vulnerable to scammers. What do I mean by "scammers"? I am referring to someone who either inflates the cost of a service or provides a service for a reasonable price but performs the job unsatisfactorily.

Many self-publishers are clueless about the costs associated with most publishing services. The truth is that these costs vary according to the difficulty of a book project and the skill level of the service provider. The amount of paid labor required will also vary widely from book to book. A well-written first draft of around 50,000 words (a standard length for adult nonfiction or fiction) will generate very different expenses than a poorly written manuscript of 100,000 words.

If you would like to get an idea of the range of costs for different publishing services, the Editorial Freelancers Association (EFA) publishes a list of editorial rates on its website (www.the-efa.org/rates). Just remember these rates depend on a number of factors and are negotiable.

Unless you have a family member or friend who is a qualified editor or proofreader, or has experience in clearing permissions, researching, or performing other such publishing tasks, be prepared to spend some money on your self-published book if you would like to end up with a product of which you can be proud. It is too hard to catch your own mistakes. An extra pair of eyes—preferably eyes that

> Your enthusiasm as a self-publisher may make you vulnerable to service providers that are less than honest. If someone guarantees you a bestseller, turn around and walk the other way.

have been trained in editing or proofreading—is needed to achieve a professional-looking project.

CONCLUSION

You should now be familiar with all the "nuts and bolts" involved in taking your final draft and turning it into the text you will use when you go to print. Moreover, even after your manuscript has been edited and proofread, and you've gotten any necessary permissions and every possible endorsement, you will still have to establish your publishing company as a business. If it all seems like a lot of work, that is because it is—but you can accomplish it. Before you realize it, you will have a completed text and may start envisioning it bound and sitting on someone's nightstand. And this is when the next phase of your work will begin.

As you are surely beginning to understand, the success of your book has almost as much to do with how it looks as it does with what it says. Part Two will teach you how to present your work to the world, from your book's cover to its interior. It is a vital lesson for a self-publisher to learn because, yes, people do judge a book by its cover—and by its layout as well. In addition to describing the intricacies of manufacturing a printed book, Part Two will also take you through the many different options at your disposal for creating an e-book or audiobook.

CHAPTER 4

COVER DESIGN 101

*The first step in designing a compelling book cover is
learning about your target market. Who is likely to
buy your book? What group of people did you have
in mind when you wrote your book? . . . Your book
needs to have a look and feel that is similar (but not
too similar) to the others in the same category so that
potential readers are not thrown off by it at first glance.*
—FIONA RAVEN AND GLENNA COLLETT,
BOOK DESIGN MADE SIMPLE

Not judging a book by its cover is good advice in general, but if
you are actually in the business of publishing books, you should
assume no one will ever follow it. Your book will absolutely be
judged by its cover. A study conducted several years ago by the
Stanford University Publishing Program found that the average
bookstore customer takes approximately three seconds to look at a
book cover. If it doesn't grab the customer's attention within three
seconds, he simply moves on to the next book.

Essentially, a book's cover tells a potential reader almost instantly
whether to buy that book. Moreover, if a book's cover makes the
book appear to be self-published, critics and other people in the
media might not bother to read it. Even if you are able to drive people to look at your self-published book through your own publicity
efforts, a poorly designed cover could stop a sale in its tracks.

Most commercial publishing houses employ art directors to handle cover designs. An art director may work with a freelance artist or an in-house artist in the creation of a book cover. The goal of a publishing house's art director is simple: To make sure the books published by that company all have covers that look professionally prepared, provide all the right information, and catch people's attention. Following certain common rules for their book covers, art directors ensure that every aspect of a book's exterior has been designed to sell that book, including its front cover, spine, and back cover. As this chapter will show you, by understanding and following these design principles, you can create a memorable and professionally complete cover, whether you are working with an experienced cover artist or by yourself.

FRONT COVER

Go into any bookstore or library and you will see hundreds and hundreds of books. At first glance, all of them look different. If you take the time to study them, however, you will see that the vast majority of these books conform to specific rules of design. Most of these rules, in fact, have been around for over a hundred years. They are not complicated or difficult to follow. Once you see what the creation of a standard front cover entails, you will begin to recognize the similarities among many book covers.

There are five important elements involved in an effective front cover. These include:

- placement and size of copy
- typeface style
- coloration
- background
- design

While there are slight differences between fiction and nonfiction front covers, the overall elements remain the same. No matter how you combine these elements, the two most important questions to keep in mind are: "Will the finished cover look as good as any commercially produced cover?" and "Will the cover stand out?" If you can answer yes to both questions, your design is a good one.

■ PLACEMENT AND SIZE OF COPY

While one cover may appear quite unlike another, almost all covers provide informational copy and arrange it in a certain way. Let's take a look at the cover copy from top to bottom.

Sell Line

A *sell line* is normally a single sentence located directly at the top of a front cover. Usually associated with nonfiction works, it briefly describes a book or the benefits a book may provide. It may stretch across a front cover on one, two, or three lines.

Quotation

A *quotation* may be used instead of a sell line. Like a sell line, it should provide a positive statement that offers the reader an understanding of what's in the book. Most often, quotations are used for works of fiction. A quotation may come from a newspaper or magazine review, an individual whose name people would recognize, or an expert on a book's subject matter. A quotation may stretch across a front cover on one, two, or three lines and should always be accompanied by a credit line set below it in a smaller typeface.

Title

There are two types of titles in both fiction and nonfiction. One specifically explains what the book is about, the other is designed to be intriguing. A title may be composed of one or two words, or even a full but short sentence. Standard placement for a title is above the midpoint of a cover, although it can extend further down.

Subtitle

A *subtitle*, or *secondary title*, of a nonfiction work is meant to clarify the focus of the book. To some degree it is similar to a sell line, although with less emphasis on a book's benefits. A subtitle falls directly below the title. It may stretch across a front cover on one, two, or three lines.

Although works of fiction generally do not include subtitles, the most commonly used subtitle in this category would likely be "A Novel," while occasionally an entire phrase may be used to enhance a title.

Author's Name

The name of a book's author normally appears at the bottom of the front cover. If an author has any professional credentials, such as a PhD or MD, he may add them to his name. (In the case of some-one with a doctorate, he may use the abbreviation "Dr." before his name instead of the corresponding professional abbreviation after his name if he so wishes.)

Every once in a while, you may see an author's name appear above the title of a book—in some cases, in a larger typeface than the one used for the title itself. This style is normally reserved for best-selling authors whose names alone can make readers stop and pick up their books. Understandably, it doesn't work quite as well for most other writers.

It is important to note that one of the most common "tells" of a self-published book is when the author's name is preceded by the word "By." Do not include this word before an author's name ever!

Author's Credit Line

When an author has an attribute that may catch the eye of a reader, it is always a good idea to place it below his name. Like advance praise, an advantageous credit can lend credibility to a book in the eyes of a potential reader. A few examples of such attributes include "Founder and President of . . . ," "Best-Selling Author of . . . ," and "Winner of the . . . Award." If you have a strong enough credit, it can enhance your profile as an author. A credit should be only one line long and set in a smaller typeface than the one used for the author's name.

Follow the Rules

- When considering the size of each part of the front cover copy, there is a simple formula to use. In order, from biggest to smallest font, the sections are title, subtitle, author's name, sell line or quotation, and author's credit line.

   Technically speaking, font size is measured in units called *points*, with a 30-point font being relatively large and a 10-point font being on the small side. Eyeballing your cover copy for size with the recently mentioned formula in mind is a quick and easy way to build an appropriate front cover.

- On most standard front covers, copy is set up to be flush left, flush right, or centered.

- When copy stretches over more than one line, never allow a word break to end a line with a hyphen, and try to keep line lengths similar. Sometimes this task requires rewriting copy to make lines fit, but the cover will look better for it.

| FLUSH LEFT | CENTERED | FLUSH RIGHT |

■ TYPEFACE STYLE

Although the terms "typeface" and "font" are often used interchangeably, technically they refer to different concepts. A typeface is a family of characters that share one basic design, while a font is a particular size and variation of a typeface.

Typefaces, also commonly referred to as *fonts,* come in hundreds of different styles. To better determine which fonts you should use, it is helpful to understand the three basic classifications of typeface.

Serif

Serifs refer to the little lines or strokes attached to the ends of larger strokes in a letter or symbol. A book's interior is normally typeset using a serif font. While there are many fonts with serifs, the following examples are relatively common in publishing:

Baskerville	Georgia
Book Antiqua	Goudy Old Style
Bookman Old Style	Minion
Centaur	Palatino
Garamond	Times New Roman

Sans-Serif

The term *sans serif* refers to letters and symbols that do not feature extended lines at their ends. These characters are designed to have a modern look. The following examples are standard sans-serif fonts:

Arial	News Gothic
Gill Sans	Franklin Gothic
Helvetica	Verdana

Display

Display typefaces are generally considered to be unusual fonts. They range from wacky-looking typefaces to beautiful scripts, from vegetables put together to form letters to people extending their bodies in the shape of letters. Display typefaces are not commonly seen on front covers, but as long as it can be read without difficulty, a display font is always an option. The following examples are popular display fonts:

𝕬rnold 𝕭öcklin   **Cooper Black**

Bauhaus   Papyrus

Bodini   **STENCIL**

Follow the Rules

- When selecting which typefaces to use on a front cover, avoid using only one style. Doing so could appear boring. On the other hand, don't use more than three different styles, which could make your cover appear too busy.

- A display typeface should be used only in a title, as it will draw attention to wherever it appears.

- Provided you are not using a display typeface, the title of a book and its author's name may be set in the same font, with the title set in a larger font than that used for the author's name.

■ COLORATION

Before the age of digital printing, the cost of using more than one or two colors on a cover could be very expensive. These days, however, advancements in printing technology have made the use of any number of colors on a cover affordable. If you would like to select a specific color for your copy or the space behind your copy, there are two ways of doing so. You can select a color from the self-publishing program you are using, or—like a cover designer—you can refer to the standard PMS swatch book of colors.

The standard book of colors used by printers to indicate the exact color ink required for their presses is based on the Pantone Matching System book, or PMS book. By selecting PMS colors and letting your printer know the number codes associated with them, you can ensure the use of your exact color choices on your cover.

Follow the Rules

- Avoid using only one color or shades of only one color, which could appear boring and make a book look self-published. The use of two or three different colors for the various lines of copy on a cover is standard.

- Try matching the color used for the title with the color used for the author's name.

- Consider using a dark color for the sell line or author's credit line.

■ BACKGROUND

The background behind a front cover's copy can be a very critical element of a cover's design. It may be composed of a solid color. When using a darker color, copy can be "knocked out" to white or filled in with any other color. A front cover's background may also be a textured image—a slightly marbleized surface, a wood grain, or anything related to a book's topic. Lastly, a photograph may be used as a background image. Photos may fill the background of a cover completely, or copy may be arranged next to or around a central image. With the right background, your cover is more likely to stand out from the crowd of other titles on the shelf.

Follow the Rules

- When using a busy photo and a good deal of cover copy, always make sure that the cover copy is easy to read. This may require adjusting the position or size of the photo, or the copy may need to have rectangular bars placed behind it to make it stand out against the background image.

- When using a photo from a stock photo company, a copyrighted photo or image, or even a friend's photo or artwork for your cover's background, make sure you have a permission letter that provides you with the right to use this material on your book's cover.

- Be sure to add a credit line to the interior text for the use of this material. Such permission credits normally appear on the copyright page.

■ DESIGN

If you would like to use a cover artist to design the cover, make sure you provide the artist with the copy that you would like to have printed on the book. Also, you should ask the artist for at least three preliminary renderings for consideration.

If you would like to do the cover yourself, you should consider the following question: Do I have a good eye for art? If the answer is yes, designing a cover can be an enjoyable experience. If the answer is no, you might want to consult with someone who does. While this book provides you with rules to follow as you design your cover, if you do everything yourself, the result may not get your book the attention it deserves, or worse, your cover might scream, "This book is self-published."

While anyone can learn the rules for designing a good book cover, not everyone has a good eye for art. If design is not one of your strengths, don't hesitate to work with an artist who can provide the striking cover that your book needs to succeed.

Follow the Rules

- When designing a front cover for your book, look at a number of commercially produced book covers that are similar in subject or genre to yours. Whether you are writing a children's book, a nonfiction work, or a novel, the covers of books that were released by large publishing houses can serve as models for your own design.

- Create three preliminary designs and show them to people whose artistic judgment you trust.

- Try to keep all your copy in horizontal positions. Sometimes a title may be tilted at an angle, but unless you have the skill to make this style work, horizontal placement is likely to be your best choice.

AUTHOR'S LAST NAME

THE BOOK TITLE

PUBLISHER'S NAME
AND/OR LOGO

**Sample
Spine Layout**

SPINE

Nearly all commercially produced books have book spines. Except for saddle-stitched titles, which are held together with the help of staples, the vast majority of books found in bookstores or libraries have spines. While a book's spine may not seem all that important, it is typically the first thing seen by a potential buyer when he is browsing bookstore shelves. It is more important than you may think.

There are four important elements involved in a standard spine. These include:

- placement and size of copy
- coloration
- typeface style
- background

The good thing about a book's spine is that its design should simply reflect most of the elements found on the front cover.

■ PLACEMENT AND SIZE OF COPY

A book's spine normally contains three parts: the author's last name, the book's title, and the name or logo of the publisher. Make the size of the copy on the spine as large as you can get it within the limited space available. Doing so will increase the likelihood that potential buyers will be able to read the title and name of the author from a distance.

Author's Name

Traditionally it is just the author's last name that appears at the top of a book's spine. When there is more than one author, their last names appear on top of one another, or their names may be placed on the same line and separated by a small circle known as a *dingbat.*

Title

The title runs below the name of the author. Subtitles are not used on spines. In the case of a particularly lengthy title, it may appear on two lines, depending on the thickness of the spine.

Publisher's Name or Logo

As a self-publisher, you may place your publishing company's name or *logo* (a graphic design identifying the company) on your book's spine if you wish to do so. Not every publisher uses a logo on its spines, but many do. Should you choose to include your company's name or logo, place it at the bottom of the spine.

Follow the Rules

- Commercial publishers normally lay out a spine by setting the title in a font that fills the width of the spine but still allows for room to place the author's last name and the name of the company, which are then sized to fit within the remaining space. Each of these elements should run centered down a book's spine. (See page 62.)

■ TYPEFACE STYLE

The typeface used on a spine is typically determined by the typeface used on a book's cover. The title on a book's spine should be set in the same typeface that is used on its cover. The same typeface may be used for the author's last name, or the author's last name may be set in a plain sans-serif typeface. Setting the author's last name in a plain font may allow the title to stand out better. The names and logos used by commercial publishers are usually set designs that appear identically on all their titles. Since you are self-publishing, you have the freedom to create your own look.

■ COLORATION

The color used for a book's title on the spine is normally the same color as that used on its cover. Either black or a complementary color may be used for the author's name and the name of the publishing company.

■ BACKGROUND

Most books displayed in bookstores are arranged "spine out" because of limited shelf space. Since the spine is the usually the first part of the book seen by a potential buyer, it should have an attractive design and readable copy.

The background of a spine may be handled in several ways. It may be an extension of the background color found on a front cover. If a front cover uses a photo, the photo may wrap around the spine, but if the image is too busy, placing a solid bar behind the copy on the spine would allow this information to be more easily understood.

As you stroll down the aisles of a bookstore, you will see some interesting choices in terms of spine layouts. There is no reason why you can't be creative. Just make sure your design stays within the general parameters previously outlined.

BACK COVER

While front covers and spines almost always follow certain design rules, back covers are generally afforded much more creative leeway in terms of design. Commercial publishers tend to develop their own ways of putting together their back covers. Their layouts may be based on book type or category (e.g., fiction, nonfiction, children's books, scholarly titles, etc.) or they may simply reflect how much freedom their art directors were given to be creative. The bottom line is that you can make your back cover as simple or as fancy as you would like it to be, if you have these four basic elements in place:

- Retail Price
- Category
- ISBN Number and Barcode
- Publisher's Name or Logo

■ RETAIL PRICE

The retail price of a book may be expressed in one of two ways. It may be listed as "$15.95 US" to indicate that the price is being expressed in US dollars, or it may be listed simply as "$15.95," omitting the US reference. So, why should you include the term "US" next to the price? If your book is going to be sold in other countries, foreign prices will likely be different from the US price. If your book is going to be sold only in the United States, it will not be necessary to include the term "US" after its indicated price.

Of course, it might occur to you to include a foreign price next to the US price. The problem with this idea is that monetary exchange rates tend to fluctuate. To deal with this issue, you could always note your book's foreign price on your publishing company's website or the websites of your chosen online booksellers and adjust it when necessary.

The price of a book is most often placed in one of the corners at the bottom of its back cover. A book's barcode often contains its price as well.

Some self-publishers, however, prefer to avoid putting a price on their back covers and within their barcodes. Barcodes that do not include book prices use what is called a "90000 designation," which indicates that a book's price is not listed. Omitting a set price on your book means not having to reset your back cover every time you wish to adjust pricing. Unfortunately this strategy can have negative consequences, as some retailers and wholesalers require pricing to appear on a book's back cover. They may charge you to sticker the cover with a revised barcode that contains the price, or they may decline to add your title to their bookstores or warehouses.

■ ISBN NUMBER AND BARCODE

Although you should already have an ISBN number for your book at this point, you will also require a *barcode* to include on your back cover when you go to print. Barcodes allow retailers to scan books for price information and keep track of their inventories. There are many websites that sell barcodes, including the same online resource you used to acquire your book's ISBN number. (See page 22.)

The ISBN number and barcode should appear at the bottom of your book's back cover.

Sample Barcode

■ CATEGORY

This item is probably one of the most overlooked elements of a back cover. It should be found on the back of any book, but it is sometimes forgotten even by commercial publishers. The Book Industry Study Group (BISG), a leading book trade association, has established and maintains a category list called the BISAC Subject Headings List. These subject headings allow you to classify your book. Once you have assigned BISAC subject headings to your book, bookstores or libraries will be able to place your book in the appropriate section on their shelves.

For example, if you see a book on learning Japanese, its subject headings should be "FOREIGN LANGUAGE STUDY/ JAPANESE," or if a book deals with interplanetary war, its subject headings should be "FICTION/SCIENCE FICTION/ ADVENTURE." It is important not to assume your book's title will make clear your book's subject headings. You can determine your book's BISAC on the BISG website (http://bisg. org). Each subject heading or combination of subject headings is associated with a BISAC code, which, once entered into a database, helps libraries, online book retailers, and brick-and-mortar bookstores place your book in the appropriate sections of their shelves and websites. For example, the combination FICTION/THRILLERS/CRIME is associated with BISAC code FIC031010.

A book's subject headings are normally located near the price of the book on its back cover. You might look at some of the books on your own bookshelves to get a better idea of where to place your BISAC listing.

A good logo can lend a great deal of credibility to your self-published work.

Logo Samples

VITAL HEALTH PUBLISHING
Ridgefield, CT

■ PUBLISHER'S NAME OR LOGO

Most commercial houses place the name of their companies next to their logos on the back covers of their books, normally at the bottom. You may do the same. The name of your publishing company may be set in a stylized or simple typeface, and your logo, if you choose to have one, may be as fancy or as plain as you would like it to be, but your goal should always be a professional-looking back cover.

■ BACK COVER OPTIONS

With the previously described four elements included on your back cover, you now have the freedom to create several layouts and designs that reflect the nature of your book, that promote it, or both. The following elements are optional. Some may be added quickly and easily, while others may take a little more effort and time, but in the long run, they will prove worthwhile.

Photograph of Author

Normally, author photos are reserved for works of fiction, but this is not to say that they may not appear on the back covers of nonfiction titles as well. Obviously, if you include a photo on the back of your nonfiction book, you should use an image of yourself that is in accordance with your book's subject matter. For example, if your book is about overcoming a health issue, don't use a photo that was taken on a beach vacation. Make yourself look as professional as possible. On the other hand, if you book is about traveling, that beach picture may work well.

If you are going to have a photo taken by a professional photographer, make sure you obtain the exclusive right to use the photo. You may also want to credit the photographer on your book's copyright page.

Promotional Copy

Promotional copy should give potential readers an idea of what's in a book, and there are a few of ways of presenting it. You can write three paragraphs of descriptive copy about the book followed by an "About the Author" heading and one or two paragraphs of biographical information on the author. You can instead provide a bulleted list of all the benefits the book has to offer. Lastly, you can combine your paragraph-style copy with a bulleted list.

Always make sure to have your copy edited and thoroughly proofed before finalizing it on your back cover. The presence of typos or grammatical errors will severely hurt your chances of having your book taken seriously.

The Cost of a Cover

Creating a cover that is distinctive and note-worthy does not have to cost a fortune. Charges for cover design can range from inexpensive (less than $100 or even free if you use students or designers just starting out and looking for a credit) to over $1,000.

Besides asking fellow authors, self-publishers, or publishers for referrals, you may find a cover designer through services such as Fiverr (www.fiverr.com), which features participating cover designers that charge as little as $5 to as much as $1,000 for an original cover design. Another resource to help you hire a cover designer is Reedsy (https://reedsy.com). And, since so many book illustrators also design book covers, especially illustrators of children's books, the membership directory of the Society of Children's Book Writers and Illustrators (https://www.scbwi.org) may be of use to you in your search. It provides basic information about illustrators and links to their websites.

If you are working with a severely limited budget, you could consider running a design contest for your book's cover at a local college, the winner of which would see his cover design officially published, have his name recognized in the book as its cover artist, and take home $50 or so.

Make sure it is clear that you will control the rights to the finished cover image. Some cover designers may not agree to this stipulation, or they may ask for a higher fee to agree to it. It may be worth it for you to get these rights, however, since you may want to feature the cover on merchandise such as t-shirts or tote bags, or on other versions of your book.

If you do not establish a formal contract with your cover designer, you should at least have a record of all key points agreed upon in an email exchange, which you may print out and keep. Of course, you could also draft a letter agreement that you both sign.

Quotations

There are few things on a back cover that can be as powerful an inducement to buy a book as advance praise, also called quotations. There are three types of quotations, or blurbs, as they are also known in the publishing world. The most important type of blurb comes from a celebrity or someone who is famous in his area of expertise. A few good quotations from newspapers or magazine reviews can also help a book stand out. Finally, a blurb from a professional who enjoys good standing in his field (but is not a celebrity) can provide a book with credibility.

The inclusion of blurbs acquired from average people who are not known outside your circle of friends but who enjoyed your

Some of the questions you should ask a cover designer before you commit to a project include:

- What is your fee?

- When do you expect payment? (Options include payment of the full amount upon completion and acceptance of the cover, payment of half the fee at the beginning of the project and the balance upon completion and acceptance, and payment in full at the beginning of the project.)

- How do you accept payment? (Options include services such as Paypal, check, credit card, or direct deposit from a checking account.)

- Do you do original illustrations or use your own photographs for your covers, or do you purchase stock photos or illustrations?

- How long will it take you to produce an initial sketch?

- How many versions of the cover will you show me as part of our fee agreement until I am satisfied with the result?

- After I approve the initial sketch, how long will it take you to deliver the final version?

- What type of digital file will I receive?

- How high will the resolution of the delivered cover be?

How much money you spend on a cover is not as important as making sure you have one that looks professional and works for your book. You could even go the do-it-yourself route if you feel you have good design sense and are not eager to hire a professional. There are many online resources that can help you in this endeavor. Many of the print and e-book self-publishing services listed in the Resources offer templates to help you create your book cover, including Amazon, BookBaby, and 48 Hour Books. (See "Print, E-Book, and Audiobook Self-Publishing Services" in Resources on page 236.)

book is highly discouraged. It will do nothing to boost your book sales and will tend to make your book look self-published. If you can't get an impressive quotation, don't worry about it. Odds are, no one will notice.

Artwork

A book that contains artwork, such as a children's picture book or young adult book, might feature one of its illustrations on its back cover. If you decide to use an illustration on your back cover, you should credit the artist on your book's copyright page.

Combination

While each of these options may be used on its own, you may combine any or all of them. You can have a quotation at the top of your back cover, follow it with promotional copy and an author biography, and place a small author photo in the bottom corner. These are your choices to make.

OVERALL DESIGN

Now that you have a better idea of what a back cover should contain, it's essential to ensure that all your elements look good once you put them together. You want your copy to be legible, not crushed together, and have a semblance of balance. You should also remember to keep the colors on your back cover in line with the colors featured on your front cover and spine.

As is also the case with a front cover, if you do not feel qualified to create a back cover, you should find a graphic artist who can help you create one. Just remember to keep the artist aware of the four elements needed to make a back cover complete.

CONCLUSION

By now you should have a better appreciation of the covers you see on your bookshelf or at your local bookstore or library. Just as important, you should be able to see the commonalities among these commercial book covers. While you may have worked very hard on your manuscript, you should not take the look of your book for granted. You should put the same amount of effort into your book's appearance that you put into your writing. The way you package your work will influence the way it is perceived by the public and potential reviewers. The information contained in this chapter will help you avoid the common "tells" found on the covers of so many self-published books. Once you've finalized the exterior of your book, you then must focus on properly formatting its interior.

CHAPTER 5

$\mathcal{I}$NTERIOR DESIGN 101

Creativity is intelligence having fun.
—ALBERT EINSTEIN, THEORETICAL PHYSICIST

When someone opens your book, she should not be able to tell that it is self-published simply by looking at its interior layout. Just like your book's sequencing and cover, its interior must make your book appear to be produced by a major publisher, such as Penguin Random House, Knopf Doubleday, or Simon & Schuster.

The text and images contained in a book should be formatted in a visually attractive manner. The interior of a book should make the act of reading it a pleasant experience, not a difficult one. As a self-publisher, you should know that there are a lot of decisions that go into a book's interior design. Publishing industry professionals (distributors, wholesalers, acquisition librarians, independent or chain bookstore buyers, etc.) who see a poorly laid-out book will immediately suspect self-publication. It is therefore crucial to understand the rules that commercial publishing houses follow when designing their pages. By adhering to these rules, you should be able to create a book that appears as well produced as a book by a major publisher.

TURNING YOUR MANUSCRIPT INTO TYPESET COPY

So, you have finally completed the last edit of your manuscript, taken a deep breath, and congratulated yourself on seeing it through. You just know it is going to look great when it finally becomes a finished book. But turning your copy into typeset pages that don't make your book appear to be self-published can be a challenging task. Even though I had worked for a commercial publisher, when I first went about typesetting my book as a self-publisher, it was definitely a learning experience. Of course, I had a general idea of how it should be done. I knew the basics of what a typeset page should look like, but I soon discovered there is a lot more to designing a book's interior than just setting margins and balancing text.

In the old days, newspapers, magazines, and books would use a process called "hot type" to typeset their copy, meaning that each individual character or word would be set by hand using cast metal fonts. It was a relatively slow and expensive way of doing business. But with the advancement of computers, words would be typed into a computerized typesetting machine, with the operator being able to see just one line at a time. As this technology evolved, text would fill a whole screen and a typesetter would be able to see what an entire finished page would look like.

Although you can find online self-publishing services that will typeset your book for you, you'll generally enjoy better results if you either typeset the book yourself or work with a professional typesetter.

Today, these typesetting machines have gone the way of the rotary phone. They have been replaced with digital programs that allow a user to set copy using the typefaces of her choice on her home computer. Thanks to these amazing breakthroughs in typesetting, writers who would like to self-publish have options from which to choose when it comes to turning their manuscripts into printed books:

- Doing it yourself

- Using a professional typesetter

While each method has its own pluses and minuses, by understanding what these are, you will be able to make a decision that should work best for you. Although some online self-publishing services may offer to typeset your book for you, relinquishing control of your typesetting may result in a book with formatting problems that you could have avoided had you done it yourself or worked with a professional typesetter.

■ DOING IT YOURSELF

If you are determined to typeset your book yourself, you will need to use the right software to do so. Adobe InDesign has become the leading software of typesetters and designers. Adobe offers a variety of monthly software plans that include InDesign. These plans cost between $20 and $53 a month if you sign up for one year in advance. If you think you might be able to typeset your whole book in one week, you could simply sign up for InDesign's free week-long trial.

Although the learning curve may be too steep for you to finish typesetting your book in just seven days, there are a number of free online tutorials that can teach you how to use InDesign and ultimately get the job done. For example, YouTube features many videos on how to use the software. If you don't mind paying for a course, there are several fee-based online courses available through Pluralsight (www.pluralsight.com), a technology training company that offers thousands of courses on a wide variety of software.

LinkedIn's learning tutorials (www.linkedin.com) are another source of InDesign training. Simply go to the website, click on "learning" at the bottom of the home page, and then type "InDesign" in the search bar. The creator of InDesign, Adobe, also has forums on its website where you can post your questions about InDesign for other users to answer. Finally, you could pick up a how-to book such as *Adobe InDesign for Dummies* before getting started.

The main typesetting alternative to InDesign is QuarkXPress (www.quark.com). Like InDesign, it offers a free one-week trial. Of course, as with InDesign, you will have to learn the ins and outs of QuarkXPress. There are tools on the company's website to help you do so, and the same learning options discussed above in relation to InDesign also apply to QuarkXPress (online tutorials and courses, how-to books, etc.).

There are also a few free typesetting software options online, including Reedsy Book Editor (www.reedsy.com) and Scribus (www.scribus.net). To use Reedsy Book Editor, you must simply create a free account on the Reedsy website. You will then be able to upload your manuscript to Reedsy Book Editor and format it using the formatting toolbar. The Reedsy website also features a free downloadable user guide entitled "How to Format a Book with the Reedsy Book Editor." Nevertheless, Reedsy recommends working with a book designer if your book is a children's book, technical, or illustrated.

The popularity of Scribus is largely due to its similarity to InDesign. It boasts an interface that functions just as professionally as the two previously mentioned typesetting programs. If you are at all familiar with InDesign, making the jump to Scribus should be effortless. The only downside to the software is that it cannot open or save typesetting files created with other design programs, so if you have any projects made with other software, you will not be able to modify or even review them with Scribus.

■ USING A PROFESSIONAL TYPESETTER

Today there are thousands of people around the world who use the professional typesetting programs mentioned above to typeset books for a living. Many of them do excellent work, while some do not. You can find professional typesetters, who may also be complete book designers, by contacting some of the "Groups and Organizations" listed in the Resources section. (See page 243.) If you have never hired a typesetter before, choosing one may seem a little overwhelming. If you know what to look for and which questions to ask, however, you should be able to make an informed decision. Here are some important questions to ask your prospective typesetters as you search for the right person for the job.

Widows and Orphans

In typesetting, the terms *widows* and *orphans* refer to dangling lines that have been separated from their paragraphs. When a paragraph's last line appears on its own at the top of a page, it is called a *widow*. When a paragraph's first line appears on its own at the bottom of a page, it is called an *orphan*. When a paragraph ends with a single word alone on a line that isn't the first line of a page, this word may also be called an orphan, depending on the style guide. Whenever possible, avoid widows and orphans by rewriting the copy.

What Is Her Background as a Typesetter?

Request the typesetter's résumé. Make sure that she has a solid background in setting book pages. Ask if she currently works with any commercial publishing houses. If she has a website, visit it to see if it looks professional. Most important, check her website to see if it includes examples of her work for review.

Which Typesetting Program Does She Use?

You may not be familiar with all the aspects of a typesetter's typesetting program of choice, but as a self-publisher, it is important simply to know the name of the program that will be used to typeset your manuscript. Why? For one thing, you want to make sure this program will interface correctly with your printer's equipment. For another, should you wish to revise your book in the future and use a different typesetter, it will be helpful to know which program was used to typeset your book originally.

Is She Able to Design a Book's Interior?

Unfortunately, just because someone can typeset does not necessarily mean she can lay each page out appropriately. You will find it helpful to use a typesetter who can also design a professional-looking interior for your book. Most experienced book typesetters should have the skills to do good design work. Their résumés and websites should give you a sense of how skilled they are. Once you have read the section on layout design later in this chapter, you should be able to identify correctly designed layouts and incorrectly designed layouts. When you find a typesetter who is a skilled designer, she should be able to work with you to help create an interior that matches the vision you have in your mind for your book.

Remember that an individual may have the ability to use a typesetting program but not know how to correctly lay out a book. Before you hire a typesetter, check her résumé and ask to see a sample typeset chapter so that you can better assess her skills.

How Long Will It Take to Complete the Job?

While some manuscripts are relatively easy to set, other manuscripts may be very time consuming and difficult to turn into set pages. If the timing of your book's release is critical, you need to make sure that you provide your typesetter with a deadline for completion. After giving her an electronic file of your manuscript, you should ask how long she thinks it will take to complete the initial work.

With timing in mind, always remember that once your manuscript has been typeset, you still need to proofread and possibly index it, so you should always build this additional time into your book's schedule.

Can She Show You a Sample Chapter?

Asking your potential typesetter to show you a sample chapter is recommended if the individual is relatively new to typesetting. While this typesetter's price may be reasonable, try not to make your decision simply on the basis of cost. Seeing a sample of her work should help you make the right call.

Can She Put You in Touch with Previous Clients?

When interviewing a typesetter, ask to talk to some of her former clients. If her previous work has been satisfactory, then your request should not present a problem.

How Much Will the Job Cost?

Typesetters can set their rates in a number of ways. Rates may be based on number of pages, word count, or hours it takes to set the copy. It may also be based on how difficult it would be to set a book. There is also the matter of time required to make any necessary corrections once a book has been proofed. As you compare prices of typesetters, make sure to ask about the costs of additional work that may be required after proofing and perhaps in the future. Without asking about these issues ahead of time, revisions can be unexpectedly costly.

Will She Provide You with a Copy of the Final Typeset Book?

Once your book has been finalized and is ready to go to the printer, the typesetter should provide you with a digital copy of your typeset book. Make sure this is part of your arrangement at the start.

As a self-publisher, you don't have to be an expert in book design, but it is important to have a working knowledge of how a standard commercial book should be laid out. Typesetting is only part of the job. If your page layout doesn't conform to the basic rules, it will broadcast your book as self-published.

HOW TO FORMAT YOUR BOOK

In the previous chapter, you learned that all commercial covers share common elements. You also learned that your book should not outwardly appear to be self-published as long as you have followed the rules for creating your cover. Similarly, if you follow the rules for formatting the interior of your book, it should not have any "tells" of a self-published book. If the pages of your book are formatted incorrectly, however, it will scream "self-published" to reviewers and other book industry professionals.

There are eight important elements to keep in mind when typesetting and formatting your book's interior pages. Once you know what to watch out for, you will see how easy it is to follow the rules to which nearly all commercial houses adhere. These elements include the following:

- Page numbers
- Section headings
- Section openers
- Headers and footers
- Margins
- Typeface
- Typeface size and leading
- Paragraph placement and indentation

Just as there are rules for designing book covers, there are rules for designing the interior of books. By keeping these rules in mind during the typesetting of your manuscript, you will help avoid the "tells" which announce that your book is self-published.

While there are few differences between fiction and nonfiction covers, there are even fewer differences between fiction and nonfiction interiors. The rules for the following elements apply to both categories of publication.

■ PAGE NUMBERS

Normally, books feature two different sets of page numbers. The first set is Roman numerals (e.g., iv, v, vi, etc.) and the second set is Arabic numerals (e.g., 1, 2, 3, etc.). The problem is that many self-publishers use only one set—the one they are used to seeing—which is Arabic numerals. In their minds, the first page of a book is page "1" and the last page of a book is whichever page number happens to apply. This page numbering style is wrong, and a major "tell."

While there is no single accepted style of page numbering across all publishers, one of the most appropriate ways to number your pages is to distinguish between the main story or content of a book and any part that might appear before it. This means that a book's introduction or prologue would be page "1" and begin its Arabic numeration, which would be used throughout the rest of the book, while the majority of the front matter would use Roman numerals. If a book does not have an introduction or prologue, Arabic numeration would begin on the first page of the first chapter.

Follow the Rules

Number the pages of your book consecutively, being sure to count all pages whether or not page numbers appear on them.

- While most front matter pages are numbered sequentially using Roman numerals, some front matter pages should not feature page numbers at all (although it should be counted in the sequence of front matter page numbers). These pages include the half-title page, title page, copyright page, contents, and dedication.

- Page numbers should not be printed on blank pages (although blank pages, too, should be counted in the sequence of page numbers).

- Whether it is Roman or Arabic, the appropriate page number should appear at the bottom of the first page of each section (e.g., foreword, introduction, all chapters, about the author, index, etc.). Placement of page numbers is discussed further in "Headers and Footers."(See page 81.)

■ SECTION HEADINGS

With the exception of the copyright page and the dedication page, every separate section of a book should begin with a heading that

When Should You Hire a Book Designer?

As noted, some typesetters are actually book designers as well. They may sound like the same job, but a book designer provides more services than just typesetting. Sometimes a book project requires the skills of a professional book designer to see it to the finish line. In many cases, a book designer may also provide illustrations, editorial and typesetting services, and final design work for both the cover and interior of a book. In the same way you would check a typesetter's qualifications, you should check a book designer's, as well. Always interview several designers for the job. Remember that this type of service may be costly. You can find a freelance book designer online by consulting a networking website such as Fiverr or Reedsy. (See "Groups and Organizations" in Resources on page 243.)

stands out. (This goes without saying, of course, for the title page and half-title page, whose sole purpose is to feature a particular heading: a book's title.) Headings provide a finished look to a commercial book, but must be set properly; otherwise, they will be obvious "tells" of a self-published work. For example, headings that are the same size as the running text are sure to make a book look self-published. As long as you have a sense of how headings should appear, you can avoid this type of mistake.

Follow the Rules

- Standard section headings should appear on the first page of almost every section of a book, including the contents, foreword, preface, introduction, chapters (if the chapters have titles), references, resources, about the author, and index. As already noted, the copyright page and dedication page are excluded from this rule.

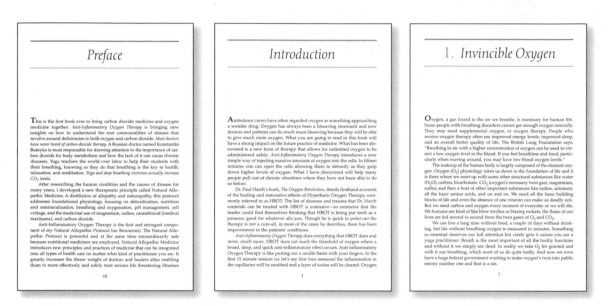

Section Headings
Samples

- The actual dedication copy itself should be set in the same style as the running copy that makes up the body of each chapter. It should be positioned approximately an inch or two higher than the center of the page, based on the length of the dedication.

- All section headings should be placed at the same height on their respective pages, as may be seen in the examples at the top of this page.

- While section headings may be set in the same typeface employed for the running copy, using a different typeface is preferred. Section headings can be set using either a serif or sans-serif font, but do not use a display typeface or any other typeface that may be difficult to read.

■ SECTION OPENERS

When laying out the sections of a book, you may wonder if you should place every first page, or opener, of a section on a right-hand page. As you will discover, the rules for section openers are much more flexible than other rules we have outlined in this chapter.

Follow the Rules

- The half-title page, the title page, and page 1 of the text should always fall on a right-hand page.

- While the copyright page should always fall on a left-hand page—on the back of the title page—you should try to have all your other section openers start on a right-hand page.

- Here's where options come into play. Some books are exceptionally long, and because of this fact, many commercial publishers start every chapter after the opening chapter on the first available page, which may be a left-hand page. This is done to avoid having too many blank pages and to cut down on a book's length.

- Publishers may also alter the positions of front matter or end matter openers to shorten the length of a book. Although these changes may go against the rules, they are subtle enough not to be noticed by most reviewers and readers.

- Now that you know more about section openers, take a look at some of the books on your bookshelf to see how they handle their openers.

■ HEADERS AND FOOTERS

All commercial books have *headers*, which refer to copy that runs within the space allotted for the top margin. This copy may include the title of a book, the section or chapter titles, an author's name, or page numbers. Headers may have a narrow horizontal line running beneath the copy. This line should always be the same length as the standard width of text below it. The addition of this line, however, is a matter of taste. *Footers* refer to copy that runs within the space allotted for the bottom margin and most often are reserved for page numbers when page numbers are not included in a book's headers.

A header, often called a running head, helps orient the reader within a book. This is especially true in works of nonfiction, where the right-hand-page header often includes the chapter or section title.

Follow the Rules for Headers

- Headers are never used on half-title pages, title pages, copyright pages, dedication pages, section openers, or any blank pages. Except for the pages listed above, headers should be used on all other pages in a book.

- In nonfiction works, the header on a left-hand page should provide a book's title (but not its subtitle). If a page number is not included in the footer below, it should appear to the extreme left of the title. An exception to these guidelines may occur when a nonfiction book is presented in the form of a narrative story. In such a case, headers may be handled in the same fashion as they would be in a work of fiction.

- In works of fiction, the header on a left-hand page should provide the full name of a book's author as it appears on the cover. If a page number is not included in the footer below, it should appear to the extreme left of the author's name.

- In nonfiction works, the header on a right-hand page provides the section or chapter title. If chapters do not have titles, then a book's title may be repeated (without its subtitle) in the right-hand header. If a page number is not included in the footer below, it should appear to the extreme right of the section, chapter, or book title.

- In works of fiction, the header on a right-hand page should provide the section, chapter, or book title. If a page number is not included in the footer below, it should appear to the extreme right of the section, chapter, or book title.

Follow the Rules for Footers

- If you have chosen not to include page numbers in your headers, then your page numbers must appear in your footers. On a left-hand page, a page number may appear on the left side (just outside the margin) or in the center. On a right-hand page, a page number may appear on the right side (just outside the margin) or in the center.

ation, and help us de-stress. Slower easier breathing improves cell-oxygen content. We call this abdominal breathing or diaphragmatic breathing because the diaphragm pushes down and the belly swells out just as we see when babies breathe.

There is no quicker way of getting oxygen into someone then taking sodium bicarbonate because it instantly releases carbon dioxide into the stomach and thus bicarbonates are thrust into the blood. In the blood, car-

The next solid to be introduced should be fruit. However, take the precautions that we make for everybody: focus on the lower-sugar, lower-glycemic fruits (the "Green" category). Do not give too much at one time and give it on an empty stomach. No point in making your baby's life a misery by bad food combining. Give fruits to your baby every day.

What about animal matter? Of course, many people bring up their children successfully as v—ians. However, staying with the Savanna Model, fish and

number, but that it is by nature a part of a whole and cannot be understood in isolation.

But 3D life tempts you—all but coerces you—into seeing 3D lives in isolation, and of course life is going to be seen as unfair, chaotic, undirected, painful, meaningless. Is that the fault of the structure of life, or of a constricted point of view?

perhaps four times that most everybody lost at each session of the workshop. Even then, people's financial losses tended to be small. And they still expressed much satisfaction with what they had learned. What seemed to be happening in these groups was two-fold. First, at the table people tried just a little too hard, which is tempting to do if there have been some losses. Second, in these few groups there were great challenges to beliefs and emotions going on for the majority of the participants in that group. All groups

Headers Samples

- As section or chapter openers should not contain headers, each section- or chapter-opening page should have a footer that contains its appropriate page number. This number should be placed in one of the positions described in the previous paragraph.

- The rules for both headers and footers are relatively standard and used by the vast majority of publishers. Some book designers, of course, use variations of these rules to make their headers or footers stand out. These fancier treatments can work well for nonstandard titles such as illustrated titles or guides. By looking at commercial titles that are similar in format to yours, you will quickly see how header and footer rules apply to your book's interior.

Remember that your page number and book title or chapter name should appear only once on a page, never in both a header and footer.

used over the abdominal area during sleep. The more hours of exposure to the chair pad and multipurpose pad, the better. At night, sleep on the magnetic mattress pad and place magnets in the carrier against the headboard. Also, sleep with a magnetic eye unit across the face.

Place a 5" x 12" double magnet, multi-magnet flexible mat over the heart and chest, held in place with a 4" x 52" body wrap around

used over the abdominal area during sleep. The more hours of exposure the Type II diabetic has enough insulin, but it cannot do its job properly in acid-hypoxic cells. Later in the disease process, the pancreatic cells also become acid-hypoxic and reduce their insulin production. However, this reduced amount of insulin is secondary to the maladaptive reactions. The failure to isolate the major cause of insulin resis-

used over the abdominal area during sleep. The more hours of exposure cals), also facilitate the elimination of toxic chemicals). Approximately 70% of the toxins from tap water enter the body through the skin; the remaining 20% of the toxins enter via ingestion. Tap water in the United States contains chlorine, aluminum, pesticides, lead, copper, and other toxic substances.[1]

used over the abdominal area during sleep. The more hours of exposure to the chair pad and multipurpose pad, the better. At night, sleep on the magnetic mattress pad and place magnets in the carrier against the headboard. Also, sleep with a magnetic eye unit across the face.

Place a 5" x 12" double magnet, multi-magnet flexible mat over the heart and chest, held in place with a 4" x 52" body wrap around

Footers Samples

■ MARGINS

Technically, a printed page's line length is measured in *picas*. (There are 6 picas to 1 inch.) For the sake of practicality, however, this book will use inches. The *margins* of a page generally measure 1 inch on the top and bottom, and $3/4$ inch on the left and right. Variations of these measurements happen all the time in commercial publishing, however, and the reason for these variations is important to understand.

When a manuscript's copy runs long, a publisher may decrease the size of a book's margins to accommodate more text per page. Instead of $3/4$-inch side margins, a publisher may use $1/2$-inch side margins. Instead of 1-inch top and bottom margins, a publisher may use $3/4$-inch top and bottom margins. Sometimes footers are avoided entirely to gain even more space. With additional room on each page, a book may lose a significant number of pages, making it less expensive to print—and no one will be the wiser.

On the other hand, if a book's margins are too small, its interior will look terrible and give away the fact that the book is self-published. If you understand how to use margins correctly in the layout of your book, your margins will not even be noticed by readers—which is the whole point.

Follow the Rules

- Once you have set your top, bottom, and side margins, they should be kept consistent throughout your book. Except for your header or footer copy, no text should be placed within margins.

■ TYPEFACE

As discussed in the previous chapter, typefaces come in literally hundreds of different styles. Unlike the creation of a book's cover, however, which requires you to be familiar with three different classifications (serif, sans-serif, and display), formatting a book's interior copy requires you to know only two: serif and sans-serif.

Margins and Page Length

When reading a commercial book, you may notice that all, or almost all, its pages are uniform in length. Copy should run from the top margin to the bottom margin. The only pages that do not follow this layout are section openers and possibly the end page of a chapter, which may not have enough text to fill an entire page. Some self-published books allow the bottoms of their pages to end irregularly, never quite reaching the bottom margins. Having the bottom of your copy jump up and down is one of the most obvious "tells" that your book is self-published.

By adding or deleting copy, you can adjust page lengths and achieve a consistent look throughout. In addition, depending on the typesetting program, you may be able to expand or contract a paragraph's length, allowing you to lose or gain a line and achieve consistency without changing any copy.

Serif

Serifs refer to the little lines attached to the ends of a letter or symbol. A book's interior is normally typeset using a serif font. While there are many fonts with serifs, the following examples are relatively common in publishing:

Baskerville	Garamond
Book Antiqua	Minion Pro
Bookman Old Style	Times New Roman

Sans-Serif

This term refers to letters and symbols that do not feature extended lines at their ends. These characters are designed to have a more modern look. The following examples are standard sans-serif fonts:

Arial	Helvetica
Franklin Gothic	News Gothic
Gill Sans	Verdana

Thankfully, when selecting a typeface for your interior copy, there is only one overriding mandate: No matter which typeface you choose, your copy should always be easy to read. Nevertheless, there are still a few other rules you should keep in mind.

Follow the Rules for Body Matter

Most books are typeset in serif fonts, since the serifs—the small extra strokes—make it easy for the eye to travel over large blocks of text. For the same reason, newspapers and magazines also make use of serif fonts.

- Body matter, including running text, chapter headings, headers, footers, and footnotes, should be set in an easy-to-read serif typeface. While some sans-serif typefaces may be used for the body matter of illustrated or large-format books, the majority of published books do not use sans-serif type in the running text.

- Within the running text, you may have section headings, sub-section headings, or paragraph headings. Usually, these headings are set in a bold version of your selected serif typeface. You may instead set these headings in a bold sans-serif typeface as long as you use the same heading style throughout your book.

Follow the Rules for Front Matter, Chapter Numbers or Titles, and End Matter

- Consistency in the presentation of your front matter, chapter openers, and end matter is an important part of creating a professional-looking book.

- All your front matter openers, chapter numbers or titles, and end matter openers may be set in either serif or sans-serif typeface.

- Once you have selected your typeface style for your front matter, chapter numbers or titles, and end matter, make sure to follow the style consistently.

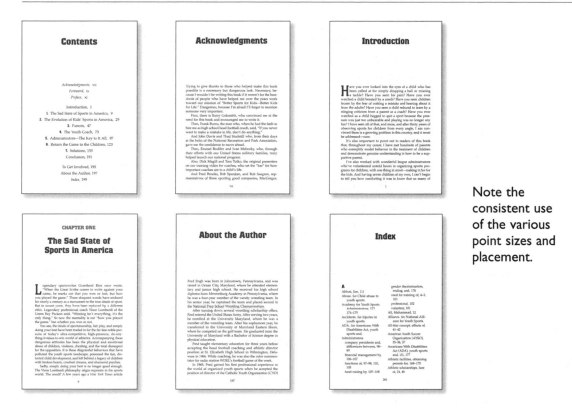

Note the consistent use of the various point sizes and placement.

■ TYPEFACE SIZE AND LEADING

Have you ever looked at the interior of a book and noticed that the typeface used for the running copy was really hard to read? Perhaps the typeface size was too small or the spacing between lines was too tight, making the copy on each page look crushed. The fact is that a number of commercial houses allow their books to have this sort of crushed appearance. Why would this happen?

In some cases, a publisher wants to fit as much copy on a page as possible. Using smaller type, tightening the spacing between lines, and reducing margin size can accomplish this task. And while doing so never serves to make a book look any better, it may reduce the final cost of production. In some cases, crushing the text may simply be the way a specific type of book is traditionally produced. Highly technical books, for example, are often set in this manner because publishers do not feel crushed that copy will deter readers, who must already have a strong interest in such subjects to seek out these scholarly works in the first place.

Unfortunately, most self-publishers don't have the luxury of producing a poorly set page that is difficult to read. By knowing just a few of the technical aspects involved in typesetting, however, you should be able to produce a legible book.

Typeface Size

Typeface size is measured in points. For normal running copy, a 10-point to 12-point typeface should be used. The larger the point size, the larger the letter. (Interestingly enough, there may be a slight size difference between two typeface styles of the same point size.)

11-point Baskerville   **11-point Univers**   11-point Times Roman

Leading

Leading (pronounced "ledding"), also called *line spacing* or *interline spacing*, refers to the distance between lines of text. Once you have determined your typeface size, simply add between two to four numbers to its point size to establish a reasonable leading. For example, if you use a 10-point font, all you need to do is add 2 to this number, giving you the point size to use for your leading: 12. This leading should then be used to set all your copy. If you want a larger leading, add 4 to the 10-point size to wind up with 14-point leading.

10-point type with leading of 12

10-point type with leading of 13

10-point type with leading of 14

Follow the Rules

* The typical typeface size of a book is between a 10-point and 12.5-point style. Some people may prefer to use a larger point size, but it is important to remember that when you use a 13-point or greater typeface, your text may look like the copy found in a "large-print" book. This type of book is specifically designed for people with poor vision. And while your book

8-point type

9-point type

10-point type

11-point type

12-point type

14-point type

16-point type

18-point type

Sample Gill Sans
Point Sizes

will be easier to read, it may be confused with a large-print title and have limited sales. The leading of your copy, as you know, should be two to four points greater than the size of your typeface.

- While, to some degree, the process of typesetting copy is relatively technical, there is a simple way to judge how your typeset page compares to a commercially typeset page. Once you have settled on your typeface, size, and leading, have a few sample pages of your text printed out and place them next to the pages of a book you would like to emulate. This juxtaposition should tell you if you are on the right track.

■ PARAGRAPH PLACEMENT AND INDENTATION

The way writers separate their paragraphs may be interesting, but it is not always appropriate for a published book. For example, some writers skip a line between paragraphs to establish separation. This may be an acceptable style in a manuscript, but it is an immediate "tell" in a self-published book. You must know the rules of paragraph placement and indentation to avoid giving yourself away as a self-publisher. And the nice thing is that fiction and nonfiction books share similar rules in this area.

Follow the Rules

- Never indent the lead paragraph in an opening section. This rule applies to front matter, body matter, and end matter.

- In a nonfiction book, the first paragraph beneath a heading should not be indented. All other paragraphs in a fiction or nonfiction work should be indented.

- Do not add an extra space between paragraphs in your running copy. The only exception to this rule occurs in fiction when a new scene is introduced within a chapter. Two or three blank lines may be added to separate sections, and ornamental dingbats may be placed in this space to signal the new scene.

CONCLUSION

While designing a book's interior may be a confusing endeavor, I hope the explanations and visual aids included throughout this chapter have provided you with clarity. Laying out your copy properly is a necessary part of making your book look professional. While an adequately produced cover may initially fool the public, the interior of a book is often where the trouble begins for self-publishers. Anything less than a well-designed layout is always a major "tell."

There is no question that designing the interior of a book requires a level of technical knowledge and practice, but by following the instructions in this chapter, you should be able to avoid the common mistakes made by self-publishers and create a book that readers and reviewers consider worthy of their attention. If you need to reread this chapter, go for it. The better you understand the rules of your book's interior, the better prepared you will be to work with a typesetter or self-publishing company, or to lay out the pages yourself.

Of course, there are exceptions to many of the rules you have just read, but the vast majority of commercial books stick to these established guidelines. The interior of a book should not be a distraction to a potential reader, nor should it cause a book to appear to be self-published. If a book's cover is meant to capture a reader's attention, a book's interior is meant to keep it.

CHAPTER 6

CREATING AN E-BOOK

This is the point. One technology doesn't replace
another, it complements. Books are no more
threatened by Kindle than stairs by elevators.
—STEPHEN FRY, COMEDIAN AND AUTHOR

At this point in the self-publishing process, you should have a final
proofread manuscript that you want to convert into a published
book. You may be publishing it only as an e-book, or you may be
publishing it in other formats as well (e.g., print, audiobook). While
this book discusses each of these formats, this chapter focuses on the
creation and distribution of e-books.

E-BOOK VS PRINT

As the tablet and smartphone market expands, so does the call for
e-books. Although print books have become easier and less expensive to self-publish, it is faster and easier to release a book in only
e-book format than it is to release it in both e-book and print. One
noticeable difference is that you do not have to worry about creating
a back cover or spine for an e-book. Most e-books include just a front
cover.

As more and more
people purchase
tablets, smartphones,
and special e-readers
such as the Kindle, the
popularity of e-books
is continuing to grow.

Of course, you still need your manuscript to be edited and
proofread, and for the interior of your book to appear professionally

designed and easy to read. But it is less demanding to format a manuscript as an e-book than it is to have the interior of a print edition designed properly.

Fortunately, you do not have to choose one format over all others when the time comes to produce your book. You may release your book in any format you please. You could always try one format first, such as an e-book, and see how it goes. If your book then gets enough of a response, you could invest the time and effort needed to create a print version or audiobook.

My preference is to release a book in all three formats, if possible. I find a book released in only e-book format often does not get the attention or the sales of a title available in both e-book and print formats. Media outlets especially like to get physical copies of books to look over and refer to when considering or conducting author interviews. Of course, you could always work around this issue by printing your e-book and mailing it to a potential reviewer.

WHY PUBLISH ONLY AN E-BOOK?

If you are struggling to finish your book because you are a perfectionist and fear you may want to make changes to it after it has been printed, publishing it as an e-book could be a good solution for you. With an e-book, you could quickly substitute a new file for the previous file. Any new e-books would include your changes.

These days, of course, changes may be made to print editions relatively quickly, easily, and inexpensively. Nevertheless, if you have hundreds of copies of the uncorrected books, you may be torn between selling them or destroying them and making the new version available, depending on the extent of your revisions.

If you have analyzed your market and feel strongly that the bulk of your sales is going to come from e-book buyers, creating only an e-book might be the right decision for your book. You could always publish an e-book first and then, if you decide you would like a print version, you can publish physical copies of your book.

Advantages

As already mentioned, it is easier to format an e-book than it is to format a print book. It is possible to get your manuscript formatted as an e-book and available for sale within twenty-four to forty-eight hours on one of the websites that sell e-books, such as Amazon, Barnes & Noble, or Kobo. Furthermore, by choosing to publish in only one format, an e-book, you will have fewer publishing accounts to monitor. (Amazon and Barnes & Noble even offer print-on-demand for e-books.) Obviously, it will also be less expensive to produce only an e-book, as you wouldn't have to deal with the costs of printing and shipping.

Publishing your manuscript as an e-book allows you to include color photographs and illustrations at no extra cost. In print publishing, four-color art is more expensive than black-and-white graphics. With e-books, you do not need to worry about page numbers in the table of contents because readers are able to "jump" to chapters. E-books do not require page numbers in their indexes either. By clicking on the concepts or words contained in an e-book's index, readers will be directed to the pages on which they appear.

There are several advantages to publishing your work only as an e-book. Compared with print versions, electronic books are usually easier to format, cheaper and faster to produce, and simpler to revise if you wish to make changes in the future.

Disadvantages

Despite the relative ease with which a self-publisher can create an e-book, e-book publishing still has its disadvantages. For example, it is difficult for an e-book to include any kind of fill-in sections or checklists, unless it features an interactive component, which most online retailers are not yet set up to offer. If you are sure you would like to publish an e-book, you should keep this limitation in mind as you finalize your manuscript.

SELLING YOUR E-BOOK

You may sell your e-book directly to buyers by engaging in direct-to-consumer email exchanges, whereby you send your e-book to a buyer as an attachment after receiving payment. (You may have the e-book file encrypted before sending it if you are fearful of piracy.)

You may instead sell your e-book directly through your website if you have hired a programmer to set up a system for automatic fulfillment.

Most authors and self-publishers, however, delegate the fulfillment of their e-book orders to a third party (or parties). The most well-known e-book vendor is Amazon, which offers Kindle Direct Publishing, or KDP, although there are other options to consider. While an e-book and its printed version should use different ISBNs, a number of vendors, including Amazon, do not require their e-books to have ISBNs at all. In the case of Amazon, it assigns its own unique identification number to each of its e-books, although you may also supply an ISBN for your title if you wish to do so.

CREATING AN E-BOOK

To create an e-book, you will need a completed, edited, and proofread manuscript that can be formatted in whichever e-book format is required by your e-book vendor. If you are going to sell your e-book directly from your website to consumers, you will likely use a PDF format for your e-book. (Be careful about this sales method, though. Unless you encrypt your files, your book could fall victim to piracy.) Online retailers such as Barnes & Noble, Kobo, Apple, and Google support the well-known EPUB format, while Amazon uses its own AZW format. In fact, Amazon will automatically convert your PDF file to its e-book format, AZW, when you create an e-book through Amazon Kindle Direct Publishing.

I personally use a third-party converter instead of these automatic conversion programs because I have had better results using the former. It is more expensive to do things in this manner, of course, since the automatic e-book conversion programs offered by large companies such as Amazon are free to use, while third-party e-book converters charge fees for their services.

You may have to experiment to find out which approach works best for you. You should also revisit vendors from time to time to see if they might have anything new to offer. They may have simplified or improved their services, making their automatic conversion programs more appealing.

Standard E-Book vs. Fixed-Layout E-Book

A standard e-book format, the most common of which is EPUB, provides a flowing text that can be adjusted in size and style according to preference. The number of words per page may be altered based on user settings or the screen size of the reading device. You may wish to employ a standard format if:

- your book is mostly text.

- you would like your book to be easily compatible with a range of devices.

A fixed-layout format may be a better choice if your e-book is composed of large illustrations, photos, or text in the margins. This format is commonly used for cookbooks, children's books, and coffee table books. It essentially features fixed digital images of the typeset pages you would find in a printed book. Readers are not able to change typefaces, text size, or margins. You may want to use a fixed-layout format if:

- you need to keep intact text over images.

- you would like to use a background color.

- you need to create pages composed of more than one column.

- you need text to wrap around images.

- you require your book to be read in landscape view.

The conversion of a manuscript into a fixed-layout format is usually more costly than creating a standard layout.

While standard e-book format is most commonly used, if your book contains images and text that need to be presented in a particular way, you may opt for a fixed-layout e-book, which would not allow readers to alter your book's page presentation in any way.

Classifying Your E-Book

Any decent publisher is aware of the significance of book placement in a brick-and-mortar store. Placement is just as important for e-books, by which I mean the placement of an e-book in a category. A badly classified e-book can be confusing or upsetting to readers and may affect sales. If a reader is expecting to read science fiction

Be careful when choosing the category in which you place your e-book. If you classify your work inappropriately, your intended audience may never know that it exists. Fortunately, most online e-book retailers allow you to select two or three classifications.

but winds up with a thriller through poor e-book classification, he may be inclined to leave an unfavorable review of the book. Remember, you are not only selling a product; you are also selling yourself as an author.

The majority of online e-book retailers allow you to place your book in up to three categories. To find your audience, it is important to place your book in the two or three categories that are most appropriate for your work.

E-BOOK RETAILERS AND AGGREGATORS

Once you have your e-book ready to go, the next step in the process of e-book publishing is getting your e-book to online e-book retailers. You will need to decide if you would like to work with each online retailer individually or use an e-book aggregator, or distributor, to distribute your e-book to retailers for you. Working with an e-book aggregator typically means having to give up a larger percentage of your profits than you might have to relinquish if you were dealing with each retailer individually, but this cost may be worth it, as a partnering with a distributor may augment your sales. If you choose to work with each online retailer directly, however, you will keep more of your profits and may have more access to marketing.

There are currently five major online book retailers from which to choose: Amazon, Kobo, Barnes & Noble, Apple, and Google. In terms of e-book aggregators, popular options include Smashwords, PublishDrive, BookBaby, and Draft2Digital.

AMAZON

Amazon Kindle Direct Publishing allows you to self-publish your e-book for free and distributes your e-book to Kindle stores worldwide within twenty-four to forty-eight hours. It is nonexclusive, meaning it allows the sale of your e-book through other online vendors, although Amazon also offers enrollment in its KDP Select program, which is exclusive but gives users access to a number of promotional tools and perks.

The advantage of using KDP is that you gain access to the largest number of e-book buyers in the United States. Of course, as mentioned previously, there are other advantages to be had if you sign up for KDP Select, Amazon's exclusive program. Most notably, KDP Select allows you to give your e-book away for free for up to five days every three months, which is the minimum number of months of participation required to join the program. Another perk of using KDP Select is that you can participate in Kindle's "countdown deals" every three months, also for a maximum of five days. These deals offer your book at a promotional price for a limited time as a means of encouraging sales.

Finally, KDP Select includes participation in Amazon's e-book subscription program known as Kindle Unlimited and the Kindle Owners' Lending Library. Nevertheless, KDP Select prevents self-publishers from selling their titles through any other service, which may be considered a drawback. If you do not sign up for this KDP exclusive program, you may list your e-book on Amazon as well as any other e-book vendor, and even sell your e-book through your personal website.

Adding a Book

You may use your existing Amazon account's username and password to sign onto Kindle Direct Publishing (KDP). If you do not have an Amazon account, you may create a KDP account on Amazon's KDP website (https://kdp.amazon.com). You will also need to have some form of bank account that accepts electronic payments so that Amazon will be able to send you any money generated by sales of your book.

Allow at least a few days, preferably a week or so, to set up your account if you do not already have one with Amazon, as your banking information will have to be verified, which Amazon does by depositing a very small amount of money in the account. Once you confirm receipt of these funds, your account is considered verified, allowing Amazon to pay you any applicable profits from your book sales in the future.

Once you are all set with an account, you may add a new title. After you've chosen the type of new title you will be creating (in this case, an e-book), the first thing you will be asked for is the language of your work. What is the primary language of the e-book you are creating? The default is "English." After you've specified your book's primary language, you will enter your book's title and subtitle, the latter of which is optional. You will also note your book's edition number and whether it is part of a series, enter its author and any additional contributors you would like to acknowledge, and add a description of your book. This description will be uploaded verbatim to Amazon's US and international websites, so make sure it is well written, interesting, informative (but not hyperbolic), and proofread.

You will then upload your manuscript and its cover. Acceptable file formats include PDF, MOBI, DOC, EPUB, RTF, TXT, and KPF. You will be asked if you would like DRM (digital rights management) enabled on your Kindle e-book. DRM is meant to prevent piracy of your e-book file by restricting the ways in which a file may be used or copied. If you would like to try to create a cover yourself, you can use Amazon's free cover creator option. If you already have a cover prepared, you may upload it. Amazon Kindle accepts covers in JPG or TIFF format.

You will then select up to five keywords that could be used to find your book in searches and up to two categories that appropriately suit your book. You will also need to note the territories in which you are able to sell your e-book. You may click on "all" or, if you have assigned one or multiple territories to one or a few other companies, you may go through the more than two hundred listed territories one by one, indicating the regions in which you have the right to sell your e-book through Amazon.

When you are deciding on your retail price, be aware that most e-books priced anywhere from $2.99 to $9.99 receive a 70-percent *royalty* on sales. The royalty rate may drop to 35 percent, however, under certain circumstances. The "List Price Requirements" on the website explain these matters in detail. If you request price conversion for your book in applicable territories outside the US, Amazon will automatically convert your US price into its equivalent in the currencies of these territories. You will be asked to confirm the copyright of your work, verify that it is not in the public domain, and provide the name of the publishing company releasing your title.

Finally, you will be asked if you would like to enroll in the KDP Select program. As recently mentioned, this program offers its authors a number of tools to encourage their readerships, including "countdown deals" (see page 97), e-book giveaways, and participation in Amazon's e-book subscription program known as Kindle Unlimited and the Kindle Owners' Lending Library, from which Amazon Prime members may choose one e-book to read for free each month (with no due dates). Minimum length of enrollment in KDP Select is ninety days, during which period Amazon will hold the exclusive sales rights to your e-book. In other words, you will not be permitted to sell your e-book through any other retailer while enrolled in KDP Select. Your participation will automatically renew every ninety days unless you request otherwise.

Once your manuscript has been uploaded, Amazon Kindle will offer an online previewer that will enable you to see your e-book exactly as the customer will see it.

Enrolling your book in the Kindle Direct Publishing (KDP) Select program has many benefits. KDP Select provides a number of tools that encourage readership, including e-book giveaways and participation in the Kindle Owners' Lending Library. Just remember that as long as your book is registered in KDP Select, you can sell it only through Amazon.

KOBO

Kobo (www.kobo.com) calls its self-publishing service "Kobo Writing Life." Its e-books are published in the EPUB format, and Kobo can convert your book into this format as long as it is a DOC, DOCX, ODT, or MOBI file. Kobo also provides an online previewer so you can review your book as it will appear to customers before letting it go live.

Adding a Book

To get your book sold through Kobo, you will have to set up a Kobo Writing Life account and have it verified. Once you have established an account, you will follow steps similar to those used to add a book to Amazon KDP, which involve describing your book, adding your book's content, providing information about the rights and distribution of your book, and setting your book's price. After you have entered all the necessary information and have been told there are no errors, you will click on the "Publish" button, and your e-book will be available for sale within seventy-two hours. Kobo allows you to keep your rights, set your price, and run your own promotions. It is also a nonexclusive service, so you will be able to use any other e-book service that interests you.

BARNES & NOBLE

Barnes & Noble's self-publishing service, known as Barnes & Noble Press, is an expansion of its former service, Nook Press, which offered only e-books. Barnes & Noble Press now offers a print-on-demand service in addition to its e-book model. In certain situations, the company even features a Barnes & Noble Press POD book in some of their brick-and-mortar stores.

Adding a Book

Once you are on the Barnes & Noble Press page of the company's website (https://press.barnesandnoble.com), you can set up an account. You will then be asked to choose to publish your book as an e-book, print book, or both. No matter your choice, as long as your book is in the system, you can opt to convert it into a different format later on. If you choose to create a print book, you will be asked your book's title, its estimated page count and page size, its interior print color, its cover format and finish, and your desired paper color. Your answers will generate the printing cost of your book, which should help you determine your book's retail price.

If you choose to create an e-book, you will submit an acceptable file format, which may be DOC, DOCX, TXT, HTML, or EPUB. You will then be asked additional questions on:

- language
- audience
- categories and keywords
- retail list price
- rights and other information
- public domain (yes or no)

- DRM encryption (yes or no)
- authors and contributors
- default book description
- publisher
- publication date

You will be able to examine a preview of how your e-book will appear when published. Once you have reviewed this preview, you will be asked to fill out vendor information and then click the "Publish Now" button. Your book will appear for sale on the Barnes & Noble website within seventy-two hours. If you are self-publishing a paperback book, you will also be given the option to preview your print version. If possible, get a physical book sent to you, as what you see online may not look the same as the physical book in your hands. The quality of certain aspects of your book, such as its spine, may be difficult to gauge if you see it only in an online preview.

Several services, such as Amazon, Kobo, and Barnes & Noble, allow you to see a preview of your e-book before it is made available to the public. Be sure to take advantage of this service when it is offered.

APPLE

Formerly known as Apple iBooks, Apple's e-book reader application is now called Apple Books. An author who wishes to create an e-book from his manuscript through Apple may do so using its "Author" application, after which he may submit his e-book to Apple Books by following the proper steps.

Adding a Book

If you are not using an aggregator to add your book to Apple Books but instead are going directly through Apple, you will need an Apple ID. If you don't already have one, go to the Apple website (www.apple.com), scroll down to the "Account" heading, and click on "Manage Your Apple ID" to sign up. Once you have an Apple ID, use it to enable "iTunes Connect" (https://itunesconnect.apple.com), after which you will be asked to choose between offering your e-book for free and selling it. (It is not possible to convert a free account into a paid account later, so choose a paid account if you are not sure. Paid accounts require taxpayer ID information, so be sure to have that on hand.)

You will then need to download the "iTunes Producer" app, through which you will upload your book in EPUB or PDF format to iTunes Connect. If you are planning to sell your e-book, you will have to create a sample for potential customers to view for free, which you may do using Apple's "Author" app. If you are submitting an EPUB file, however, a sample will be created automatically when you publish to Apple Books.

GOOGLE

In order to sell books through Google's e-book service, known as Google Play Books, you have to join the Google Books Partner Program (https://play.google.com/books/publish). Currently, however, the program is accepting only a limited number of new publishers. If you are interested in joining the program, Google asks that you make a request to do so through its online interest form, which may be found at the web address recently mentioned.

SMASHWORDS

Not all e-book services accept all file formats for conversion. Double-check the types of files that your chosen company permits before sending in your submission.

Smashwords is an e-book distributor that was founded with independent publishers in mind. Authors may upload their manuscripts to the Smashwords' website, and the company will then convert them into a number of file formats that may be sold through multiple online e-book retailers and read on different types of devices. As a distributor, the company will take a percentage (typically 15 percent) of net sales.

Adding a Book

To add your book to Smashwords, first set up a Smashwords account on the company's website (www.smashwords.com). Then download the "Smashwords Style Guide," which provides instructions on how to format your manuscript as a DOC file prior to uploading it to Smashwords. If you aren't able to format your manuscript properly on your own, Smashwords features a list of low-cost e-book formatters and designers, which it calls "Mark's List." If you already have a professionally prepared EPUB file, you may submit it to Smashwords directly.

When you are ready, simply click on the "Publish" button on the website and you will be guided through the process of uploading your book and its cover. The company takes pride in the notion that no technical experience is necessary to get your book into the Smashwords system.

Initially, your book will be availble through the Smashwords e-book retailer as it is reviewed for inclusion in what Smashwords calls its "Premium Catalog," which includes distribution to major bookstore retailers and library distributors such as Apple Books, Barnes & Noble, OverDrive, bibliotheca, and Odilo. Payment is on a monthly basis and royalties are 60 percent of list price for sales through major e-book retailers, and up to 80 percent of list price for sales through the Smashwords store.

How much of your profits will you have to relinquish to your e-book retailer or aggregator? Since these percentages vary greatly from company to company, it's important to understand exactly what you're signing up for before you make a commitment.

PUBLISHDRIVE

PublishDrive (www.publishdrive.com) is an e-book aggregator that is free to join but takes a cut of 10 percent of your e-book's list price on each sale. It distributes e-books to over four hundred online retailers, including major retailers such as Amazon, Apple, Google, Kobo, and Barnes & Noble, and hundreds of thousands of digital libraries all over the world.

Adding a Book

To learn how to upload your manuscript to PublishDrive, you can watch the demonstrational video featured on the company's website, or you can simply sign up for an account and follow the prompts to enter your content. PublishDrive requires a properly formatted EPUB version of your title for distribution and can convert your Word DOC, InDesign file, RTF, or HTML file into an EPUB for a fee if necessary. This fee is based on the number of characters and graphics in your manuscript.

Once your file is ready to go, you will need to provide information that includes your book's title, subtitle, and language, and then you will be asked to upload your EPUB and cover. If everything meets PublishDrive's specifications, you will be asked to fill in the rest of the required information, which includes page count, ISBN number, book description, publication date, and price.

BOOKBABY

This self-publishing platform enables you to create e-books as well as print books. BookBaby's business model differs from that of most other self-publishing services, in that it does not take a percentage of sales. BookBaby derives its income from upfront fees. Among its service packages is an all-inclusive option that provides interior and cover design, creation of e-book and print versions of your title (twenty-five printed books), ISBN number assignment, and worldwide distribution.

Adding a Book

Once you have landed on BookBaby's website, follow the prompts to get a quote for the services you desire. You could use BookBaby solely to create your e-book. Acceptable file formats include DOC, DOCX, TXT, HTML, and PDF files, as well as files created with Pages, Quark, or InDesign. If you are also interested in BookBaby's distribution service, just check the corresponding box when you fill out the online quote form. In addition to distributing your book to online retailers on your behalf, BookBaby also places your book in its own online bookstore, BookShop, which is able to offer your book in both e-book and POD formats. BookShop is free to all BookBaby authors.

DRAFT2DIGITAL

Draft2Digital is an aggregator that partners with Amazon, Apple Books, Barnes & Noble, Kobo, Playster, Scribd, Tolino, 24Symbols, OverDrive, and bibliotheca. The company does not charge any fees for formatting or distributing your e-book. It simply keeps about 10 percent of the retail price. Draft2Digital allows its authors to set the prices of their books and even lets them give their books away for free.

Adding a Book

Before you upload your manuscript, you will need to sign up for an account, at which time you will be asked for your book's title, description, sales categories, and search terms. When it comes to uploading your manuscript, Draft2Digital will accept a Word DOC, RTF, or any other file type that can be read by Word. You don't even need to have a title page, copyright page, contents page, or "About the Author" page. The service can create these pages for you.

If you have cover art, you can upload it, and Draft2Digital will resize it appropriately. As the website boasts, "any tall rectangle will do." Of course, the service will accept a properly formatted EPUB, too. Once your book has been uploaded, you will choose your vendors and set your list price.

CONCLUSION

While the thought of seeing your book in print might have been the one thing that kept you going as you were writing it, the actual printing of your manuscript may not be necessary to its success in the marketplace. E-books have entered the mainstream and are here to stay, and your book could do very well simply in its digital form. Of course, you don't really have to choose between producing an e-book and a print version, unless finances are a factor, in which case, creating only an e-book would be the more affordable option. Even then, the ability to print on demand has essentially rendered the cost issue obsolete.

Whichever path you decide to follow, there are so many great online retailers and aggregators out there that self-publishers shouldn't find it all that difficult to get their books to their potential readers. You need only consider which production and sales models most appeal to you and start uploading your book to the company or companies with which you choose to do business.

CHAPTER 7

---

*P*RINTING YOUR SELF-PUBLISHED BOOK

If there's a book that you want to read, but it hasn't been written yet, then you must write it.
—TONI MORRISON, AUTHOR

Many of us grew up reading books and being drawn to local bookstores and libraries to check out new titles. There are still lots of readers who enjoy browsing these wonderful establishments, preferring to read printed books rather than e-books. They like the feel of a book in their hands, the sensation of real paper on their fingertips, and the experience of turning pages. If you have decided to offer physical copies of your book for purchase, you will then need to choose between using a print-on-demand service and doing what is known as a short run.

Although e-books have some advantages over paper books, many readers prefer the experience of reading a traditional book—which is why so many authors choose to offer physical copies of their works.

SHORT-RUN PRINTERS VS. PRINT-ON-DEMAND SERVICES

As a self-publisher, one of the biggest decisions associated with the production of physical copies of your book involves how to go about doing so. Will you produce a short run of books, which is the more traditional way of printing, or use the *print-on-demand (POD)* model, which allows customers to print one copy of your book at a time?

The reason this is such a key decision is that it can impact the availability of your book in bookstores, some of which do not use the print-on-demand model. Some companies, however, allow you to have it both ways. For example, Lightning Source allows you to do a short run of books and store your inventory in its warehouse for fulfillment of future orders, which it will manage, while also enabling you to offer your book as a POD title.

Short-Run Printers

If you frequently speak to groups, you have the opportunity to sell your book at events, or you want large quantities of your book to sell to organizations or give to clients, it makes sense to invest in a print run. Otherwise, print-on-demand services might be a better choice.

Short-run printing allows an author to order a specific number of books per batch. The size of a batch generally ranges from at least fifty copies to thousands of copies. The advantage of short-run printing is that the unit price of a book is reduced as the number of copies requested is increased. This price drop occurs because the main expense of a short-run printing lies in its initial set-up at the printer.

When I started my small press twenty-three years ago, our first titles were produced as short runs. I had a distributor who was warehousing the printed books, which were delivered right to them directly from the printer. Since they were handling all the sales to wholesalers, such as Ingram and Baker & Taylor; handling sales to additional bookstores or libraries; and dealing with any returns, I only had to make sure they had enough books to sell and to promote my book so there were orders to fill. For *Friendshifts,* I did two short runs of 3,000 hardcover copies per run. When I lost the distributor and I decided to do a paperback edition a few years later, going the print-on-demand, non-returnable route seemed the more realistic course for that book, as I did not want to pay the thousands of dollars up front to print thousands of additional copies of the book or to pay to warehouse those books. For me, using Lightning Source (see page 115), a POD printer that is affiliated with Ingram, the wholesaler, seemed like the best course of action.

As you will learn in this chapter, however, there are pros and cons to either way of printing: short-run versus POD. Each self-publisher has to judge the best way to print her book based on a number of factors. Neither way of printing is better or "right" compared with the other method.

Print-on-Demand Services

Print-on-demand services allow an author to order only the number of books needed at a particular time, meaning books are printed when customers submit orders and not beforehand. While the unit price of books produced in short runs generally decreases over time, the unit price of a book that uses POD never decreases.

FINDING A SHORT-RUN PRINTER

If you decide you want to do a short run, the next step is finding a printer. Once you find a printer, you will also need to determine how many copies to print.

It is advisable to procure a few bids for the job, as prices may vary widely among printing companies. In addition, the way one company handles its short runs may differ considerably from the practices of other companies. It is crucial to learn these details, as they are bound to impact your print job and its delivery. Also ask to see book samples from the companies under consideration. If they want your business, they should be more than happy to fulfill this request so that you may judge the quality of their products. You may also want to get referrals from other self-publishers before making your decision.

If you decide to do a short run, don't be afraid to get a few bids for the job. Prices can vary widely from company to company.

Domestic Versus Overseas Printing

Most of the time, printing your job domestically rather than internationally will save you money due to the lower shipping costs associated with having your book produced in your home county. However, if you are producing a book that contains four-color artwork, such as a children's book, or a specialty book such as a board book, you should consider the cost and time involved in having it printed overseas, in China, India, or Eastern Europe. When looking into international production, be careful not to spend more in customs and shipping charges than you will save in printing costs, and double-check your estimated delivery date, as the international company you are using may decide to save money by shipping your books by boat instead of air.

Of course, when figuring out the cost of doing business internationally, remember that you may be going back and forth with proofs in your need to approve the final book. Who will pay for the overseas shipping charges? You? The printer? Will the cost be shared?

Another consideration that might tip you in favor of printing within your own country rather than in a distant one is the ease with which you will be able to communicate with your account manager. It would be helpful if you could speak to someone who lives in or close to your time zone. If you still want to print overseas, find out if your printer has a local representative to whom you can address any questions.

Standard Black-and-White Print Runs

Keep in mind that short-run printers usually bind their own paperback books but do not handle the binding of hardcover books in-house.

In regard to standard black-and-white books, short runs usually become more affordable than POD services once you print at least 1,000 copies at a time. If you print 5,000 or more copies of a black-and-white book, the per book cost could be very low—as low as $1.00 a book, compared with as much as $2.50 or $3.00 a book for POD printing. You may have to pay a greater upfront cost in this case, though, and, unless you are lucky enough to have advance orders, you will need a strong belief that you can sell this many copies. You may save money on each copy but find yourself stuck with thousands of books, which you must then store in your closet or garage, or in a warehouse to which you will have to pay storage fees.

On the bright side, printing thousands of books could motivate you to get out there and hustle for sales. If you know you will be printing only one book at a time, you might become complacent about the part of self-publishing that involves becoming a salesperson for your work. If, on the other hand, you invest money in a print run, it is likely that you will devote time and energy to selling your book.

Estimate Sheet

When deciding on which short-run printer to use, you will be asked to fill out an estimate sheet, which you should find on the printer's website. You will be asked for the trim size of the book you are printing as well as the page count. Trim size refers to the final size of a printed page after excess edges have been removed (e.g., a 6-inch by 9-inch trim size). For short runs, as well as for POD, page count is a pivotal issue when it comes to pricing. Understandably, it will cost more to print a 352-page book than it will to print a 160-page book.

In addition to trim size and length, you will be asked to designate the type of book you would like to print: hardcover or paperback. Printing a hardcover book is more expensive than printing a paperback, but you can also charge more for a hardcover. You will also be asked to choose the finish of your cover: glossy or matte. If your book is a black-and-white print job, you will be asked if it includes any photographs or illustrations. While printing a book that contains four-color artwork can be expensive, having photographs or illustrations in a black-and-white book should not affect the cost. It could, however, influence how professional it looks. Be aware of the resolution of the photographs or illustrations you wish to include. If the resolution of an image is too low, it may look blurry in print.

If you are producing a hardcover book, you will have to decide if you would like to have a book jacket, also known as a dust jacket, which will add to the cost of the job.

Prior to hiring a short-run printer, ask about how you will be charged for any corrections you might need to make before your

> Although most self-publishers choose to produce paperback books, hardcover books remain an option, albeit a more expensive one.

Converting Your E-Book into a Printed Book

If you have already created an e-book and now wish to go the printed route, it is best to go back to the original digital file that you had converted into an e-book and use this document to create a version in print. This advice is particularly worthwhile if you have photographs or illustrations in your book. The original file should have these materials at their highest possible resolutions, while the e-book file likely will not.

book is officially printed. This is a key difference between printing short-run jobs and POD jobs. When you use POD, even if you change one word or one letter in your book, you must provide your POD service with an entirely new digital file of the book. This file will replace the previous file for future print jobs. You may even be charged a new set-up fee to update your file.

FINDING A PRINT-ON-DEMAND SERVICE

When I first turned to POD printing in 1999, I was one of the initial customers of Lightning Source, the POD printing arm of Ingram wholesalers, which is still going strong after all these years. At the time, it was a lifesaver for me, since I had almost sold out of the 6,000 hardcover copies of my first self-published nonfiction book, *Friendshifts*, with only about 200 books left in inventory. Rather than print another 2,000 or more copies as a short run, which would have cost thousands of dollars up front, I decided to try POD since I was unsure just how much demand there would be for the two-year-old book. Alas, it turned out that there would soon be a groundswell of demand. Ironically, even before I could make the book's file "live" on Lightning Source, I was asked to appear on *The Oprah Winfrey Show.* I flew out on a Monday, the show taped on Tuesday, and I was told it was going to air two days later, on Thursday.

As I sat at the airport, waiting for my flight back to New York City, instead of calling friends and family about the taping I had just done, I called my account manager at Lightning Source. Although I had submitted everything that was needed to print the new paperback POD edition of my book, I had not made the file "live" yet. I told my account manager that I had just taped *Oprah* and that it was due to air two days later. I needed the book to be ready for sale as soon as possible.

Within a couple of days, my book could be ordered, which was extremely fortunate, as the phone was ringing off the hook with orders immediately after my interview on *Oprah* aired. This experience has always represented to me a perfect example of the value of print-on-demand services.

The following companies represent some of the most popular POD services available.

AMAZON KINDLE DIRECT

Amazon Kindle Direct (https://kdp.amazon.com) allows self-publishers who have created e-books for Kindle to make paperback versions of their titles on demand, as well. As with its e-books, Amazon lets self-publishers set separate prices and distribution options for each supported marketplace for their paperbacks. Any sales will be included in your Kindle monthly sales accounting and payments.

BARNES & NOBLE

While Barnes & Noble Press (https://press.barnesandnoble.com) has been providing e-book creation and distribution for a number of years, it took the company until 2018 to offer a POD service. Now authors can create POD titles that are immediately offered for sale on the Barnes & Noble website.

A POD title, however, is not guaranteed physical shelf space at brick-and-mortar Barnes & Noble stores. To have your book sold in Barnes & Noble retail locations, it must meet certain criteria, which include offering your book on a returnable basis for up to 180 days, having your book with a wholesaler or distributor, and offering at least a 50-percent discount off the retail price. Furthermore, to be considered for in-store placement, you will need to provide reviews from trade publications (*Publishers Weekly*, *Library Journal*, *Booklist*, etc.) as well as a marketing plan.

BLURB

This self-publishing creation and distribution platform specializes in photo books and illustrated books, especially those in color. In regard to trade books, Blurb (www.blurb.com) offers two printing qualities: standard and economy. Self-publishers may opt to sell their books in hardcover, with or without a dust jacket, or paperback, in a variety of trim sizes.

In the last few years, the quality of digital printing has improved so much that most consumers can't tell the difference between a book produced on a printing press and one produced with print-on-demand technology. This is just one of the many factors that make print-on-demand services so popular.

Blurb's website lists pricing information by book size, format (hardcover or paperback), paper and printing quality, and page count. Blurb also offers the choice of square, portrait, or landscape formats for photo books. Although these flexible options mean that a self-publisher should be able to create the print version she desires, they also mean that the author must have a very clear vision of the final printed book.

Blurb enabled Judy Smith, a successful self-publisher of numerous gift books, to get her start, beginning with *Dear Granddaughter: Life Lessons from Your Grandmother*. When she was asked about her self-publishing experience, Judy explained, "It started out that I did one book for my granddaughter as a gift. That went so well that I decided to make the granddaughter book more generic so it would work for all granddaughters and not just mine. Blurb worked really well for me because I used a lot of photos, but it allowed me to format the book so I could give the book to my designer, who could see the basics of what I wanted done."

Blurb is a good choice for the serious self-publisher who wants to control every detail of her book's layout. It also offers a wide range of format options and luxury paper choices.

BOOKBABY

BookBaby (www.bookbaby.com) is a well-known self-publishing platform that offers a number of services, including cover design and interior formatting. Its print-on-demand service may be used to print a wide variety of book styles, including hardcover books, paperback books, photography books, children's books, and more.

Customers are able to order and pay for self-published books online through vendors such as Amazon or Barnes & Noble, as well as wholesalers such as Ingram or Baker & Taylor. BookBaby prints, binds, and packages these orders, and then ships the books to the appropriate retailers or wholesalers, allowing them to fulfill their orders. BookBaby retrieves payments, deducts its fees, and then distributes the net dollar amounts to its self-publishers for their sales.

INGRAMSPARK

With facilities located around the world, IngramSpark (www. ingramspark.com) boasts the ability to get your book to retailers, warehouses, libraries, distributors, and individual readers quickly and reliably through its print-on-demand service. IngramSpark is a subsidiary of Ingram, a major US book wholesaler, and an alternative to its Lightning Source print-on-demand company. It is geared towards self-published authors with fewer than thirty titles, while Lightning Source is aimed at midsize to large publishers with over thirty titles.

This company's print-on-demand services promise to produce books that are indistinguishable from traditionally published titles. You can print books in a variety of formats, trim sizes, color types, and binding types.

LIGHTNING SOURCE

As already mentioned, Lightning Source (www.lightningsource. com) is a self-publishing platform owned by US wholesaler Ingram. It allows self-publishers to print quality books on demand in a variety of formats, bindings, and trim sizes. It promises to put books through ten quality control checks before sending them out. It also promises to use some of the most advanced print technology in the world, so that the text and graphics found in its books are comparable to those found in traditionally printed books.

Espresso Book Machine

When it comes to print-on-demand books, brick-and-mortar stores or libraries may feature the Espresso Book Machine, which, according to its slogan, offers "books printed in minutes at point of sale." This machine is able to print, collate, cover, and bind a paperback book in a few minutes, eliminating the need to warehouse or return unsold books. It also grants customers the luxury of obtaining any title they desire in the database, even if that title has gone out of print.

OUTSKIRTS PRESS

Outskirts Press (www.outskirtspress.com) is another self-publishing service that prints paperback and hardcover books on demand. It is a full-service self-publishing company that charges flat rates to authors in exchange for wholesale printing, order fulfillment, and distribution to major vendors, with authors keeping 100 percent of the rights to their books and any earnings. Pricing starts at a little under $1,000 for economy black-and-white books and can hover around $2,000 for full-color publishing.

THOMSON-SHORE

Thomson-Shore (https://thomsonshore.com) offers a number of print-on-demand models. Using its "Publisher-Driven Order Fulfillment" model, self-publishers receive orders through their own websites and collect payments themselves. They then send their order information to Thomson-Shore, which prints and ships the ordered books.

Using the "Direct-to-Consumer POD" model, self-publishers use links to direct their shoppers to the pages on Thomson-Shore's online store, through which their books may be ordered. Thomson-Shore collects payments and then prints and ships the books directly to the shoppers. Self-publishers receive detailed monthly statements and royalty checks.

If you opt for the "Trade POD" model, Thomson-Shore will make your book available to major wholesalers such as Ingram and Baker & Taylor, and manage your online sales through Amazon.com. These sales platforms will send Thomson-Shore their orders, and Thomson-Shore will then print the requested number of books and handle fulfillment.

While Thomson-Shore prints books only when orders are received, it also allows self-publishers to print large quantities of books whenever they might need them. Its distribution team also offers to help self-publishers analyze demand for their books and decide when they should switch to short-run printing.

CONCLUSION

If you are disappointed by the prospect of never being able to hold your book in your hands—of having only a digital version of your title to show for all your hours of toil—chances are you are going to create a print version of your text. Thankfully, as mentioned at the outset of this chapter, there is no shortage of readers who still want physical books. Whether you choose to do a short run of books or simply use a print-on-demand service, your title could one day sit on bookshelves next to the works of authors you grew up reading and from whom you have drawn inspiration. Print is not dead. Even if you are publishing an e-book, there is no reason to feel you cannot also produce a print version. Moreover, you may not want to stop there, as the growing popularity of audiobooks suggests that this third format might also be worth your consideration.

CHAPTER 8

CONVERTING YOUR BOOK INTO AN AUDIOBOOK

Audiobooks speak for themselves.
—PAUL ACAMPORA, AUTHOR

Although experts might disagree on which book format is most desirable, they are all in agreement that audiobooks have become a very important part of overall book sales. In recent years, audiobook downloads have increased substantially. More and more, people who might be too busy to read a physical book are turning to audiobooks to fulfill their literary needs, and audiobook services are making it easier and easier for them to do so. According to the Audio Publishers Association (APA), the number of Americans who listen to audiobooks each year has surpassed 67 million and continues to grow. Yet I am astonished and bewildered by the number of authors and self-publishers I know who are still on the fence about whether they should turn their books into audiobooks.

These days, the decision to convert your book into an audiobook should be a no-brainer. Of course, it took a decade for authors, publishers, and the public to recognize the value of e-books. As audiobooks become increasingly simple to access and use, I am confident that they will one day enjoy a status on par with e-books and print books.

Developments in technology—including smartphones, smart speakers, and AirPods, as well as improved audiobook production—have contributed to the growing popularity of audiobooks. In fact, both audiobook sales and digital audiobook library borrowing are on the rise.

AUDIOBOOK NARRATION

Narration can make or break an audiobook, so take the time to consider the essential elements of good narration when creating your own audiobook.

One of the signs of a successful audiobook is when a reader listens to it and thinks, "I could listen to this narrator forever." This thought means that the narrator is reading the dialogue in a way that draws the listener in and gives emotional weight to the words.

The narration of a book can have a major effect on the success of an audiobook. There are essential narration elements that should be considered in the creation of an audiobook. You should make sure:

- the narration is smooth, free from interruptions or pauses.

- the narrator sounds engaged and energetic, as if he is enjoying the story.

- the accents sound authentic.

- the narrator crafts a believable voice for each character without overdoing it.

Narration forms the foundation of a good audiobook. The audiobook version of a best-selling book may not sell well if it is poorly narrated, while a less successful book may sell well as an audiobook because it has engaging narration.

Narrating Your Own Audiobook

Some authors think they should be the narrators of their own audiobooks. Unfortunately, many authors do not have the time, interest, or skill to do the job. Often, rather than delegate this task to a voiceover artist or professional book narrator, they end up doing nothing. Others are unaware of the fact that it is possible to get their audiobooks created and distributed on a royalty-sharing basis, without any upfront costs.

Nevertheless, there are some self-publishers who narrate their own audiobooks and are terrific at it. (I have even been told by some authors that their publishers paid them to narrate their own books.)

As a self-publisher, you will either perform tasks yourself or, when advisable, delegate them to other people. As a result, you will need to be mindful of your expenses and your time—two key concerns when it comes to getting the most out of your self-publishing experience without going broke or burning out.

You have already taken on the job of self-publishing your book. It is up to you if you would like to narrate your book yourself. But try not to feel compelled to take every step of this publishing journey on your own. If you are looking for a way to make your self-publishing life a little easier, getting someone else to narrate your book just might do the trick.

Getting Your Book Narrated

I have converted dozens of books into audiobooks using a service called ACX, or Audiobook Creation Exchange, which is part of Audible, a producer and vendor of audio entertainment and a subsidiary of Amazon. I have done all of these audiobooks on a royalty-sharing basis, which means the narrators, also called "producers" on ACX, receive a percentage of income from each sale, but ACX offers three different payment and distribution options to its customers:

- **Royalty Share.** This option grants exclusive distribution rights to Audible for a term of seven years. Royalty payments are shared between the rights holder (author) and the producer (narrator) at a rate of 40 percent of retail sales. This royalty rate is split evenly between the rights holder and the producer.

- **Pay for Production (Flat Fee) with Exclusive Distribution.** This option grants exclusive distribution rights to Audible for a term of seven years. Instead of sharing royalties, however, the rights holder pays the producer a flat fee for production of the audiobook. In this scenario, the rights holder receives the entire royalty rate of 40 percent of retail sales.

- **Pay for Production (Flat Fee) with Nonexclusive Distribution.** This option grants nonexclusive distribution rights to Audible for a term of seven years, which means the rights holder is allowed to grant distribution rights to parties other than Audible in any market or format. The rights holder pays the producer a flat fee for the production of the audiobook and receives the entire royalty rate, which in this scenario is 25 percent of retail sales.

An additional source of income on sales is what is called "Bounty Payment." This payment refers to a $50 earning that is generated any time your audiobook is the first audiobook purchased by a member of Audible's subscription service. If you have opted to share your royalties, this payment will be divided equally between the rights holder and the producer. If you have opted for the flat-fee method, this entire payment will go to the rights holder.

When deciding between sharing your royalty rate and paying a narrator a flat fee, you should consider the length of your book and the time it would take to produce its audiobook version. For example, let's say you opt for the flat-fee method, and the narrator you would like to use charges $100 an hour. In this case, a production job that takes approximately five hours to complete would cost you $500. Consider how many units it would take for you to earn $500 in royalties at the rate of 40 percent. If your audiobook ends up being priced at $15.95, at a 40-percent royalty rate, you would get $6.38 per sale. You would have to sell approximately seventy-eight units to earn in royalties what you paid as a flat fee to your producer.

If you opt for a royalty-sharing arrangement at the previously mentioned sale price, you would get $3.19 per sale, but you would not incur the $500 upfront cost. According to these numbers, as long as your audiobook ends up selling at least 157 copies, the flat-fee arrangement would be the better choice for your bank account. If your audiobook ends up selling fewer than 157 copies, however, sharing your royalty rate would be the most profitable option. It all depends on how well you think your audiobook might sell. Of course, if you have a number of books to convert into audiobooks, the flat-fee option might seem like more of a risk to your bottom line.

Audiobook services sometimes allow authors to choose from different payment and distribution plans. To select the best option, you should consider several factors, including the length of your book (and, therefore, the time it will take to produce its audiobook version), and how well you think your audiobook might sell. Be as realistic as possible when making this decision.

ACX

If you choose to work with ACX, you will need to register for an ACX account, which you may do using your Amazon account. If you do not have an Amazon account, you will need to sign up for one in the process of registering for an ACX account. Once you are

Should You Narrate Your Own Book?

The decision to narrate your own book is a major one. A narrator can help make or break an audiobook. Here are some questions to ask yourself as you decide whether you should narrate your own work:

1. Over the years, have friends or classmates told you that you have a great voice or that you should do voiceover work or narrate a book?

     Yes_____ No _____

2. Do you have the time it will take to narrate your book?

     Yes_____ No _____

3. Do you have the skills to complete book-length narration?

     Yes_____ No _____

4. Do you have the technical ability and equipment to make sure your audiobook meets all expected sound and quality standards?

     Yes_____ No _____

5. Are you financially and psychologically comfortable with the possibility that you might not sell enough audiobooks to compensate yourself for the time spent recording and editing your audiobook?

     Yes_____ No _____

   If you answered yes to these five questions, then narrating your own audiobook could be the right step for you to take. If you answered no to one or more of these questions, consider what your answers suggest about the idea of producing your audiobook on your own.

all signed up, you may put a book up for auditions. If your book is already listed on Amazon in print or as an e-book, you may do a search for it and import its cover and description to the ACX site.

On the ACX site, there is a drop-down menu that asks several questions about each audiobook project. A description of your book goes at the top of the page (and may be taken from the Amazon listing of your book), where there is also room to add additional information that might cause a producer to want to convert your book into an audiobook, including genre, language, gender, character age, accent, and vocal style.

After you fill in this information, you will have some additional questions to answer before your book is put up for audition. You will need to list the length of your book—the number of words, not the number of pages—the name of the rights owner, and whether you would like to hire a narrator on a flat-fee or royalty-sharing basis.

One very important step is adding a sample from your book for producers to narrate in the audition process. After adding this sample, auditions should start to roll in for review. You may listen to each audition file directly on the ACX website or download it to your computer or smartphone to listen to at a later time.

In addition to waiting for producers to contact you, you can click on the "Producers for Hire" button at the top of the ACX website and contact any of the listed producers to request an audition. ACX allows you to see the names of its narrators and learn a little bit about them through their ACX profiles, including their genders and the regions in which they live. This could be useful information if you would prefer to hire someone who lives in a certain area—near where you live, for example—because you would like to meet your narrator in person and discuss the project. Most narration and production work, however, is done remotely, so don't count on meeting your narrator. You will also be able to see if they have a royalty-sharing option under their pictures. If they accept flat fees, you should be able to see their ranges—such as $100 PFH (per finished hour), $200 PFH, etc.

After you listen to the auditions, you should have a good impression of which voice you would like to use as your narrator. If you need more options, however, just wait until you get more submissions. If you hear a narrator you like and want to hire, you may send him a contract. When sending a contract to a narrator, you will be given the option of granting this individual twenty-four, forty-eight, or seventy-two hours to respond. If the contract is not accepted within the time period selected, it will be automatically cancelled. If the contract is accepted, you will be able to communicate with the producer through the ACX website or, if the narrator has provided you with his email address, over email.

You will need to pick a date on which you would like to receive the first fifteen minutes of your audiobook as a sample, and a second date on which you will expect the completed audiobook. Many producers have told me it takes one to two weeks to complete a fifteen-minute sample, and approximately three months to finish an entire audiobook. Keep in mind that most producers work on multiple projects at a time, so they would prefer to have more time rather than less.

Once you have received your sample, you may accept it or ask for revisions. If this fifteen-minute sample does not meet your expectations at all, you may instead cancel the contract at this point. If you accept the first fifteen minutes, it is assumed that you will accept the completed audiobook. If you are completely dissatisfied with the final version of your audiobook or the process is being unacceptably delayed, you may want to cancel your contract with your narrator. Cancellation can be done, but it is a very formal process that requires you and your narrator to agree that the contract can be cancelled. Unless the contract is formally cancelled, including the receipt of an email from your narrator which states that he agrees to the cancellation, ACX will not allow your book to be put up for audition again.

Some producers send their work chapter by chapter to authors for review. Others prefer to send only completed audiobooks. The way in which you would like to review your audiobook is a matter you can discuss with your narrator. Once you've accepted the final audiobook, ACX will give it a thorough review. If it has any objections to it, you and the producer will get a detailed explanation of the elements that need to be fixed.

Some audiobook companies, such as ACX and Spoken Realms, involve the author in the selection of a narrator. You may be able to learn a little bit about the available narrators through profiles and listen to their auditions before granting approval.

It takes anywhere from one to three weeks for ACX to approve your completed audiobook for sale. Once it has been approved, it will go on sale on audible.com, amazon.com, and itunes.com within one to three business days. It is important to note that the process may be slowed down if your cover has not been reformatted to fit ACX's specifications. If you have trouble reformatting your cover to ACX's specifications on your own, consider hiring a graphic designer or cover designer to help you.

SPOKEN REALMS

An alternative to ACX, Spoken Realms offers to connect authors with its "featured voices," which refer to narrators who are already part of Spoken Realm's production system. It does not intervene between author and narrator. After an author contacts a featured voice directly, the two parties then work out a production arrangement, whether a royalty-sharing deal, flat-fee deal, or some sort of combination of the two. Once the details have been ironed out, the project will be set up in the Spoken Realm system. There are no additional costs beyond what an author and narrator have agreed to in advance.

Spoken Realm also does a limited number of in-house productions at Spoken Realms Studios each year, and self-publishers may submit their works for consideration through the Spoken Realm website. (See Resources on page 231.)

Spoken Realms places audiobooks into online and physical distribution chains, but content owners retain their right to sell digital or physical copies of their audiobooks without Spoken Realms. The company also claims to match or beat the royalty rates offered by ACX.

Selling Your Audiobook Rights

I have spent a lot of time discussing ACX because I find its royalty-sharing option such a blessing for those self-publishers who would like to have audiobooks but cannot afford to pay narrators or production companies. Nevertheless, I would like to provide information about other ways to get an audiobook produced, as this book is all about self-publishing options and helping you determine which choices might yield the best outcome for you and your book.

The companies discussed below pay authors to option the audio rights to their e-books or print books. They have their producers create audiobooks of the books they've acquired. This field is super competitive, though, and you might find your submission declined. Your book will need to have excellent reviews, decent sales, or just the luck of someone at one of these companies falling in love with it for you to be offered one of these sought-after deals.

BOOKS ON TAPE

A subsidiary of Penguin Random House, its editorial staff accepts manuscripts and advance reading copies from agents, other publishing houses, and authors. It determines which titles it will make available as audiobooks to its customer base and then produces these audiobooks in its own studios, which are located in New York and Los Angeles.

BLACKSTONE PUBLISHING

Building upon its long history as a producer and distributor of audiobooks, Blackstone Audio became Blackstone Publishing in 2015. It now seeks to publish groundbreaking books in both the fiction and nonfiction categories by talented writers in print, e-book, and audio formats.

BRILLIANCE AUDIO

Now owned by Amazon, Brilliance Audio began in 1984 by recording best-selling books and selling these recorded versions to retail stores at affordable prices. Of course, back then, these recordings were not called "audiobooks" but rather "books on tape." Unlike Amazon's other audio-publisher, ACX, which publishes only downloadable audiobooks, Brilliance Audio produces audiobooks in multiple formats, including compact disc, MP3-CD, and downloadable files. According to its website, it offers 6,500 titles.

It's not easy for authors to land a contract with major audiobook publishers such as Books on Tape and Brilliance Audio. In this competitive field, excellent reviews and good sales records—and, of course, great writing—are needed to convince an editor that your print or electronic book would make a profitable audiobook.

TANTOR MEDIA

Founded in 2000 in California and now based in Old Saybrook, Connecticut, Tantor Media produces unabridged fiction and nonfiction audiobooks as both physical discs and downloads. In 2012 it began to offer print and e-book versions of its titles. It works with 150 of the industry's best narrators, taking care to match the right voice to each of its books. It is open to book submissions through publishers and literary agents.

Hiring a Narrator and Producing an Audiobook on Your Own

Even if your audiobook is available through major outlets, you will want to promote it through as many means as possible, including your own website and websites and magazines that focus on audiobooks.

You could hire a narrator completely on your own and book time in a recording studio with a producer to create your audiobook. You could then distribute your audiobook through your website and send it to other online outlets using an audiobook distributor such as ACX, Author's Republic, or Findaway.

But where does one find a narrator? Well, you could always take a look at the narrator listings and samples provided on the websites of some of the companies mentioned in this chapter, such as ACX and Tantor Media. *AudioFile* magazine's website also maintains an extensive collection of narrators' samples.

Finally, many narrators have websites and actively promote their narration services online. An online search for "audiobook narrators" should yield a large number of names.

PROMOTING YOUR AUDIOBOOK

Although having your audiobook available for sale through the major outlets mentioned in this book will be beneficial to your cause, it is still critical to promote your audiobook and drive traffic to the places where interested readers may purchase it. Promoting it on your personal website goes without saying, but garnering notice from audiobook reviewers is the best way to spark sales.

Audiobook Reviewers

Do an online search for "audiobook reviewers," and you should find a number of great websites such as Audiobook Reviewer, *AudioFile* magazine, Audiobook Jukebox, AudioGals, and The Audiobook-worm, which might review your audiobook. If you are able to create a press kit for your audiobook, which should include a press release about your book, your author bio, and your author photo, send it along with your audiobook whenever a website allows you to do so. If you have created your audiobook using one of the services described in this chapter, you should be given access to enough free downloads to meet your promotional needs.

Promotional Websites

Once you have had your audiobook reviewed, you may then seek out websites that focus on promoting audiobooks, such as AudaVoxx, Audiobook Boom!, and AudioBookRadio. If possible, send these promotional websites your press kit along with any other information the websites might require.

CONCLUSION

If you were sitting on the fence about whether to produce an audio-book, hopefully you now see the value in creating one. Of course, deciding to do an audiobook means having more choices to make. You may choose to narrate your book or have your book narrated for you. If you opt to hire a narrator, you will have to decide on which payment and distribution structure you'd like to use. Once your audiobook has been created, you will need to contact reviewers and promotional websites that might help you get the word out.

Yes, doing an audiobook means giving yourself more work to do, but having a good audiobook also means that your work will be able to reach as many people as possible, as there will always be those who prefer to listen to a book, whether in the car, at the gym, or even right before bed. It's a growing market that is worth the work.

CHAPTER 9

*U*NDERSTANDING THE *M*ARKETPLACE

So many books, so little time.
—FRANK ZAPPA, MUSICIAN

Do not confuse a book's *marketplace* with its *audience*. A book's audience refers to its potential readership, specifically the demographics for which a book has been designed. These demographics are based on factors such as gender, age, religion, race, politics, and profession. A book's marketplace, on the other hand, refers to the means by which a book reaches its audience. As it turns out, one of the most challenging parts of being a self-publisher is getting your book into the hands of the people who might be interested in reading it.

This chapter looks at various marketplaces for books and explains which are relatively easy for a self-publisher to access and which are more difficult, and why this is so.

One of the most common mistakes an author can make is to think she has completed most of the hard work of self-publishing simply by producing a professional-looking book. Unfortunately, while having a well-made book is important, it is just one of many pieces of the puzzle when it comes to self-publishing. By understanding the marketplaces that are available to you, you should be able to select the best ways to reach these marketplaces and, in turn, your book's audience.

MARKETPLACES

The two terms most often used when describing a book's market-place are *trade* marketplace and *non-trade* marketplace. As you will see, there is a world of difference between them.

Trade

In publishing, the expression "selling to the trade" refers to selling books to bookstores and libraries. Most large commercial publishers consider themselves trade publishers, with the bulk of their sales going to bookstores and libraries. These publishers may, however, have divisions, departments, or individuals that focus on selling their books to the non-trade marketplace.

The trade marketplace includes the following:

- College bookstores

- College libraries

- Military libraries

- Online retailers

- Physical (so-called "brick-and-mortar") retailers

- Private or specialty libraries

- Public libraries

- School libraries

Each of these aspects of the trade marketplace has a well-established distribution system from which it purchases its titles. Some of these distribution systems overlap, and some of them market and sell to only one or two of these book buyers. In addition, in terms of the trade marketplace, it is important to know that all books sold to the trade are returnable for full credit. This is actually one of the key elements that could make it harder for a self-publisher to sell a book to the trade. As a self-publisher, you need to seriously consider if you will make your book returnable or non-returnable.

Non-Trade

If there is a Wild West of book marketplaces, it would be the non-trade marketplace. In a nutshell, the non-trade marketplace refers to every possible bookseller who is not considered part of the trade marketplace—and this definition encompasses quite a lot of places. And whereas access routes to the trade marketplace have been well established for decades, the non-trade marketplace is open to anyone with a book that meets a specific outlet's needs. The non-trade marketplace includes the following:

- Association sales
- Book fairs
- Catalogs
- Corporate sales
- Crowdfunding
- Direct mail
- Direct online sales
- Gift shops
- Government agencies
- Infomercials
- Lectures
- Museum shops
- Specialty retailers that carry books for their specific shoppers, such as pet stores, health food shops, sewing centers, cooking equipment stores, etc.

While your focus will likely be on the trade marketplace when you are trying to sell your book, don't overlook the potential of the non-trade sector. While some non-trade opportunities may seem a little out of left field, you never know where your book might find a foothold in the market.

The non-trade marketplace presents self-published authors with many opportunities to find the perfect outlets for their books. Unlike the trade, though, books sold to the non-trade marketplace are typically non-returnable. As noted, the trade marketplace has a tradition of allowing returns. Since the non-trade marketplace allows non-returnable books, it may be the better option to pursue as a self-publisher.

REACHING MARKETPLACES THROUGH TRADITIONAL MEANS

While some retailers and libraries may occasionally order books directly from publishers, the vast majority of the trade—and to some degree, a number of non-trade outlets—use wholesalers, distributors, or both to obtain books. Traditionally, the terms *wholesaler* and *distributor* refer to two different types of operations.

Distributors

A distributor is a company that has an exclusive agreement with a publisher to sell its books to bookstores, libraries, or wholesalers. In some cases, the publisher is free to sell its titles to the non-trade marketplace. In other cases, the distributor controls all sales.

When a publisher signs an exclusive arrangement with a distributor, typically the distributor would:

- warehouse the bulk of the publisher's titles.

- have a sales force to sell the titles.

- market the books in its catalog, on its website, and in promotional emails.

- ship all orders, invoice customers, collect money owed, and take back returns. (If returns are in good enough condition, they will be placed back in the warehouse and resold.)

In exchange for providing these services, the distributor collects a percentage of net sales shipped to customers (minus returns), a monthly fee for warehousing the books, and perhaps even handling fees on both outgoing shipments and returns. In regard to payments made to publishers, distributors generally take ninety to one hundred and twenty days to pay publishers for titles sold (again, minus returns).

If you have an interest in working with a distributor on an exclusive basis, learn as much about the company as possible. Look at its website to see which publishers it represents and the types of books it handles. Once you know the names of some of its publishers, email or phone a few of these companies, ask to speak to their marketing directors or sales managers, and ask them what they think of the job their distributor is doing. Making a commitment to a distributor is a major business decision, usually requiring a two-year exclusive contract, so be sure that when you sign an exclusive sales arrangement, you have done all your homework.

Wholesalers

A wholesaler is a company that has an arrangement with a publisher to sell a publisher's books to bookstores and libraries on a nonexclusive basis. Distributors may also use wholesalers to sell the titles of the publishers they represent. (If you sign with an exclusive distributor, however, you will not deal with the wholesaler. The distributor will do that for you.) After a publisher signs a deal with a wholesaler, the wholesaler will generally:

- hold a large or small stock of titles in its warehouse, based on their sales.

- ship all orders, invoice customers, collect money owed, and take back returns.

- offer means of promotion, such as ads on its website, ads in its promotional pieces, or emails to its customer base.

As a self-publisher, it is important to understand the details of any deal offered by a wholesaler or distributor—two terms that seem to be used interchangeably these days despite the fact that they refer to different systems.

In return for providing these services, the wholesaler would collect a percentage of net sales shipped to customers (minus returns, if applicable). It would also reimburse itself for the total cost of shipping returns back to the publisher. Wholesalers generally take ninety to one hundred and twenty days to pay publishers or distributors for titles sold (minus returns and shipping).

Over the last decade, the terms "wholesaler" and "distributor" seem to have become interchangeable, although the two systems still exist independently of each other. So, even if a wholesaler calls itself a distributor, it is still a wholesaler. Nevertheless, some wholesalers may also have distribution divisions that work with their wholesale operations. While these distinctions may be confusing, as a self-publisher, it is important for you to understand them—especially since both wholesalers and distributors take back returned books from the trade and deduct these returns from any money they might owe you.

If you would like to sell your book to the trade marketplace, you must produce enough physical books to show a traditional wholesaler or distributor that it would be able to meet its sales needs if orders start coming in. As long as a book is deemed returnable by the trade marketplace, it has a chance of being sold through one of these entities. There are, however, exceptions to this rule. Ingram, one of the largest wholesalers, will sell non-returnable print-on-demand titles, especially if they have been printed through its own print-on-demand subsidiary, Lightning Source.

How Much Will You Make?

There are a number of distributors that are happy to work with self-published authors. When a distributor takes over sales functions and becomes the exclusive seller of a book, it may receive 60 to 70 percent of the retail list price of the book, depending on the negotiated commission rate in its contract.

Although a distributor's or wholesaler's commission might seem to take a big bite out of your profits as a self-publisher, your earnings would actually be far smaller if your book were to be released by a major publishing house, which would likely offer you a 10-percent royalty rate at best. Of course, the seemingly low amount offered by publishers reflects the fact that they take care of every facet of publishing, from editing and typesetting to promotion, order fulfillment, and shipping.

If a distributor is working with a wholesaler, it may pay the wholesaler 50 to 55 percent of its 60- to 70-percent commission in warehousing fees, as well as a percentage to sales representatives, who are tasked with presenting books to buyers. Wholesalers typically give bookstores a discount of 40 percent, while some publishers that deal directly with libraries or bookstores might offer only a 20-percent discount.

If a self-publisher works directly with a wholesaler, the percentage of the retail list price paid to the wholesaler is typically between 50 and 55 percent, although some publishers may try to offer only a 40-percent commission. Even if a wholesaler accepts this lower commission rate, doing so may limit the bookstores or other venues to which it may sell your book. Some wholesalers require a non-negotiable rate of 55-percent commission on retail. Depending on who pays for them, the costs of shipping books from self-publisher to wholesaler can make a big difference in a self-publisher's earnings through a wholesaler.

When working directly with a wholesaler, in most cases, a self-publisher's earnings are calculated by taking the retail list price of a book, subtracting the wholesaler's commission, and then subtracting any shipping costs. To illustrate: $16.95 (retail list price) minus $9.32 (55% commission) minus $3.50 (shipping costs) = $4.13 profit on the sale of one book through a wholesaler.

Yes, this profit might seem small. But remember that if you were to publish a book through a traditional trade publisher, your earnings as an author (if you were lucky enough to get a 10-percent royalty rate) would be just $1.69 per book. And if the publisher were to offer this royalty only on net income, your profit could wind up being less than $1 per book.

REACHING MARKETPLACES ONLINE

The Internet is not only a tool that self-publishers can use to research and connect with brick-and-mortar booksellers in the trade marketplace, but also a huge part of the trade marketplace itself. Online retailers sell millions of physical books, e-books, and audiobooks to people all over the world. As a self-publisher, it is helpful to know the main reasons why online book retailers are such an important aspect of the business these days. Online book retailers are able to:

- carry tens of thousands of different titles, ranging from bestsellers to niche titles.

- deliver e-books immediately and physical books within days.

- display cover images, author images, promotional copy, and reviews.

- sell books throughout the world.

While online book retailers focus on books, there are other online retailers that sell various lines of products and offer product-related books for sale as well. For example, a website that sells slow cookers may also sell slow-cooker cookbooks, and a website that sells camping equipment may sell books related to anything dealing with the outdoors. By understanding how your book fits into the marketplace, the Internet can provide you with the means and opportunity to get your book seen by more people.

There are a number of ways to get your title picked up by an online book retailer or an online retailer that specializes in other products but also carries books. Each outlet, however, comes with its own payment structure and set of rules to follow, and each has its own pros and cons. It is important to note that, in most instances, online book retailers demand return privileges. The more you understand an online retailer's terms, the less likely you are to be surprised by the amount of income you receive from sales.

Distributors

As previously noted, if you are going to have the book printed yourself, you may choose to work with a distributor. A distributor would normally have the sole right to sell your book to the majority of sales outlets, which include all the normal online book retailers. It may also place your book on non-bookstore websites that may have an interest in carrying your title. Your distribution agreement would likely include the e-book version of your title. With your input, your distributor would provide each online retailer with the elements necessary to sell your title.

While this approach may take a good deal of work off your shoulders, it also provides the smallest monetary return, since a distributor will take as much as 70 percent of the list price of your book from sales.

Wholesalers

Some wholesalers may provide the service of contacting online retailers to sell your physical book. Some may also offer the service of converting your physical book into an e-book. On the other hand, you are likely to find that you can sell books directly to online retailers by making connections yourself and letting online retailers know that your book is available through a specific wholesaler. Once the ordering system has been set up, your wholesaler will receive book orders directly from your online retailers.

Just like working with a distributor, of course, using a wholesaler results in a smaller return on each sale for the self-publisher.

Self-Publishing Services

As the number of self-publishing services continues to grow, so do the number of services they offer. Some self-publishing services include the option of producing physical books in various quantities, printing single copies on demand, or creating e-book versions of books. Many of these companies also act as traditional distributors while also being physical book or e-book producers. Many self-publishing services use their websites as a platform to sell the titles they have produced for self-publishers. They may also direct readers to online book retailers or wholesalers.

Depending on the type of publishing agreement you sign with a self-publishing service, it may be more financially lucrative for you to use this type of company than it would be for you to partner with a traditional distributor or wholesaler, in that your portion of net sales would be greater.

DIY

Although this may not come as a surprise, if you do all the work yourself—that is, handling the printing or e-book conversion of your book yourself—you may wind up with a larger return on your investment than you would otherwise. This doesn't mean you are going to make a fortune. It means that you may make a larger percentage of net profit—in other words, the money placed in your hands after costs have been deducted. In doing it all yourself, however, you may encounter problems with the policies of certain online book retailers. For example, some online companies may purchase physical books only from wholesalers. Thankfully, most take e-books directly from authors. To learn the policies of an online retailer, look on its website for a "Publisher Information" page, which should contain this information.

Beyond just online book retailers are other online specialty retailers that may carry your title. By exploring the world of online retailers that may have some interest in carrying your book, you can create a list of potential contacts, email or call them, and learn how they select the books they sell. Once you have the appropriate information, you should be able to see if your book would be a good fit for their websites.

Of course, you also have the opportunity to reach the marketplace with your book using your own website. Selling your book through your website should provide you with the highest percentage of

Doing all the work yourself almost certainly means making a larger percentage of net profit, but you may run into problems with certain online retailers that purchase physical books only from distributors or wholesalers. An online retailer's policy should be listed on its website under "Publisher Information."

returns per sale, but you will need to make sure your website looks professional and functions properly in order to get any sales in the first place. When creating your website, you should:

- hire a website designer or use an online service that allows you to build a website on your own.

- establish a means to download e-books or take print book orders.

- have a payment method for your customers to use.

- place links on your website to other online book retailers that sell your print book or e-book.

There are now over 200 million active websites, and many of them were created by "novices" with no special technical skills. For help in creating your own website, check out the do-it-yourself website builders listed in the Resources section of this book.

If you don't want to be responsible for shipping physical books to your customers, you could always sell only the e-book versions of your book. And if you do not wish to take the time to build your own website, hiring someone to build it for you may be the right choice, although it is sure to be the more expensive option.

If you have the time to build your own website and are somewhat computer savvy, there are a number of do-it-yourself website design programs that you might consider using to cut down on your start-up costs. (See "Do-It-Yourself Website Builders" in Resources on page 239.) No matter who creates your website, however, the real trick is getting people to visit it. (See Chapter 11.)

REACHING MARKETPLACES IN THE REAL WORLD

Selling is not for everyone, but to some people the act of selling comes naturally, like talking to an old friend. For others, it's an intensely disconcerting experience, something that they would like to avoid completely. For all self-publishers, however, the act of selling a book to the appropriate marketplace is a matter of presenting the book's sales sheet, creating a solid sales pitch, and being prepared to answer any questions. Meeting with distributors, wholesalers, brick-and-mortar retailers, librarians, or any other entity that purchases books might be a daunting task, but you'll thank yourself for doing so once you see your self-published book's sales increase.

Large and midsized publishers usually have their own sales-people who go out regularly to independent bookshops, chain bookstore buyers, and wholesalers and provide these sellers with sales sheets that focus on new and top-selling titles. In many cases, they also have salespeople to handle what is called *special sales.* This term refers to the sale of any book in large quantity (and typically at a great discount) to a company that will not resell it to the trade marketplace. Special sales focus on the many outlets found in the non-trade marketplace, which would not be covered by trade book sales forces. Over time, these salespeople are able to establish working relationships with these buyers, and if you know what to do, you can do the same thing.

Distributors

Most distributors schedule two sales meetings a year, one for the fall season and one for the spring season. Attended by the publishers' sales representatives and, more rarely, by their editors, these meetings are scheduled six months in advance of their associated seasons so that new books can be pitched and pre-ordered before their official publication dates. Due to the large number of new books that most distributors handle and the limitations of time, the standard policy is to present new titles only once within the sales season in which they are scheduled to be released.

At a sales meeting, the sales reps and editors discuss the publishers' new and forthcoming titles. Sales sheets describing forthcoming books are handed out, along with advance reviews and copies of the books, if available. The publishers provide overviews of their titles and describe the target audiences of their books. They then explain their promotional plans for launching their titles. All of this is done in an effort to give the distributor's sales force a clear understanding of the sales potential of each book they will be distributing.

As a self-publisher, you could always ask your distributor if you can make a presentation to its sales team at one of its sales meetings. Not every distributor will allow a self-publisher time to talk to its sales force, but it is important to ask. If you can attend a meeting, ask your distributor what information it would like you to present.

Wholesalers and Bookstore Chains

Many wholesalers and bookstore chains have buyers who deal with small publishers. In some instances, using the term "small publisher" to describe yourself may afford you an opportunity to set up an appointment with a wholesaler or bookstore chain to present your book. To learn more about how their buying systems are set up, call wholesalers or chain bookstore headquarters to see if you can schedule a meeting with their buyers.

It's important to point out that few, if any, chain store buyers order titles directly from small publishers. Even if they love a small publisher's book, they will ask the publisher to work with a wholesaler with whom they have a relationship. If you, as a small publisher, are able to get a buyer to commit to ordering your book once you've partnered with a wholesaler, it is very likely that any wholesaler you approach will immediately pick up your book.

As exciting as it may be to have your book bought by a bookstore chain, it does come with sizeable downsides. For one, you will have to sell your book to the chain at a large discount; you will have to pay to ship books to your wholesaler's warehouse; you will be required to take back all returns; you will have to pay to have your books returned; and you will have to wait for ninety to one hundred and twenty days from the time your wholesaler ships the books out to stores to get paid.

Is getting your book into a bookstore chain worth the time and effort it will take to do so? The answer is a lot simpler than you might think. If your book has received high praise from legitimate reviewing journals and you've seen strong online sales, then you have a good idea of how your book might do in a chain store. On the other hand, if your reviews have been limited and your online sales have been slow, approaching a book chain may not be worth the trouble.

Individual Bookstores and Retailers

Whether you have a wholesaler to work with or not, as a self-publisher you can go into any bookstore—chain store or independent—and ask to speak to the owner, store manager, or book buyer. In large bookshops, there may be several people handling each position. By talking to the right person, you can learn a great deal about how a bookstore decides on the titles it would like to carry. You can also learn whether it orders books from wholesalers, from distributors, or directly from publishers.

Once you have a clear idea of who is in charge of ordering books and how it's done, you will be in a better position to talk about your book. There are a few considerations, however, to keep in mind. Trying to talk to a manager of a store when the staff is busy serving customers is not a good idea. If you can make an appointment for an appropriate time, do so.

Not all bookstore management will be receptive to having a conversation with an unknown self-publisher. When you are met with resistance, instead of trying to sell your book, ask questions about what makes some books sell while others wind up on the returns table at the back of the store. If you are able to get a manager talking, you can learn a great deal about this very important marketplace.

If you are able to arrange a talk with a store's book buyer, you should introduce yourself, learn about how she orders books, and then go into your sales presentation. Provide her with your book's sales sheet, pitch your book in regard to its subject matter and audience, and explain why you think your book will sell.

A bookstore is the place to learn how to sell a book from the people who sell books to readers every day. This education is harder to come by when dealing with an online retailer. The more you talk to the right people, the better you will understand how to sell a book—not only to bookstores but also to readers.

Of course, while you are at a bookstore talking to its manager or book buyer, you should also ask about the possibility of your doing an author signing or lecture. (See page 145.)

Whether or not your title finds a place in a brick-and-mortar shop, it might be a great fit for a non-bookstore retailer that carries books. In relation to these establishments, you should approach them exactly as you would a bookstore. Ask to speak to the owner or manager of a store, and inquire about how she orders titles for the store. If she orders books directly from publishers, carry on your conversation as though you were selling your book to a bookstore buyer. Learn, listen, and ask questions.

If a bookstore manager does not seem open to having a conversation with an unknown publisher, don't try to sell your book. Instead, ask why some books sell while others just sit there. Managers can provide a great deal of good advice and insight, and your sincere interest in the retail world might just pique their interest in your book.

If an owner or manager orders books from a specialty distributor or wholesaler that only handles certain types of titles, ask for the name of the company so you can look up its contact info and give them a call later. Such a specialized book service can help you gain entrance to many other retailers through its own established sales operation, whether they are fishing equipment retailers, home decorating stores, gift shops, or health food stores. Since you might find the right retailers for your book and gain access to their customers, give it a shot. You never know how your book might reach its audience.

Corporate Sales

If a corporation is interested in using your book to provide information for its employees or to act as a sales incentive for its customers—and if the proposed order is large enough—consider customizing your book to meet the company's specific needs.

Given the right title, corporations can be excellent sales outlets for a book. There are two distinct channels for corporate sales. One is for books designed to help companies' employees perform better at their jobs. For example, books on improving management skills, productivity, workplace relationships, or selling can help increase a company's bottom line. Then there are books that can act as sales incentives for customers or as a means to increase a company's visibility. As an incentive, if a firm manufactures barbecues, a barbecue cookbook might be the perfect free item to go along with its product. If a company produces juicers, a complimentary how-to juicing book would be a great customer perk. Given the size of a book order, you could offer to customize your book for a company's product.

Sometimes a corporate sale may be based on a particular holiday. For example, having a company give away a book on saving the planet with its name on it could be a great way for it to celebrate Earth Day, or a company might give away a book on American war heroes on Memorial Day. If you establish the right partnership with the right company, it could really help your book find its audience.

And who would be the person to contact in a corporation to see if your book could fit into its operation? Based on the size of a company, it could be the marketing director, the media director, or the person in charge of in-service training. By first learning about a company's history and operation, you would be in a good position to see if your book is appropriate for this type of sale.

Author Signings and Lectures

One of the most direct ways to reach your audience is through author signings and lectures. This platform can be utilized in several outlets. These outlets include the following:

- Book clubs
- Bookstores
- Business groups
- Fairs
- Libraries
- Men's or women's clubs
- Professional meetings
- Schools
- Special interest groups
- Specialty shops

Although a few of these places may not sound suited to book sales, they actually are. They represent locations that attract potential book buyers, making them all good environments in which to sell your book. Each of these outlets has its own way of being contacted. Some may be easier to reach than others, but once you understand how it's done, you may find that selling books directly is the most profitable of all methods.

Book Clubs

Book clubs have become a simple and accepted way of keeping in touch with book-reading friends. Once a book group has selected a title to read, copies are either purchased by members of the group, or library copies are placed on reserve for them to pick up and read. If the group enjoys the title, members may tell non-member friends about the book, post their thoughts on their book club's blog, or give it a positive review on book-related websites.

A number of local book clubs are now inviting authors to talk about the books they have written. By providing motivation to read their books, authors can have them become monthly selections. Being a guest of a book club may be the first step in exposing your work to a wider audience. As these clubs thrive on new titles, there is no reason your book shouldn't be on a reading list or two. If you cannot appear in person, the club may be open to an interview over the Internet or on speakerphone.

Bookstores

Your local bookstore may be a great place to hold a book signing. Just be aware that not all bookstores adequately promote their events, so if a store agrees to host a signing, it's vital to do all that you can to make it a success.

Many bookstores hold author signings frequently. Some signings are much more successful than others. While a number of shops send off large email blasts announcing all their author signings to their customers, some specify that authors are responsible for notifying friends and neighbors about their upcoming events. A few bookstores have author signings but do little to promote them. The more aggressive stores will send off emails, have authors draw in their friends, and have signs made promoting these events. Sometimes signs are paid for by the store, and sometimes, by the authors.

While visiting a bookstore to see if it might carry your title, you should also ask how an author can set up a book signing. In the larger stores, you may be directed to someone whose only job is to plan author events. If this is the case, she would be able to provide you with answers to all your questions. In smaller shops, it may be the owner or store manager who does all the event planning. When discussing these matters during your visit, consider the following questions:

- How many months in advance does the store establish a date for a signing?

- Does the store have a place for an author to lecture on a book?

- How does the store promote book signings, and what can you do to help?

- Does the store hold multi-author signings, which tend to bring in more people?

- If your book is not carried by a distributor or wholesaler, would the store purchase titles directly from you, and at what discount? (If your book is carried by a distributor or wholesaler, remember that all unsold books may be returned for full credit.)

Keep in mind that unless your book is a bestseller, attendance and book sales at your signing will likely be modest. If you put some time and effort into drawing attention to the event, however, you may be surprised by how many people show up. The bottom line is that by understanding how to set up a book signing at a bookstore, you can repeat these steps at other book outlets.

Fairs

There are literally hundreds of various fairs held throughout North America. Country fairs, state fairs, antique fairs, book fairs, ephemera fairs, food fairs—you name it. Track down fairs that seem like good venues at which to sell your book, learn what it would cost to set up a table at each of these fairs, and find out how many people usually attend each event. Also, go visit a similar fair beforehand to understand what you may need to bring to catch your audience's attention. Sitting at a table next to a stack of books might not be a crowd pleaser, but with a little bit of creative thinking, your presentation could make an impact at a fair.

Libraries

Many libraries offer regular speaking engagements, which allow patrons to listen to authors talk about their books. Some programs are administrated through a main library, while others may be run by a local branch library. All you have to do is call to find out if the ones nearest to you have such programs. If they do, make sure you ask if they will allow you to sell and sign books at such events.

Many libraries host book signings and lectures on subjects of interest to their patrons. Check with your library to see if they would be willing to host an author visit—which should include a book signing, of course.

Men's or Women's Clubs and Business Meetings

Many men's clubs, women's clubs, and business groups sponsor local meetings and dinners on behalf of charitable causes. In many instances, they hire speakers to provide interesting and, in some cases, inspiring talks. If your book offers the type of positive thinking that may be of interest to one of these groups, you should contact the individual in charge of getting speakers for their events. To do such a talk requires work and practice, though, so if you are going to pursue such an opportunity, make sure you are prepared.

If you are good at this type of speaking engagement, you may discover that word will spread from one affiliate group to the next, leading to more and more talks of this nature. For many authors, this type of speaking goes hand in hand with selling their self-published books.

Professional Meetings

Many authors make their living in other specialty professions—doctors, lawyers, social workers, nurses, librarians, historians, coaches, and acupuncturists, to mention just a few examples. Each of these specialties should have national, regional, or local organizational meetings that are directed at other like-minded professionals. Normally, these meetings take place in exhibit halls, where companies hoping to sell to these particular groups set up booths and tables to promote their products and services. If your book is designed to appeal to certain professionals, consider renting a table at one of these events. Again, as with fairs, it is important to learn how much it costs to exhibit and to walk through the exhibit hall of a meeting or two before you decide to attend one yourself.

Schools

Many elementary schools pay for authors of children's books to come and talk about their books to the students and faculty. In many cases, these authors may be published by commercial houses. By calling schools and asking if they hold such events and, if so, how they work, you may discover a new way of selling your children's book to the very children and professionals who read and recommend these books. There may also be opportunities to talk about your book at middle schools, high schools, colleges, or graduate schools, which sometimes host author lectures for parents and students.

Specialty Shops

Specialty shops offer a unique opportunity to make your book known to people who are already interested in its subject. A crafts store, for instance, would be a great place to discuss your crafting book; while a health food store would be a natural setting for a discussion on improving wellness through nutritional supplements.

In the same way that bookstores have book signings, many specialty stores conduct author lectures and signings. As previously discussed, you should visit these stores and ask about holding one of these events. Stores that sell cookware would be a natural fit for cookbook authors, knitting shops for authors of knitting and sewing books, and so on. If you have a book that has a strong focus on a product, don't be afraid to reach out to the retailers that sell this product.

BUILDING A FOLLOWING

One of the most exciting new marketplaces takes the form of a group of individuals who "follow" you and keep track of what you say on social media. In the publishing business, this is called an author's platform, and in many instances, commercial publishers are on the lookout for authors who already have a large platform of followers. Before some writers publish their works, they use the Internet to connect with as many like-minded people as possible. They do this by using Facebook, Twitter, Instagram, LinkedIn, Listservs, blogs, and their own websites. While we will cover these social media platforms in greater detail in Chapter 11, it is important to note that the ability of an individual to capture the attention of thousands of followers is now available to anyone who can use social media effectively.

Once you have built a large enough platform, you can formally announce to your followers that you have a forthcoming book. By providing them with the book's title and release date, as well as the places where it can be found for purchase, you have the potential to sell a lot of books to people who are already interested in reading what you have to say. Ask them to also tell their own followers about your new title. And don't forget to ask the people who buy your book to post their reviews wherever and whenever they can. Many of the most successful self-published books became successful by using these very techniques.

CONCLUSION

The long history of book publishing actually began when writers worked with printers to produce their works. While the marketplace may have been limited, this fact didn't stop them from going out and finding places where they could sell their titles. As a self-published author, you have access to a far greater number of outlets than they had—either through traditional channels, non-traditional venues, or the Internet.

If your title offers what a particular marketplace wants, you will find that you have it within yourself to go out and sell books. While selling your book may be tough to do at first, the more you do it, the more comfortable you will feel as a salesperson. And once you hit upon an audience that responds positively to your work, you will thank yourself for your efforts.

Still, knowing about marketplaces doesn't mean that your book will fit into every sales channel. Trying to have a health food store carry a novel (unless it has a health-related theme that might make it especially appealing to its customers) or trying to sell a math book to a book club, is not going to work. As a self-published author, you must have a clear understanding of your book's position in the marketplace and make sure that it will fit in it nicely.

Once you understand how to use the marketplace to reach your intended readers, you must consider another important piece of the puzzle: promotion.

CHAPTER 10

$\mathcal{S}$ETTING THE STAGE
FOR YOUR RELEASE

---

*One of the biggest mistakes most new authors make
is to spend all their time and energy writing the book,
without sufficient thought to how they'll market it.*
—JACK CANFIELD, AUTHOR

At this point, you should have a more complete understanding of your book's marketplace: the means by which your book—whether physical volume, e-book, or audiobook—can be made available to its intended audience. It is now time to learn how to garner some attention for your book. Over the years, publishers have developed useful strategies and tactics to get their titles in front of the reading public. While some of these methods have worked well over the years, recently there has been a revolution in book promotion.

In this chapter and the next, you will read about each aspect of book marketing, from the prepublication stage through the release stage and ongoing publicity. I hope to provide you with insight that can put you on an even playing field with any commercial house. Keep in mind, however, that successful promotion doesn't happen without preparation, hard work, and financial investment. But by knowing what to do, you can save both time and money, as well as avoid a number of pitfalls that may sound like marketing opportunities to the uninitiated.

A BRIEF HISTORY OF BOOK PROMOTION IN THE UNITED STATES

It is interesting to look at the ways book publishers have promoted their titles over the last century or so—especially in light of the recent revolution in book promotion. In the 1880s, a number of nationally distributed magazines—some owned by book publishers—would take excerpts from their writers' books and reprint them in their journals. At about the same time, publishing houses would print small book posters promoting individual titles. Publishers' representatives and independent book peddlers—who sold books to stores and individual customers from their horse-drawn wagons—would ask stores to put these posters up where they would be seen by shoppers.

One of the staples of early book promotion was the use of lecture tours. From Mark Twain to Admiral Richard Byrd to Amelia Earhart, well-known public figures would hit the road, talking to thousands of people throughout the United States and discussing their latest titles. Prior to the advent of radio and television, it was a form of entertainment that drew big crowds to theaters and lecture halls located in many of the larger American cities—and sold a good number of books.

In the 1920s, one or two enterprising publishers began to promote their titles on billboards—first in the Times Square area of Manhattan, and later in the downtown areas of major cities. Newspapers began to provide their readers with book reviews along with book ads, and then papers began producing full sections devoted to new books. Publishers would also produce seasonal catalogs to announce their forthcoming titles. These catalogs would be mailed to bookstores, libraries, and newspaper and magazine reviewers. With the advent of radio, and later of television, authors were given the opportunity to be interviewed and speak about their latest titles, reaching millions of potential book buyers.

In 1947, the American Booksellers Association (ABA) held its first formal book convention in Washington, DC, in the basement of a hotel. Initially, it was a place for well-established publishers to show off their new titles to bookstore owners. Publishers would simply display their new titles on tables. By 1970, the growing number of independent and smaller publishing houses participating in the event forced the ABA to hold the convention in a few DC hotels. While the ABA convention had started as a low-key gathering of publishers and bookstore owners, by the following year, it was moved to New York City and attracted a then-record number of attendees—6,000 people. Something had evidently happened during the previous decade—something that had awakened the reading public and turned the image of the publishing industry on its head. No longer seen as a stuffy old-fashioned business, it was thought of as a hip and happening scene.

In the 1960s, author Jacqueline Susann came across a new approach to promotion: the high-profile book party. She and her publisher would throw parties to release her latest book, and to each gathering she would invite Hollywood celebrities, best-selling authors, socialites, and the press—especially, the press. The people on her A-list were happy to write about her, her new book, and her fabulous fetes.

Other publishers soon got wise to this promotional technique and would go on to spend thousands of dollars on elaborate book parties, making them a quick way to get the press to promote their writers and their books. But by the end of the 1990s, although the idea of book release parties had become somewhat of a staple for certain publishers, the era of the big, glitzy, glamorous party had come to an end. The press had simply stopped showing up.

With the advent of the Internet, publishing was about to undergo an immerse change. In 2000, renowned author Stephen King decided to take a major leap into the future of marketing books. He chose to sell his latest work, *The Plant,* chapter by chapter, directly to his fan base, using his own website. Despite the fact that the project was shut down by Chapter 6, it forced the publishing world to recognize the potential power of the Internet. By 2010, email, websites, and social media outlets were allowing publishers to reach the public directly. Publishers, who had concentrated their marketing efforts using traditional means of promotion, began to focus more and more attention on using the Internet to spread the word.

While the Internet helped major publishing houses in their promotional efforts, it also opened the door for anyone interested

Stephen King forced the publishing world to recognize the potential power of the Internet when in the year 2000, he decided to sell his new novel, *The Plant,* chapter by chapter through his own website. Although the story was never completed, King later revealed that he had made nearly half a million dollars through his experiment.

in selling his own book. As the technology for producing books in short runs and as e-books improved, the ability of self-published authors to promote their own titles exploded, as they now had access to many of the web-based resources used by the largest commercial publishing houses.

CREATING A TIMELINE FOR YOUR BOOK PROJECT

Anything worth doing requires the right planning, so setting up a schedule of tasks to complete as a self-publisher is critical. By creating a timeline, you will be able to determine when to start marketing your book. By using the Book Project Timeline provided on pages 155 and 156 as a model, you can adjust each step to fit your own situation.

As you can see, the timeline of any book project involves a number of important steps, many of which have been covered in previous chapters. The following information focuses on those subjects not yet covered, which include timing, sales seasons, publication date, metadata, sales sheets, and prepublication reviews.

Timing

It is essential to create a schedule for your book project. A realistic timeline will insure that all the necessary tasks are completed and will help you determine when you should start marketing your book. (See the model timeline on pages 155 to 156.)

As you can see, I filled out the third column in the Book Project Timeline. I based my projections on my own experiences in publishing and the priorities of my day-to-day life. The time periods you use should be realistic. They should reflect the amount of time you will be able to put into these tasks in light of your other responsibilities. For example, some people will be able to dedicate enough of their time to complete a 250-page manuscript in six months, while others with less spare time on their hands will need a longer time frame, perhaps a year or two. The same idea holds true for each of these steps.

Working against a deadline you've created for yourself can make all the difference in your quest to become a successful self-published author. On the other hand, unexpected things can happen, so don't be afraid to revise your timeline when necessary. If you need to change your book's release date, it's okay. Large companies are no strangers to changing release dates—even for books by best-selling authors.

BOOK PROJECT TIMELINE

STEPS	ACTIONS	TIMING
1. Establish a "soft" publication date.	Set a date far enough in the future to accommodate the remaining steps.	6 months to 1½ years.
2. Develop and complete your manuscript.	Give yourself enough time to complete your work.	3 to 6 months.
3. Create a sales program.	Consider whether you will be working with a wholesaler or distributor, or using your own sales program.	Upon completion of your manuscript.
4. Edit and finalize your manuscript.	Work with people who can help you produce the best version of your work.	2 months.
5. Create your book's cover.	Design a commercial-quality cover on your own or with the help of a designer.	Upon completion of your manuscript.
6. Design the interior of your book, typeset, and proof.	Work with people who can help you produce the best version of your work.	1 to 4 weeks.
7. Begin a social media campaign.	Based on the topic of your book, begin to build a platform of followers interested in what you have to say. Consider creating a website through which to sell your book or direct readers to booksellers that carry your title. Consider hiring a social media consultant.	Upon completion of your manuscript.
8. Get advance praise.	If you decide to seek advance praise, aim for half a dozen quotations.	Upon completion of your manuscript.
9. Establish a "hard" publication date.	At this point, you should have a clear idea of when your book will be in print. This is the date you will use in all future announcements.	6 to 8 months later.
10. Print advance reading copies (ARCs).	Determine who will be receiving ARCs, and produce enough ARCs to meet your needs, plus a few additional copies just in case.	1 to 2 weeks.

STEPS	ACTIONS	TIMING
11. Create a sales sheet.	Along with copy about your book, include necessary metadata on the sheet.	Upon ordering ARCs.
12. Send ARCs for review.	Include a cover letter and sales sheet along with each ARC.	2 to 5 months prior to publication.
13. Place your book's metadata online.	Provide all relevant websites with information on your title.	Upon confirmation of all the details.
14. Focus on publicity.	Set up ways to publicize your book, which may include interviews, book signings, and reviews. Consider hiring a publicity consultant on a full- or part-time basis.	Upon completion of your manuscript until 1 year after publication.
15. Send your electronic file to your printer.	Any changes to the material should be made before submitting the file to your printer.	Upon completion of your book's interior design.
16. Announce the publication of your book.	Use social media to announce the publication of your work.	Upon day of publication.
17. Register your book with the US Copyright Office.	Although registration is not mandatory, it is necessary to enforce your copyright in a court of law.	Upon publication to within the first 3 months of publication.
18. Send printed copies to reviewers and interviewers.	Implement your publicity strategy by sending copies of your book to anyone who is likely to provide you and your book with greater visibility.	Continue to send out review copies as required.
19. Continue to promote your book.	Based on your book's sales, you will be able to see if your publicity strategy is helping your book find its audience.	1 year.
20. If you would like to produce an audiobook, do so now (or simultaneously with e-book and print versions).	Work with people who can help you produce the best version of your work.	At any point after finalization of edited and proofread manuscript.

Sales Seasons

Historically, publishers would release their new titles according to three *sales seasons*. These new books would become part of the fall list, spring list, or summer list. Because it would take a year or more to turn out a new book, making sure a book was scheduled to be released in the appropriate season was important. For example, a particular title may have been suited to a publication date at the beginning of the school year, or designed for a specific holiday, or considered a perfect summer read. It was usually sales departments that set up publishers' seasonal lists, which made perfect sense, since sales reps knew which types of books sold better in which seasons.

It also fell on the shoulders of sales reps to inform chain stores and independent bookstore buyers of their companies' forthcoming books at least six months prior to their release periods. This was done through ads and reviews in trade journals, mailed-out sales sheets and catalogs, phone calls, personal visits, and the distribution of *advance reading copies*, or *ARCs*—all necessary tasks to complete in advance of a book's release.

While a book's release is still referred to by its season—a winter book or a summer book—things have changed greatly in this area. Now, the required dissemination of information regarding the release of any new book may be done within minutes. By going online and placing a book's metadata (see page 158) on the appropriate websites, a self-publisher can make this information available to all libraries, brick-and-mortar bookstores, and online book retailers. Nevertheless, if you want your book to get some traction in the marketplace, you will still need to plan its release well in advance and select the most appropriate sales season for its publication. So, how is this done?

Consider your book's subject matter. If your book is a nonfiction title on elder abuse, having it ready for sale in the month of June—which happens to be Elder Abuse Awareness Month—would make it a summer book with a June release date. Or perhaps it's a book on dieting. The three months that follow New Year's Day—January, February, and March—would work perfectly for its release, as all the people who promised themselves to lose weight as their New Year's resolutions will need some guidance. Your book would then be a fall book with a January release date. By looking at some of

Your book's subject matter can be an important consideration in timing its release. For instance, self-help, dieting, and exercise books are generally best received in January, right after many people make their New Year's resolutions. Travel books are usually most popular in May, when people are planning their summer getaways.

the release dates of other published titles similar to yours, you can learn a great deal. Of course, some titles may not pair naturally with certain dates on the calendar, so you may choose to schedule your book's release date to suit your own needs.

Publication Date

If you intend to have your book reviewed in the trade media, it is important to make sure that your publication date allows you enough time to send ARCs to the appropriate parties. Most journals ask for a four-month lead time prior to a book's publication to review it. So, as you prepare your time frame, make sure to choose a release date that reflects this fact.

Metadata

If you are going to promote your book effectively, you will need to compile your book's *metadata*—basic descriptive information such as title, author, ISBN, retail list price, and page count. This metadata should eventually be sent to all relevant websites.

Before the existence of the Internet, what is now called *metadata* was simply known as a book's specifications, which provided a description of the book. This information would be included in a publisher's catalog and on a book's sales sheet. It would also be given out to wholesalers, distributors, and libraries. This information was first stored on paper index cards, and then, when computers became available, it would be entered into a company's database.

With the advent of more sophisticated online programs, most retail websites began to require this information, now called metadata. As a self-publisher, you need to compile your book's metadata in order to promote your book.

So, which details make up your book's metadata? While many websites request the same data, some request more information. I've included the metadata for this book as an example.

- **Title:** How to Self-Publish Your Book: A Complete Guide to Writing, Editing, Marketing & Selling Your Own Book
- **Author:** Dr. Jan Yager
- **ISBN number (paper edition):** ISBN 978-0-7570-0465-0 (pb)
- **ISBN number (e-book edition):** ISBN 978-0-7570-5465-5 (eb)
- **Retail paperback list price:** $19.95
- **Number of pages:** 272 pages

- **Publication date:** May 15, 2019

- **Index:** Index included

- **Photographs or illustrations:** Illustrated

- **Trim size:** 7.5 x 9-inch quality paperback

- **Weight:** 1.5 lbs.

- **Case quantity:** 36 copies in a carton

- **Genre:** Nonfiction, How-To

- **BISAC:** Reference/Writing

- **Audiobook details (if any):** None at this time.

New title information may also include information on how a book will be distributed, the wholesaler or distributor that will be handling it, and a selected or comprehensive list of retailers from which the book can be purchased. If it will also be available through the self-publisher's website, this information may be listed, too.

Metadata may also contain the publisher's contact information, such as:

- **Name:** Square One Publishers, Inc.

- **Address:** 115 Herricks Road, Garden City Park, NY 11040

- **Website:** www.squareonepublishers.com

- **Email:** sq1publish@aol.com

- **Telephone:** 516-535-2010 x100

- **Fax number (if any):** 516-535-2014

Metadata should also include a summary of the book and an author biography, which may feature the same copy found on the sales sheet. (See "Sales Sheets" on page 161.) If you will be producing a physical book, some metadata may not be available prior to your book's publication. For example, you will not know its weight or how many books will fit in a carton. You can fill in these lines as "not yet available." If changes need to be made, as long you have kept a record of all the websites into which you have entered your metadata, you can update your metadata to reflect the latest information.

AVAILABLE

$19.95 US

272 pages

7.5 x 9-inch quality paperback

2-color

Reference/Writing

ISBN 978-0-7570-0465-0 (pp)

ISBN 978-0-7570-5465-5 (eb)

REFERENCE/WRITING

HOW TO SELF-PUBLISH YOUR BOOK

A Complete Guide to Writing, Editing,
Marketing & Selling Your Own Book

Dr. Jan Yager

A new world has opened to writers who wish to have their words turned into finished books. With technological advances in typesetting, printing, distribution, and sales, self-publishing has become a reality. But while converting your writing into a commercially available title may sound relatively easy—based upon the claims of the companies that offer this service—there are many important considerations you should be aware of before going to press. Book publishing expert Dr. Jan Yager has created an easy-to-follow guide that will take you from conception to production to selling—and everywhere in between. Whether the work is fiction or nonfiction, there are many crucial decisions to be made and pitfalls to avoid. *How to Self-Publish Your Book* offers sound and proven advice at every turn.

The book is divided into three parts. Part One takes you through the initial manuscript preparation—setting your goals, writing, sequencing, editing, and proofing, as well as creating a business plan for your book's eventual release. Part Two focuses on the actual production of your book. It explains the importance of cover design and interior design, what you need to know about producing physical books and e-books, and how to turn your title into an audiobook. Part Three provides key information on how to market and sell your book—the very areas most writers understand least, even though they are essential to a title's success. Also included is a valuable resource section that you can to turn to time and time again for helpful websites that offer essential information on self-publishing service providers, including freelance editors, proofreaders, book marketers, publicists, printers, and related associations.

Today, numerous workshops and lecturers charge hundreds of dollars, promising to turn self-published books into bestsellers. The fact is that to create the best book possible, you have to start at its conception, not with the finished product. Here is a complete road map to what lies ahead for the self-published author—not based on hype or wishful thinking, but based on Dr. Jan Yager's lifetime of experience in the world of publishing.

ABOUT THE AUTHOR

Dr. Jan Yager received her MA in criminal justice from Goddard College, and her PhD in sociology from the City University of New York Graduate Center. She began her publishing career at Macmillan, and then moved on to Grove Press, working directly under the company's founder, Barney Rosset. There she learned to do everything from selling foreign and subsidiary rights to acquisitions, publicity, and sales. She is the author of more than forty books and has been published by such houses as Simon & Schuster, Penguin Random House, Scribner, Wiley, and Doubleday, as well as self-published by her own company, Hannacroix Creek Books.

Dr. Yager has been featured on *The Oprah Winfrey Show, The View, Today, Good Morning America, CBS Sunday Morning,* CNN, MSNBC, and BBC television. Her award-winning titles include *Foreign Rights and Wrongs; Effective Business and Nonfiction Writing; Career Opportunities in the Publishing Industry* (with Fred Yager); *Business Protocol; Victims; When Friendship Hurts; Friendshifts; The Pretty One; Untimely Death* (with Fred Yager); *The Quiet Dog* (illustrated by Mitzi Lyman), *Work Less, Do More;* and *Put More Time on Your Side.* She and her husband, Fred, reside in Stamford, Connecticut.

Sales Sheets

A good sales sheet is of primary importance when it comes to marketing your title. A *sales sheet* refers to a one-sheet presentation of a book's basic information. Essentially, it is a book's metadata delivered in a pleasing and easy-to-read fashion, whether as a properly formatted PDF or printed sheet. It provides the recipient with the necessary details to convey what a book is all about, including publication date, number of pages, trim size, BISAC subject headings (see page 162), ISBN (of both the paper and e-book editions), list price (of both the paper and e-book edition), title, book summary, author biography (typically called "About the Author"), and publisher or distributor name. (See this book's sales sheet on page 160.)

Sales sheets may vary slightly in format as long as the basic information they contain is clear and easy to understand. A sales sheet should always be prepared in advance of a book's publication, which means that a number of specifications may change—from the number of pages to the price. As a result, be sure to keep your sales sheet up to date.

Your sales sheet should be prepared well in advance of your book's publication date, but its specifications may change before your book's release. Be sure to amend your sales sheet over time so that it reflects up-to-date information.

Prepublication Reviews

With just a few exceptions, the art of getting your book reviewed has been the anchor of nearly every successful publisher. Many books are beautifully written and packaged, but if no one knows about a wonderful book, it is not likely to sell very well. It's no wonder that one of the most common questions a self-publisher asks is, "How can I get my book reviewed before it goes to press?" The answer is simple: While there is no guarantee that your book will receive a good review, if you know which book trade journals to contact and what their submission rules are, you can absolutely increase your odds of getting your work reviewed.

And how important is getting a decent review to the sales of your book? It is very important. These book reviews are read by three influential groups: acquisitions librarians, bookstore owners, and, to some degree, the general reading public. Although the journals listed on the following pages are aimed at industry professionals, a good or outstanding review in one of these publications may also reach a wider audience.

BISAC Subject Headings

As explained in Chapter 4, the BISAC Subject Headings List is a collection of categories that are meant to designate the main subjects or topics of your book. All commercial books are assigned BISAC subject headings, which normally appear on a book's back cover. Without these headings, a book might appear to be self-published. BISAC categories are created and updated by a nonprofit organization called the Book Industry Study Group, or BISG. The BISG includes members of various aspects of the book publishing industry, who come together to discuss and update the BISAC subject headings, among other issues related to publishing.

As previously mentioned, each subject heading or combination of subject headings is associated with a BISAC code, which, once entered into a database, helps libraries, online book retailers, and brick-and-mortar bookstores place your book in the appropriate sections of their shelves and websites. Amazon, Barnes & Noble, Bowker, and Ingram (including Lightning Source, the POD and e-book

company owned by Ingram) are some of the distribution outlets that require at least two BISAC subject headings for each title.

You can determine your book's BISAC subject headings and associated code on the BISG website (http://bisg.org), which provides detailed instructions on how to do so. In short, you will pick a main code, or primary code, and then a secondary code, which should narrow down your primary category. A third code may also be chosen to narrow your topic down even further.

For example, if your book is a fictional crime thriller, its main subject would be FICTION, while its secondary subject could be THRILLERS, and its third subject could be CRIME. This combination, FICTION/THRILLERS/CRIME, would result in BISAC code FIC031010.

Don't try to be too creative when it comes to choosing BISAC subject headings. A confusing or incorrect BISAC code can greatly limit your sales if it prevents outlets in the marketplace from knowing where your book should go.

It is important to recognize that a negative review can stay with your book for a long time, as well. Because of the Internet, a number of these reviews get reposted on online bookstore websites, as commonly happens on Amazon.com. So, even if you get a negative review that you want to bury, you may not be able to hide it.

ARC Submissions

In Chapter 7, you learned how to set up a short-run printing of your book. The very same method may be used to produce the ARCs you will need to send out for review. Once you know the number of ARCs you will be sending out, you may want to add a few additional copies to this number, just in case.

Prior to printing your ARCs, you may add the words "Advance Reading Copy. Not for Resale." to your book's cover, title page, or back cover. You may also include a disclaimer on the title page that states, "This is an uncorrected edition." If your book has an index but this index has not yet been done, it is acceptable to add a last page that states, "Index: To be finalized prior to publication."

Along with the requested number of ARCs, you should include an introductory letter and sales sheet in each package you send. The letter shouldn't be longer than one page, much like the sales sheet. Fold the letter and sales sheet in half and place them on the front cover of your ARC to avoid their getting crushed during mailing.

While you can use more expensive means of getting ARCs to journals, editors are not impressed when having to sign for a hand-delivered package. Using the US Postal Service is fine and will allow you to keep track of your packages, as well. Also, make sure that each package can be opened quickly. Having an editor spend ten minutes trying to open a box that has been secured by half a roll of tape does not make a good first impression.

Most journals schedule their prepublication reviews to appear prior to a book's date of publication. Because of this fact, they request that advance reading copies be submitted approximately four months before a book's actual publication. If you find that your ARCs are going to be available only one or two months before your book's release, push back your book's pub date to follow the required submission dates of prepublication review journals. Otherwise, it's unlikely that any prepublication reviews will be written.

> Advance reading copies, or ARCs, are critical to getting prepublication reviews. Make sure that your ARCs look professional in every way and show no "tells" of self-publishing. A short-run printer can help you produce good-looking bound copies that are suitable for submission to potential reviewers.

Prepublication Journals

The majority of mainstream magazines, journals, and newspapers will not review a book prior to its publication. While there are some exceptions made for a few best-selling authors, self-published authors have little chance of getting their books reviewed in mass market periodicals. On the other hand, there are a number of prepublication trade journals that can positively impact a self-published book's visibility by letting the industry know about a forthcoming book that is worth noticing and buying.

It is important to point out that these publications receive thousands of submissions annually, and it has become increasingly more difficult to get reviews—not only for self-published books but also for commercial presses. Some publications have started separate reviewing options for self-published books. Others choose to review self-published books on a case-by-case basis.

It is possible to purchase reviews from certain prepublication magazines through paid review divisions. While the practice of buying a review was very controversial when it was first started about a decade ago, it is now an acceptable form of obtaining a review. A paid review will not have the clout of a traditional prepublication review, but it could still provide a beneficial quotation or two for publicity purposes. Think of it as a "book infomercial." Of course, there is no guarantee that your book will receive a positive review, even from a paid reviewer. You might get a glowing, wonderful endorsement of your book, a so-so review, or, even worse, a negative review. Many of the publications and services listed below will not pull a negative review, so you need to go into the submission process with your eyes wide open and prepare yourself for the possibility of having to counter a bad review at the very outset of your book's publicity campaign. Moreover, prepublication reviews often get reposted on major bookstore websites, including Amazon.com. It can be hard to bury a bad review.

A poor review is a common risk all publishers face. As a self-publisher, you need to believe in your book and have the courage to understand that there is always a chance of getting a bad write-up.

The following journals are the most popular periodicals that provide free prepublication reviews.

BOOKLIST. *Booklist* was established by the American Library Association (ALA) in 1905. This prepublication review journal offers critical reviews of books and audiovisual materials for all ages. *Booklist* is a respected resource for librarians, booksellers, and educators, helping them decide which materials are best suited for students and patrons. In addition to its print version, *Booklist* can be found online at www.booklistonline.com.

- **Submission requirements.** If you would like to have your book reviewed, send one ARC to *Booklist's* mailing address, which may be found on its website, at least fifteen weeks before publication. Include a brief introductory letter and sales sheet in your package. If you do not have any ARCs, a photocopied manuscript, page proofs, folded-and-gathered sheets, or other form of prepublication copy is acceptable. Address your package to the editor in charge of your book's category, such as adult books, children's and young adult books, or graphic novels. A complete list of editors may be found on the company's website, in addition to descriptions of submission requirements specific to each category.

  If you are submitting an e-book only, *Booklist* accepts solely those accessible to libraries via a digital distributor of e-books, such as OverDrive or Axis 360. You may want to send an email to the relevant editor requesting instructions on e-book submissions.

Unless a reviewer specifically requests an electronic ARC, send a hard copy. Most reviewers actually prefer a paperback ARC. Moreover, if you send the book in digital form, you run the risk of ending up with a free copy of your work on the Internet.

CHOICE. *Choice* magazine publishes five hundred reviews of academic nonfiction titles each month, in addition to editorials, features, and bibliographic essays. It is part of the Association of College & Research Libraries, a division of the American Library Association. Geared towards librarians working in academia, the magazine aims to help them curate comprehensive collections of academic publications.

- **Submission requirements.** *Choice* primarily evaluates books and electronic publications that belong in libraries which serve undergraduate students, as well as graduate-level materials suitable for advanced undergraduates. *Choice* does not accept ARCs, uncorrected proofs, or PDFs, so you will have to send a finished book to the address specified on its website, www.ala.org/acrl/choice/, along with an introductory letter and sales sheet. Only 25 to 30 percent of submitted titles are chosen for review.

KIRKUS REVIEWS. *Kirkus Reviews* is a biweekly American book review magazine based in New York City. Since its establishment by

Virginia Kirkus in 1933, *Kirkus Reviews* has been a respected source of critical, comprehensive book reviews, which may also be accessed on the *Kirkus* website, www.kirkusreviews.com. In 2014, the Kirkus Prize was established, bestowing $50,000 in prizes to fiction, nonfiction, and children's authors each year.

● **Submission requirements.** To submit your work to *Kirkus*, you must mail in two ARCs addressed to the appropriate editor. Check its website for a complete list of editors and its mailing address. As usual, include a short introductory letter and sales sheet in your package.

LIBRARY JOURNAL. *Library Journal* was founded in 1876 by Melvil Dewey, the inventor of the Dewey Decimal System. The magazine reports on news in the library world, particularly public libraries, and features articles about all aspects of the profession. It is a key prepublication trade journal for librarians in public, school, and special interest libraries. Its reviews are written with librarians in mind, highlighting books that librarians may or may not wish to add to their collections.

● **Submission requirements.** Authors must submit their materials to the address noted on the company's website, https://lj.library-journal.com, three to four months in advance of publication. Your submission package should include an introductory letter and sales sheet. Authors with books in the following categories may submit their titles for possible review up to three months after publication: reference books, illustrated coffee table books, art books, graphic novels, craft and DIY books, library science books, and poetry books.

PUBLISHERS WEEKLY. Established in 1872, *Publishers Weekly,* or simply *PW,* is a trade magazine targeted at publishers, literary agents, librarians, and the publishing community as a whole. It alerts its readers to the latest news in the book industry. Other features include bestseller lists, author interviews, and, of course, book reviews.

Publishers Weekly offers prepublication reviews of thousands of new trade books each year. These reviews span a wide range of genres and include audiobooks and e-books. Its monthly supplement, *PW Select,* is devoted to the self-publishing industry and highlights independent authors.

● **Submission requirements.** Self-publishers hoping for a review in *Publishers Weekly* must submit their material through BookLife, a website from *Publishers Weekly* dedicated to indie authors. Click on a link called "PR Reviews," which is located in the bottom-right corner of the homepage, https://booklife.com. Review consideration is free, although only a very small number of submissions receive reviews. To submit your book, you must first register for a BookLife account. Then create a new project in your account, click the "Submit Project for PW Review Consideration" button, and follow the submissions process. BookLife encourages self-publishers to include sales sheets and promotional information with their submissions.

There are separate submission guidelines for traditional publishing companies, which may be found on the *Publishers Weekly* website, www.publishersweekly.com, and if you would prefer to send your material in under the guise of a publisher, you may do so.

SCHOOL LIBRARY JOURNAL. Associated with *Library Journal*, *School Library Journal* is a subscription magazine that specializes in children's, teen, and young adult literature, as well as professional development titles for educators and school and children's librarians. The journal provides book reviews as well as articles on literacy, best practices, technology, and education policy. Over the past sixty years, its coverage has expanded to include digital content and databases. Reviews in the *School Library Journal* inform teachers and educators on which newly released books and educational materials are recommended for inclusion in their libraries, classrooms, and curriculums, and which are not.

● **Submission requirements.** Types of material accepted for review include children's and young adult books, original paperbacks, and reference books. Two finished copies of each book must be sent to the address specified on the company's website, www.slj.com, at least three months before publication. Advance reading copies are acceptable as long as they are followed by two copies of the finished book. Submission packages should include sales sheet information and a brief introductory letter. A limited number of

Before sending a submission to a journal, always make sure that your book is appropriate for that publication. For instance, *School Library Journal* specializes in books for children, teens, and young adults, as well as professional development titles for educators and children's librarians. A romance novel intended for adults would not make a suitable submission for this journal.

submissions are selected for review. Book reviews are published in both the monthly journal and online, where they may be viewed by librarians, educators, book distributors, and book vendors.

Self-Publisher-Friendly Reviewers

Certain periodicals, such as *Foreword Reviews,* are particularly friendly to self-published books and small presses. While sending them a submission doesn't guarantee a review, it will certainly increase the odds of getting your book noticed.

While the journals I've just discussed do review self-published works, the vast majority of titles they accept for review come from commercial houses. To give your title its best shot at getting reviewed, your ARC must avoid looking like a poorly constructed self-published work, of course, but you would also do well to know which periodicals are particularly friendly to self-published books. The following entries are good examples of such journals.

FOREWORD REVIEWS. *Foreword Reviews* was created in 1998 with the indie publisher in mind. It reviews and promotes books from independent publishers, self-publishers, and university presses, and may be found in print and online. Besides book reviews, it features resources for authors, including marketing services and advertising opportunities.

- **Submission requirements.** Authors must send review copies of their books, either in print or digital format, to the address specified on the company's website, www.forewordreviews.com, at least four months prior to publication. The managing editor will then carefully critique each submission to determine whether it meets editorial standards. About one quarter of submissions will be accepted for review per issue. If your book is not selected, *Foreword Reviews* offers a fee-for-review service under the name *Clarion Reviews.* (See page 169).

  In addition to an ARC, each submission package should contain a sales sheet and letter describing why the book should be considered for review. Please note that *Foreword Reviews* does not review titles that are published only as e-books.

MIDWEST BOOK REVIEW. Started in 1976 by James Cox, the *Midwest Book Review* is every self-publisher's friend. The organization, which is devoted to promoting literacy, libraries, and small presses, publishes an array of monthly book reviews targeted at public and academic libraries, booksellers, and the reading world at large. These reviews may be found on the *Midwest Book Review's* website, www.midwestbookreview.com, along with informative articles and resources for readers and writers alike.

- **Submission requirements.** Although the number of titles accepted for review each month is limited, the *Midwest Book Review* gives priority consideration to self-published authors and small presses. Your submission package should include two print copies of your published book, accompanied by a sales sheet and cover letter, which should note a physical address or email address to which your review may be sent should your book be chosen. If you wish to submit an e-book, PDF, or uncorrected proof for review, you will be charged a "Reader Fee."

Pay-to-Review Services

As mentioned earlier in this chapter, it is a new world when it comes to getting reviews. Certain prepublication magazines have paid review divisions for those willing to pay a sometimes hefty fee to have their books evaluated by professional reviewers. These pay-to-play services may be a reasonable option to consider as you put together your marketing plan.

CLARION REVIEWS. *Clarion Reviews* is a pay-for-review service offered by *Foreword Reviews,* a magazine devoted to the independent publishing industry. *Clarion* promises authors comprehensive critiques and evaluations written by qualified professionals. Each book is rated on a scale of one to five stars for excellence, and its review ultimately appears on the *Foreword Reviews* website, www.forewordreviews.com. *Foreword Reviews* also shares its reviews with companies such as Ingram, Baker & Taylor, and Bowker.

- **Submissions Requirements.** *Clarion* regularly charges $499 per book review. After setting up an account on the *Foreword Reviews* website and paying the review fee, you will be sent instructions on how to upload your book in any format. Reviews are emailed to authors within four to six weeks after submission.

INDIE READER. Created by Amy Edelman, *Indie Reader* is a pay-for-review service for self-published authors and independent publishers.

- **Submission requirements.** Located at www.indiereader.com, *Indie Reader* charges $250 for a review that will be provided in seven to nine weeks. For a rush review, the fee is $325, which will get it to you in four to six weeks.

KIRKUS INDIE. Launched in 2005, *Kirkus Indie* is a pay-for-review program created by *Kirkus Reviews*. Independent authors can submit their works to *Kirkus Indie* for review and the opportunity to have their reviews published on the *Kirkus* website. *Kirkus Indie's* impressive list of reviewers includes librarians, prolific journalists, PhD holders, and creative executives in entertainment and publishing.

- **Submission requirements.** Submission guidelines state that authors should submit their books online through the *Kirkus* website, www.kirkusreviews.com. Once a review is ready, *Kirkus* will email the author a link to it. If a book does not receive a favorable review, the author has the option not to publish it on the *Kirkus* website. The cost of submitting material for review ranges from $425 to $999, depending on the requested package. A complete list of review packages may be found on the *Kirkus Reviews* website under "Indie Reviews."

SELF-PUBLISHING REVIEW. Founded in 2008, *Self-Publishing Review* functions as both an online book review periodical and a pay-to-review service for self-published authors hoping to gain exposure for their books. The website, www.selfpublishingreview.com, contains a number of resources for independent authors, including editing and marketing services, and even a paid feature to turn a book into a movie.

- **Submission requirements.** *Self-Publishing Review* offers three review packages, each with more features than the previous one as the price per package increases. All packages include a professional review as well as an Amazon editorial review, which will appear underneath your book's Amazon listing. *Self-Publishing*

Review accepts submissions in a number of formats, including PDF, EPUB, and DOC. After you purchase a package, the website will prompt you for more information regarding your book before you send it for review.

Preparing and Sending Out Electronic ARCs

A shift has occurred that has enabled self-publishers to take part in a revolutionary new aspect of book reviewing: the *digital review copy*, or *DRC*. DRC services are paid to add digital versions of finished books to their databases and make them available to thousands of potential reviewers. Despite their user fees, DRC services offer self-publishers the advantage of avoiding the high costs of printing and shipping physical ARCs.

EDELWEISS+. Edelweiss+ is a comprehensive digital cataloging service that links publishers and authors to librarians, educators, and booksellers. Potential book buyers and professional reviewers can peruse the database's extensive collection of books and advance copies from a number of authors and publishers. The platform streamlines communication between publishers and booksellers, and includes extensive sales and marketing services.

- **Submission Requirements.** After signing up for an account on the Edelweiss+ website, www.abovethetreeline.com, publishers and authors can upload digital copies of their works for reviewers to read using the Edelweiss+ digital review copy service. Digital copies must be in PDF or EPUB format. Authors may promote their books directly through the Edelweiss website or share their listings on social media.

NETGALLEY. Started in 2008, NetGalley is a connection point for book publishers, reviewers, librarians, booksellers, and educators. It enables self-publishers to send digital ARCs to professional readers of influence at a fraction of the cost of sending out physical copies. Reviewers may request, read, and recommend books they find on the NetGalley website, www.netgalley.com, and then submit feedback directly to authors and publishers.

Some prepublication journals, such as *Kirkus Reviews*, have paid review divisions for authors who want to have their books evaluated by professional reviewers. Although the price can be hefty, if you have room in your marketing budget, this may be a worthwhile option.

- **Submission Requirements.** Publishers around the world use NetGalley to connect their books to a large audience. There is a sign-up fee and monthly subscription rate, but NetGalley offers a package created especially for independent authors. You must submit a query directly to NetGalley for more information on terms and pricing specific to your needs.

CONCLUSION

As you can see, there is a good deal of work necessary to get to this stage of your book's journey. With your timeline planned out, your metadata set up, your sales sheet in place, and your advance reading copies ready, you will be in good shape for your book's release and promotion. You will find that this information may be used time and time again as you attempt to bring attention to your work.

CHAPTER 11

$\mathcal{G}$ETTING PUBLICITY

Authors have to promote their books, and they have
to be flashy about it. Especially these days.
—JAMES PARKER, JOURNALIST AND AUTHOR

In the previous chapter, I laid out the fundamental information you will need to have finalized and readily available before you begin to promote your book and yourself. You have a timeline to follow; you have a sales sheet with which to introduce your book to the trade, non-trade, and media; and hopefully, you also have a number of positive reviews that may help open some doors. In this chapter, I will provide you with a number of methods that can help you bring greater attention to your work.

Publicity involves generating attention for your book in as many ways as possible, including speaking engagements, reviews, ads, socia media, and more. Some people are natural-born speakers, while others are very uncomfortable talking in public. Still others may learn how to address a crowd comfortably even when faced with a steep learning curve. It's important for you to have a firm grasp of how you would like to approach the process of getting attention. As you will see, there are a number of ways for your book to reach an audience without your being front and center. I suggest you consider using any means of publicity with which you are comfortable.

There are many ways to publicize a book. Some of them, such as speaking engagements, put you front and center. Others, such as social media, do not. Consider using any type of publicity with which you feel comfortable.

I have been very fortunate in my career as an author to have appeared on a number of major—i.e., nationally aired—network television shows. That was a few years ago, though, when there were more opportunities for self-published authors to get this type of exposure. As the Internet began to threaten established communication channels of mainstream media, it became far more difficult for self-published authors to secure guest appearances on these types of shows. Luckily, there exist today many other ways for self-published authors to reach out to potential readers. Of course, this does not mean that it will be easy to get the word out on your book. But by knowing which avenues of promotion are open to you and keeping realistic expectations for what you can accomplish, you can have an enjoyable and hopefully successful journey seeking and securing various types of publicity as a self-published author.

USING PREPUBLICATION REVIEW QUOTES

If your book receives a favorable review as a result of your sending out advance review copies to some of the publications mentioned in the last chapter, you will have a powerful tool in hand that may help bring exposure to your work. After you've shared this review with your friends and family and have taken a few moments to appreciate it, the question you will ask yourself is, *What should I do next?*

Well, the first thing you need to do is convert your good review into an accessible digital format. Using Microsoft Word, for example, type the full review into a DOC file after placing the publication's name at the top of the page. (If possible, you should also add the reviewer's name directly beneath the review.) Then create a *review quote,* which abridges the review to place focus upon its most positive points. To get a better idea of what I am talking about, take a look at the full review of *Black Broadway* that appeared in *Library Journal* (see page 175), and then read the review quote that was culled from it.

Sometimes, a book review is written in a very neutral style. It essentially encapsulates the point of a book without being negative

LIBRARY JOURNAL (STARRED REVIEW)

Lane, Stewart F. *Black Broadway: African Americans on the Great White Way.* Square One. Feb. 2015. 224p. illus. notes. bibliog. index. ISBN 9780757003882. $39.95. THEATER

The history of the participation of African Americans on the Broadway stage as actors, directors, producers, composers, and playwrights is presented in this handsomely illustrated volume. Ranging from William Alexander Brown's founding of the African Grove Theatre in 1816 through Stephen Byrd and Alia Jones-Harvey's revival of Horton Foote's *The Trip to Bountiful* with an African American cast in 2013, award-winning Broadway producer (*Thoroughly Modern Millie; La Cage aux Folles*) and author (*Jews on Broadway; Let's Put on a Show!*) Lane gives an impressive overview with rare production stills, playbills, and posters making his study an essential reference work. Of particular note are the individual short essays on such stage pioneers as Charles Sidney Gilpin, who originated the eponymous role in Eugene O'Neill's *The Emperor Jones* and a lovely tribute to Diana Sands, whose credits include the original production of *A Raisin in the Sun* and *The Owl and the Pussycat.* Of interest to students is the time line of African American history running at the bottom of each page and providing valuable social and cultural context.

VERDICT This volume's superior presentation of visual theatrical elements makes it essential for any theater collection.

—John Frank, Los Angeles P.L.

Review Quote:

"The history of the participation of African Americans on the Broadway stage as actors, directors, producers, composers, and playwrights is presented in this handsomely illustrated volume. . . . Lane gives an impressive overview with rare production stills, playbills, and posters making his study an essential reference work. . . . Of interest to students is the time line of African American history running at the bottom of each page and providing valuable social and cultural context. . . . This volume's superior presentation of visual theatrical elements makes it essential for any theater collection."

—*Library Journal* (Starred Review)

A Full Book Review and the Extracted Quotation

or positive. When this happens, try to excerpt the most positive copy. If it is not a favorable review, there still may be some hope in using a short quote. If that can't be done, just don't use the review at all. As a rule, though, you should never change the words to make the review more favorable. The quickest way to consign your self-published book to the ash heap of ignored writing is to play fast and loose with the rules of the game.

When a Stranger Calls
(After a Book Review Appears)

There are companies out there that track down authors or publishers—trade and self-published operations alike—that have received reviews from any number of publications throughout the year. These often online-only companies typically request a single chapter or some other such excerpt from a reviewed book in digital format so that they can then make it available and searchable in the online catalogs of various booksellers, distributors, and libraries across the country.

While there are reputable companies such as Firebrand Technologies in Newburyport, Massachusetts—whose free "Preview-a-Book / PAB" service plugs book excerpts into bibliographic databases of companies such as Barnes & Noble, Baker & Taylor, and NetGalley, among many others—it is important that you always do your due diligence by requesting the names of at least three other US-based entities with whom the company in question has worked. Do yourself a favor and make sure the references they provide also carry your book. If your book is not currently represented by one of these companies, this service may not be for you.

With your review quote in hand, you should now consider your placement options.

Retail Websites

By now you have established yourself as a self-published author on online book retailer websites such as Amazon and Barnes & Noble. You will want to include your review quote anywhere your book is being sold online. (Note that it is best to use a review quote instead of the entire review. Although people don't want to read a long review, they will read one or two sentences of praise.) It's possible that your prepublication review will wind up on a book retailer's website without your putting it there, but the reviews of books from major publishers are typically the ones given the spotlight.

Of course, not every publication's reviews wind up on every retail website. Keep an eye on online retailers to see if any of them have added one of your reviews to your book's entry. As your reviews become available, if you see that there are online retailers that do not include any mention of them, do your best to add your review quotes to their websites through your established account access, or contact these companies and request that your review quotes be added to their websites.

Sales Sheet

Any review quote you might have should also find a place on your sales sheet. You can also attach the entire review on an accompanying hard copy page or digital file attachment. If you find yourself with a book review—or any print media coverage, for that matter—that extends beyond one side of a sheet of paper, it is always best to place the additional material on the reverse side of the page rather than putting it on a second sheet. There is nothing that turns off the media more than receiving a bundle of pages that have been stapled together. Less remains more in this area of presentation.

Although sales sheets and media releases look similar, they have different purposes. A sales sheet (see the sample on page 160) is designed to "sell" the book to bookstore buyers and distributors. A media release (see the sample on page 186) is designed to win the attention of the media.

Book Cover

You may feature your prepublication review quote on either the front or back cover of your book before you send it off to the printer or release the e-book into distribution. With an especially outstanding review—if room permits—you might consider placing it in its entirety on the back cover or the half-title page. Keep in mind that you may need to acquire permission from the publication responsible for the review before you reprint it. Most publications need to be contacted in writing before they grant formal permission to anyone who wants to reprint something of theirs in its entirety elsewhere. More often than not, they will not charge a reprint fee for use of a complete review. You stand a strong chance of being granted the right to reprint your review as long as you take the proper and respectful steps to do so.

Social Media

Even if you've received a stellar review, avoid posting it in its entirety on your own website or on social media outlets. Instead, post the strongest quotation you can extract from the review, and provide a hyperlink that will enable people to read the full review if they wish to do so.

You should post any review quotes you may have on all your social media outlets—whether it is your own website, Facebook, Twitter, LinkedIn, Instagram, or anywhere else. It is always wise to beat the drum regarding your book's earned accolades wherever people go to learn about new things and embrace ideas. Once again, brevity is important—it is far better to share a short review quote in a post, together with a hyperlink that takes folks to a website page where the entire review may be read.

Traditional Media Release

A *media release*—also called a *press release, news release,* or *press statement*—is a written communication directed at members of the news media for the purpose of drawing attention to your book. Although a media release should describe your book and also include positive review quotations, its chief focus should be on an important newsworthy issue.

You may want to incorporate the full review or review quote into any media-related information you send out. The best spot on a media release for some bragging rights is near the top of the page, or placed in bold font somewhere within the release itself. Unlike a sales sheet, though, you always need to make sure that any featured review quotes do not appear in place of or compete with the reason you are sending a release sheet to the media in the first place. Always remember that story comes before promotion when you are looking to get yourself and your book some coverage. Even when the story is your story, as is the case with a novel or short-story fiction, you need to make sure your primary reason for contacting a reporter or producer is not to brag about how positively your book was reviewed. That being said, you should always make sure you let media contacts know that you have been reviewed—it's all in how you let them know. Remember that less is more—more or less.

As I will explain more fully later on in this chapter, you need to do everything within your power to make a bold and positive impression upon the media. Nothing ensures mainstream media attention more than the proof that your book has already started to gain notice and approval from elsewhere in the industry. These days, there is so much "noise" being generated by other publishers that it's hard to get your own voice heard as you seek to gain attention for your book. But if members of the media see that your book has begun to garner publicity from others within their community, they will be more responsive to whatever you might have to say. That's all you are looking for at this point: a way in.

GETTING YOUR BOOK REVIEWED AFTER PUBLICATION

It is understandably difficult for an author with only one published book and no real contacts to master all that goes into a successful publicity campaign, but that is what you must try to do. By the time you publish your next book, you may have built a steadier path to media coverage or decided to hire someone else to take care of promotion for you. Nevertheless, the following information should familiarize you with the core steps involved in getting your book reviewed after publication.

This book has established just how helpful the Internet can be to self-published authors. Once you have finished copies of your book in hand, you may find that your next best step involves online book reviewers or book review bloggers. There are a number of sources that can point you in the right direction in your attempts to learn what it takes to get reviews and coverage after publica-tion—and how to keep getting coverage once you have received your first exposure.

Help a Reporter Out (HARO)

Located at www.helpareporter.com, this free service offers a three-times-per-day free electronic newsletter of media queries and inter-view opportunities to which you may want to subscribe. Cision, which remains the single largest subscription-only digital database of media contacts and outlets, owns HARO. Only journalists or bloggers who meet a certain criteria—i.e., they need to generate a certain minimum number of page views monthly—are allowed to post queries to HARO's data team regarding potential publicity opportunities.

By regularly reading HARO queries, you may find that your book is suited to some of the offers of publicity from journalists or

Doing It Yourself

More often than not, the publicity process is the point at which self-publishers drop the ball. After putting all that time, effort, and money into writing and producing your book, it is very easy to feel like you have nothing left to give. Nevertheless, you must push yourself further to promote your book. You cared enough to create your book. Now you have to care enough to bring attention to it.

It is realistic to devote one entire year to promoting a book—this includes the prepublication phase, the first month of your book's publication, and the post-publication phase. In actuality, however, there is no end to the post-publication phase. What many self-publishers might find interesting is the fact that typically the lion's share of a trade publisher's annual income comes from its *backlist*, which refers to titles that are more than six months old. You will get more attention and sales for your book if you continue to regard it as a fresh and relevant source of information and inspiration.

bloggers. Before you sign up for the HARO newsletter service, however, you need to know how to write an effective email response. This is a pivotal skill that can help increase the likelihood that a mainstream media journalist or blogger will pick your book to review or provide it with some other form of coverage.

The competition to get interviewed by a media outlet is fierce—especially if it's a major TV, radio, online, or print outlet—so submit your well-written pitch as soon as possible. (See page 181.)

PitchRate

Just like with HARO, you can join PitchRate (http://pitchrate.com) for free and check the daily publicity opportunities that are posted. Over the years, I have noticed far more bloggers using this service to request review copies of new books than you might find in HARO's posts.

The Indie View

This website (www.theindieview.com/indie-reviewers) provides a list of individuals who review independently published books. To appear on the list, reviewers must actively post reviews, review e-books, not charge any fees for reviews, not be affiliated with any publisher, have submission guidelines in place for submissions, and place a link to The Indie View on their websites. If a reviewer requests a fee to review your book, the list maker asks that you let her know so that she can take the reviewer off the list. There is also a section on the website that focuses on self-published authors. All the authors listed, along with their websites, have received at least one four-star review by one of the reviewers on the indie reviewer list.

CREATING A PITCH

Whenever an occasion arises in which you need to describe your book to someone else in order to get some type of promotion, the description you offer is called a *pitch.* When you are gearing up to go out and pitch your book, there is one important thing that you must do first: Figure out where your book would work best as part of a media news story.

If your book is a work of fiction, your search for publicity is going to be much tougher than it would be if you were a non-fiction book author. The majority of national media focus given to fiction works these days is reserved for those writers who are recognizable names. Year after year, the morning news shows air short segments with well-known authors like John Grisham, Nelson DeMille, James Patterson, Jodi Picoult, and Nora Roberts. It's tough, although not impossible, to break through as an unknown. If, however, your book is a nonfiction title, then your chances of successfully pitching your work for publicity and presenting yourself as an expert in your book's chosen subject increase dramatically.

When you are trying to get coverage for your book, media outlets will generally give you only a few minutes in which to convince them it's worth covering. If you've prepared your pitch properly, you should be able to make a case for your book briefly and clearly.

As you prepare to pitch your book for media coverage or yourself for show appearances, it is helpful to memorize what you would consider the key data from your book's sales sheet. Most of the time, you will be given only a few minutes—via email, phone call, or face to face—to pitch your book. Competition for media coverage is intense, and you need to be ready to provide compelling reasons why an editor or segment producer should cover you and your book as a story of interest and value. It is very easy to become flustered while talking about your book, but pitching is a necessary part of getting publicity, and a task for which you should prepare.

Having participated in various writers' workshops over the past several years, I have watched dozens of motivated and seemingly confident self-published authors turn nearly speechless when asked to pitch their books or themselves in only a few minutes' time. Many authors have been there, including me—but in order to survive and thrive within the publicity process, you are going to have to learn a few new tricks.

The foundation of any book pitch should be five to eight talking points, each of which focuses on a dynamic aspect of your book. By memorizing your talking points and practicing them out loud, you will be better able to make your pitch confidently and effectively.

I suggest that you always be prepared to deliver your pitch by having committed to memory five to eight concise yet dynamic topics to discuss in relation to your book and yourself. These topics are called *talking points,* and they are the foundation upon which all pitches should be built. When coming up with talking points, many of which you can draw from your book's sales sheet, it is best to write them down and speak them out loud. Doing so will help you determine if your topics are clear and understandable. Something that is brilliant on paper can become awkward and confusing when spoken—do all you can do to trim all the fat away from your core points. Practicing your talking points out loud will also bolster your confidence and ease any anxiety you might have about public speaking.

The talking points on page 183 are for a fiction book. As you will see, they are meant to bring focus and direction to a pitch, and to help potential interviewers find topics to discuss with the book's author.

By way of comparison, the talking points on page 184 are for a nonfiction book and provide a secure underpinning to any discussion with the media.

The Path of the Wind: A Novel
James A. Misko

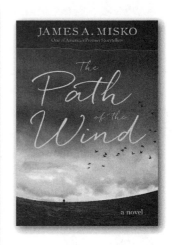

TALKING POINTS:

1) *The Path of the Wind* is the story of Miles Foster, a young newly-wed whose "can-do" spirit and educational ideals are put to the test when he is assigned to teach at an underfunded school in a remote central Oregon town.

2) Although it is a work of fiction, *The Path of the Wind* is based on the author's own brief stint as a teacher in the rural Pacific Northwest.

3) Set during the late 1950s, Misko's newest novel—his fifth—seeks to return readers to a time in America when life was simpler, dreams were bigger, and public discourse was not bound so tightly by the confines of political correctness.

4) Misko hopes that *The Path of the Wind* might bring about a renewed appreciation of teachers in this country—especially at a time when teachers remain grossly underpaid and often unappreciated for their care and commitment to the education and overall lives of their students.

5) Misko considers his creation of a key female character in *The Path of the Wind*—Eleanor Foster, the wife of Miles Foster—a pivotal moment in his continuing evolution as a novelist; so much so, in fact, that his next novel, *Tomorrow Is My Day*, will be his first novel in which the main protagonist is a woman.

Talking Points for a Work of Fiction

As you further refine and target your book's pitch, try to be aware of what is going on in the news each day. More often than not, a story pitch becomes more attractive to the media when it is shown to be relevant to a story that has just hit the news cycle.

**Talking Points for a
Work of Nonfiction**

Unsafe at Any Meal
What the FDA Does Not Want You to Know About the Foods You Eat
Dr. Renee Joy Dufault

TALKING POINTS:

1) *Unsafe at Any Meal* tells the true story of how Dr. Renee Dufault, former food investigator for the Food and Drug Administration (FDA), first detected alarming levels of heavy metal contaminants (mercury, in particular) in the plumbing systems of many US-based food manufacturing plants—and upon further examination, also found those same toxins in a number of popular processed foods commonly sold in supermarkets.

2) When she revealed these disturbing findings to her superiors at the FDA, Dr. Dufault was told in no uncertain terms to stop her investigation. Caught in a crisis of conscience, Dufault chose to take an early retirement from the FDA and soon thereafter founded the Food Ingredient and Health Research Institute (FIHRI)—a nonprofit organization devoted to food ingredient safety, education, and continued research.

3) With her ongoing studies and publication of her book, Dr. Dufault is trying to make the general public aware of the fact that exposure to toxic substances in processed foods continues to serve as a gateway to a variety of serious health issues, including cancer, type 2 diabetes, metabolic dysfunction, organ damage, decline in sperm count levels, cardiovascular disease, and a far higher prevalence of autism and ADHD among young children in the United States and Canada.

4) It was announced in October 2017 by the Clean Label Project that alarming levels of "arsenic, lead, and other heavy metals" were found in around eighty percent (80%) of infant formulas sold on the market. Dr. Dufault's own research, however, turned up this data in 2005, twelve years earlier. She has been trying to inform the public of these matters ever since.

5) If the American public were to stop eating the food ingredient known as high fructose corn syrup (HFCS), its potential for recovery from the woeful effects of the Standard American Diet (SAD) would increase significantly.

The press release on page 186 was generated one day after a new scientific study offered additional support to the claims made by an author in a newly published book. As you can see, the lead-in to the pitch of the book is a nationally released story containing specific health statistics that would be of interest to almost anyone.

CREATING A PRESS KIT

Your press (or media) kit is often the way a member of the media first meets you—and it can make an impact on the media even more readily than can your book. As such, you must write your press kit with the same amount of care and precision that you employed in writing your book. A good and solidly presented press kit can help open the door to publicity just as effectively as a bad and sloppily constructed press kit can close it. In addition to your full contact information, which should appear on every piece of promotional material you include, every author's press kit should include the items discussed on pages 187 and 189.

Every press kit should include the following:

- A media release
- A short author bio and headshot
- Copies of book reviews and press coverage
- A list of suggested interview questions

To "E" or Not to "E" Your Press Kit

When it comes to the media, many of its members prefer to receive their materials in a digital format as opposed to hard copies sent through the mail. Since you will always do better in promotion when you accept and embrace the preferences of those with whom you hope to connect, it is a good idea for you to use your materials to create an *Electronic Press Kit*, or *EPK*. Your EPK should include all the items associated with a traditional press kit. But in this digital version, you can add links to any websites mentioned, which, when clicked on, will take the reader directly to these websites. While there may always be a portion of the population, media or otherwise, that will want to read through your press kit in its printed form, the EPK is here to stay.

**A Sample
Media
Release**

FOR IMMEDIATE RELEASE
Contact Info: Anthony Pomes, VP – Marketing/PR/Foreign Rights
                Square One Publishers (www.squareonepublishers.com)
                Phone#: 516-535-2010

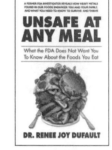

Mercury on the Menu

*Square One proudly presents an important new book that uncovers an
alarming and ongoing problem in America's processed foods industry*

Each year, Americans consume food products that contain heavy metals,
pesticides, and harmful additives—with the blessing of the FDA. Why is
this happening and why haven't you heard about it? In *Unsafe at Any
Meal,* Dr. Renee Dufault, former food investigator for the Food and Drug
Administration, provides the startling answers. While at the FDA, Dr.
Dufault discovered toxic mercury residue in the plumbing systems of
food manufacturing plants and in processed foods sold in supermarkets.
When Dr. Dufault revealed these disturbing findings to her superiors, she was told to stop her
investigation. She retired early and devoted her energy to making the public aware of the
insidious dangers that contaminate our food. To expose what still seems to be a well-kept secret
by the FDA, she has written *Unsafe at Any Meal* to provide consumers with the information
they need to know.

The book begins with the author's story leading to the creation of this work. It then describes the
toxic substances most commonly found in our food supply, and explains how they affect your
genes and health. It goes on to examine the Standard American Diet and the country's trend
toward consuming ingredients that can contain heavy metals, exposure to which can contribute to
conditions such as ADHD or autism. Also included is a guide to reading food labels, recognizing
misleading marketing tactics, and knowing what to look for—and what to *look out for*—in your
grocery store.

Over fifty years ago, Rachel Carson's book *Silent Spring* exposed the dangers of DDT in our
food supply. Unfortunately, it seems that the problem of food contamination has actually become
worse. Backed by research and first-hand experience, Dr. Dufault reveals how the FDA has
failed us, and outlines how you can protect yourself and your family by filling your kitchen with
food that is free of toxic substances. *Unsafe at Any Meal* is a book whose time has come.

ABOUT THE AUTHOR: *DR. RENEE JOY DUFAULT* earned a B.S. degree in Environmental Policy Analysis
and Planning at the University of California, Davis and a doctorate in Health Education. She worked as an
Environmental Health Officer for the National Institutes of Health, the Environmental Protection Agency,
and the Food and Drug Administration. In 2010, she founded the Food Ingredient and Health Research
Institute (FIHRI). A popular worldwide speaker, Dr. Dufault has had numerous articles published in peer-
reviewed journals. She resides in Hawaii.

If you would like more information about *Unsafe at Any Meal* or would like to arrange an
interview with Dr. Dufault, please contact Anthony Pomes either by phone (516-535-2010),
fax (516-535-2014), or email (sq1publish@aol.com). Thank you for your consideration.

BOOK SPECS: $16.95 USD * $25.95 CAN / 240 PGS. / ISBN 978-0-7570-0436-0
6 x 9-INCH QUALITY PAPERBACK

115 HERRICKS ROAD   GARDEN CITY PARK   NEW YORK 11040

Media Release

Your press release can still provide much of the material about your book as it appears on your sales sheet, but it should read slightly differently, as the information should be focused on your pitch, which should be presented in your press release as part of a news-related "hook" rather than just a straight-ahead description of your book.

Short Author Biography and Headshot

An in-depth "About the Author" biographical page is the perfect place to provide details about you and your life, including the city and state in which you live. Your location is important for two reasons. If you are pitching to the media in a place where you are a resident, you may have a better chance of getting coverage because of your local status. If you are pitching to the national media, your location will help outlets decide if you should appear in person or via satellite instead. (Keep in mind that a national media booking for a self-published author is improbable, but you could still give it a try.) Depending on the nature of your book, you may not feel it necessary to include an author headshot on your biography page. The decision is yours, but it is always better to have a photo than not.

When writing the "About the Author" copy for your press release, it's important to include the city and state in which you live. This serves two purposes: It lets local media know that you are available for coverage, and it tells national media whether you can appear in person or via satellite.

Book Reviews and Assorted Press Coverage

On the chance that you already have reviews or feature coverage for your book by the time it has been published and you are actively pitching to the media, be sure to include any assemblage you have of these items (either the full review or review quotes) in your press kit. Make sure that everything you include in the kit features your name or your book's title. (If you lack reviews but have some advance praise or endorsements, include one or two of these in lieu of reviews.) Remember that you always stand a chance of receiving more publicity for your book as you continue to pitch to the media. Be sure to scan and save copies of this new coverage

Interview Questions for *Unsafe at Any Meal*

Author: Dr. Renee Joy Dufault

1. How did your previous work for the FDA, from which you took an early retirement, lead you to write your new book, *Unsafe at Any Meal?*

2. The revelations you make in your new book about pesticides evoke the same kind of shock that Rachel Carson's watershed book *Silent Spring* did in 1962. Do you hope to incite change in our culture the way that Carson did—and if so, what would you want that change to look like?

3. Please tell our audience a little more about the frightening correlation made in *Unsafe at Any Meal* between increased exposure to chemicals and the development of disorders like Alzheimer's disease, dementia, and autism.

4. What are "heavy metals," anyway? They appear to be a sort of silent threat to human health in the sense that although we aren't aware of what they are, they have a profound effect on our risk of developing heart disease and diabetes. Tell us more.

5. Based on your observations, the average diet of American children tends to be rich in processed foods that ultimately damage their health. What advice would you offer to parents who want to introduce more organic and nutritious foods into their children's diets?

6. What is the general impact of food coloring on children's development? Aside from the research you've published an accompanying model for, what studies are being performed to examine this issue more closely?

7. While you speak on the neurological impacts of pesticides, can you please also discuss the general threat that pesticides pose to the health of children and adults alike?

8. As we work to improve public health by making lifestyle changes at the individual level, what recommendations do you have for those at federal level—specifically, the FDA—to improve public health?

9. If readers of *Unsafe at Any Meal* hope to achieve a healthier way of living, what might be the most important piece of information they should take from the book?

10. Finally, people can purchase *Unsafe at Any Meal* on Amazon.com or by visiting the publisher's website at SquareOnePublishers.com. You can call Square One directly at 516-535-2010 as well. The book is also available at Barnes & Noble and your local bookstore.

as it is published so that you can include it in your media kit. To paraphrase what they say in Hollywood, you're only as good as your most recent publicity. The media, whether major or minor, wants to see action.

List of Suggested Interview Questions

Ideally, you should provide ten to fifteen interview questions that encompass the five to eight talking points you have memorized about your book from the sales sheet. The most effective interview questions are the ones that cannot be answered with a simple "yes" or "no" response. The questions you prepare and present to media contacts for potential interviews should afford you the opportunity to touch on all your main points so that you don't get lost while being interviewed. Make sure, of course, to ask any media contacts with whom you wish to establish a good relationship whether or not they would like to be provided with a prepared list of interview questions. Most journalists or show hosts will be pleased to have some of their work done for them. Those who wish to do their own research and prepare their own questions will nevertheless appreciate the consideration you displayed in asking.

The interview questions presented on page 188 are a good example of how you can arrange your questions to suit the style and content of your book.

Over time, as long as you keep pitching your book to the media, you are likely to receive more publicity. Be diligent about scanning and saving copies of this new coverage so that you can continue to improve your press kit.

REACHING OUT TO THE MEDIA

So, you have crafted your publicity-geared pitch. You have all your promotional ducks in a row. You are ready to go. Your next step is to interact with the media. The mainstream media functions on three levels: local, regional, and national. When you are just starting to reach out, you may be most comfortable contacting local media. You have the hometown advantage. There is a greater likelihood that they will want to write about you and your book because you are a newly published local author.

By moving the focus of your publicity efforts from local to regional media, you will be expanding the potential audience, and buyers, of your new book. Regional media are often confined to one state, but some regional media may reach an audience across a cluster of adjoining states or even an entire coastline. Your book could be covered by reporters at high-circulation publications or the regional studios of major television broadcast networks, such as ABC, CBS, or NBC.

With a growing base of know-how and a little bit of luck, the performance you show in the regional media phase might very well set the stage for a shot at national media coverage. The national media stage is where all your hard work can pay off, but it is also where the stakes are highest. You need to be able to pitch hard and fast at any number of editors or producers, all of whom will be looking carefully to see if there is anything in your pitch—your story—that might not suit their promotional outlets. This is the big time, with morning, afternoon, and evening shows all getting ready to roll their segments out in front of millions of people across the country. You need to be prepared to face whatever may come your way.

A shot at exposure through a national media outlet could be a game changer for you and your book—or it may be just a one-time thing. Whatever happens, keep playing the publicity game as long as you feel you have the stamina to do so. Publicity has its ups and downs, and just because you are down doesn't mean things won't turn around again. If publicity is not something you'd like to pursue for yourself, you may want to hire a publicist to help you out on an occasional or steady basis. But more on that later.

Newspapers

Like most people, you probably know the name of your local newspaper, being a subscriber or, at the very least, having caught a glimpse of its front page at your nearby deli or coffee shop. Whether you purchase it for the local news, weather report, sports stats, or crossword puzzle, a newspaper is an important source of both information and entertainment.

When you are ready to pitch your book to a newspaper, your first step should be familiarizing yourself with its writers and their articles. The more acquainted you are with what is being written in a newspaper and who is writing it, the more prepared you will be to aim your pitch at the right person at the right time for the right kind of coverage.

If you would simply like to get your book reviewed, you should email your pitch to a writer or writers associated with a newspaper's Books section. In this section, you will find journalists with titles such as *book reviewer, book review editor,* and *books columnist.* A hardcover book of fiction stands the greatest chance of being reviewed in a Books section—even more so if its author is a member of the community served by a particular newspaper. A nonfiction paperback, however, stands a better chance of getting coverage in a section that either addresses the same general subject matter of your book or is in some way related to it. For example, a book on how to treat rheumatoid arthritis without the use of conventional drugs might be of interest to a newspaper's health reporter. Similarly, a book on how to minimize symptoms of ADHD through dietary adjustments might get the attention of a columnist who deals with parenting issues.

In the uphill battle to get newspaper coverage for your self-published book, you may find that one of your best friends will be the online versions of newspapers. More often than not, coverage that cannot be granted in a newspaper's print edition may instead be provided in its digital version. Rather than think of online-only coverage as a consolation prize, you might actually be able to do more to promote your book by having an easily accessible write-up on a respected newspaper's website.

If you do your homework before pitching to newspapers, you should find yourself in a better position in your overall promotional game. In fact, starting your promotion with newspapers can be a good warm-up to pitching to more nuanced forms of media such as magazines, radio, television, or streaming services.

DEVELOPING A SOCIAL MEDIA PLATFORM

The social media platform is still a relatively new phenomenon, but it has become a major aspect of our everyday lives. While

Consider beginning your campaign for newspaper coverage by pitching to your local paper, where you have a hometown advantage. Newspapers are often willing to write articles on newly published authors who live in the community that's served by the paper.

Countless people around the world have social media "followers," but not all of them are social media "influencers." A social media influencer is someone who is perceived as having insight or knowledge in a certain area and whose online posts can affect the purchasing decisions of her audience as a result of this perception. If your book gets the recommendation of a social media influencer, your readership could grow almost overnight.

it may seem daunting at times, publicizing your book on social media is an excellent way to gain traction and build a following. Many writers, artists, musicians, and entrepreneurs today might not have attained their levels of popularity and success had it not been for social media. Best of all, social media websites are currently free to use. While you may choose to buy advertisement space on some of the platforms listed here, you don't have to pay to set up accounts on any of them.

You don't necessarily need to create a profile on every social media website listed here in order to market your book successfully. The most important component when it comes to promoting yourself and your writing on social media is learning which websites are used most frequently by your target audience. For example, Facebook is hugely popular among a wide range of people, but younger generations now tend to favor Twitter or Instagram. Goodreads, of course, is a social media website that is devoted entirely to the world of books, and would prove useful to any author, while Pinterest is more popular among graphic designers, visual artists, and homemakers.

Social Media Websites and Applications

Social media websites and applications, or apps, have changed the way we interact with public figures, which include authors. Creating an account on at least one of the following services is a good way to begin putting yourself and your work out there. Moreover, having an account on each of these digital platforms will allow you to gain a better idea of what they are all about. It may also be helpful for you to study successful social media profiles that are similar to yours. You will be able to see what seems to be working with their large groups of followers.

Amazon Author Page

An Amazon Author Page is a personal profile page belonging to an author whose books are sold on Amazon. Every author on Amazon

Do You Need to Hire a Social Media Manager?

When it comes to the effectiveness of social media managers in generating hard sales of any given product, the jury is still out. Nevertheless, if you feel that active engagement with social media is a crucial part of how you would like to publicize yourself and your title, you might want to look into hiring someone to handle your social media for you, particularly if you are not a tech-savvy person. If you are able to manage your social media on your own, you will probably be fine posting a steady variety of comments and announcements about your book across different platforms. By taking care of these matters yourself, you will be able to keep an eye on how your social media presence may or may not be growing. If you should one day find yourself with several thousand or more online followers, hiring a social media manager might make sense.

is represented by an Amazon Author Page—even William Shakespeare. Amazon Author Pages typically include an author biography, social media links, a bibliography, and a list of each of the author's books that may be purchased through Amazon. Amazon users can also "follow" an author to receive updates when they sign in as customers.

Thousands of books are bought on Amazon every day. Amazon Author Pages give readers a chance to learn more about their favorite authors and find (and buy) other books written by them. As an author, you can control every aspect of what is displayed on your Author Page. You can post updates in the form of blog posts or videos, create event pages, and link your profile to any of your other social media pages.

After listing your books for sale on Amazon, you will be able to create an Author Page by signing up for an Author Central account (https://authorcentral.amazon.com/gp/help) Once your Author Page has been set up, you will be able to log in to Author Central at any time to make changes to it.

Facebook

Facebook (www.facebook.com) is a highly popular social media platform that connects friends and family members using a simple interface. Of all the platforms listed here, Facebook is definitely the largest, with over two billion active users around the world. It is an excellent marketing tool for companies, brands, public figures, or anybody who is interested in spreading the word about something. Just about anything and anyone you can think of has a Facebook page, from places to products to celebrities. Facebook users can show their support for their favorite musicians, brand names, political figures, and more by "liking" a page, "liking" or commenting on that page's posts or pictures, or even sharing that page's posts on their own profiles for their Facebook friends to see.

Setting up a Facebook "page" is different from setting up a Facebook "profile." Facebook profiles are personal pages run by everyday individuals who want to connect with friends and family. Facebook pages are run by individuals but often represent bigger entities, such as companies, brands, or authors. Facebook profiles are private to other Facebook users until you add each other as "friends." The information on a Facebook page is available to everyone on the website, and people can choose to see the page's posts directly on their timelines by "liking" it.

By creating a Facebook page for your book, you will be able to share information on its release date, reviews, and other news with anybody who "likes" the page. You can post status updates, photos, videos, and more. Many authors also create Facebook pages under their names—separate from their personal Facebook profiles—in order to brand themselves as professional writers and share information with their audiences.

Goodreads

Goodreads (www.goodreads.com) is a "social cataloging" website designed to help book lovers find and discuss good books. Each Goodreads user starts with three default "bookshelves," where they can keep track of the books they've already read, are currently reading, or are planning to read. However, a customized bookshelf can also be created. Users can rate books on a scale of one to five stars, and can directly express their opinions by writing reviews. Other social aspects include adding other Goodreads users as "friends" to follow their updates and view their bookshelves, and engaging in discussion boards on a variety of book-related topics.

Goodreads is a great way to expose your work directly to the book-loving community. If a book isn't listed on the Goodreads website, anybody—not just the author—may add it to the database and start the reviewing and rating process. It's a good idea to at least create a Goodreads account so that you can keep an eye on how the general public is reacting to your book if it is listed on the website. As an added perk, authors on Goodreads have the opportunity to manage their own book listings, advertise and promote their books, and engage with readers through an "Ask the Author" feature.

The world's largest social media website designed for people who want to find and discuss books, Goodreads offers a great way to expose your work to the reading community. If your book isn't already listed there, you (or anybody else) can add it and start the reviewing process.

Instagram

Instagram (www.instagram.com) is a popular photo- and video-sharing service. People share photos of their friends, family, pets, travels, and just about anything else on their Instagram profiles. Users can follow the accounts whose posts they want to see in their newsfeeds. Many businesses, celebrities, and public figures use Instagram to promote themselves and build their brands.

Instagram is well suited for someone who thinks visually. Depending on how public or private you want to be, you may use Instagram to engage directly with your audience, or simply to advertise your books. Many established, popular authors use Instagram to share personal photos, which their followers appreciate as a peek into their favorite authors' lives.

Instagram is a smartphone app (which may be downloaded from an online app store), and as such, it is generally viewed on the go by users at various points throughout the day.

Pinterest

Pinterest (www.pinterest.com) is an image-sharing and cataloging site. Pinterest users create "pinboards," each of which is a collection of images related to a single topic. People create pinboards for just about anything: their interests, their hobbies, recipe ideas, DIY projects, arts and crafts, and much more. Many businesses also use Pinterest to promote their companies, with pinboards that display their products in a sort of "virtual storefront." It remains a bit of a specialty social media network, so certain kinds of books may do a better job of tapping into the Pinterest community than others.

There is no one right way to market yourself on Pinterest—it is truly something you can make your own. If you upload excerpts from your book and images related to it as pins, users will pin them to their pinboards, starting a chain reaction that can spread information about you and your work across the platform. Depending on how you choose to use Pinterest, your followers can browse your pinboards to learn more about you, your books, your writing process, and so on. They can then re-pin the images you've posted onto their own pinboards. Some ideas for author-related pinboards include writing tips, lists of books to read, and quotations and images from your book.

Twitter

A major social network and news source, Twitter provides you with an easy and effective means of communicating with your readers. And the more you tweet, the more followers you may gain.

Twitter (www.twitter.com) is a social networking service designed for sharing short status updates and messages known as "tweets." Over the past few years, Twitter has evolved into a major social network and news source. It is a quick, easy way for users to share and spread their thoughts and ideas. By creating a Twitter account, you can choose whom you would like to follow and as a follower see their tweets directly on your timeline. You can also show your appreciation for someone's tweet by "liking" it or "retweeting" it to share on your personal Twitter page. The more you tweet, the more followers you may gain, and the more people you may reach.

By joining Twitter, you may learn more about your audience by engaging with people directly. Twitter is also an effective networking tool—you can follow and communicate with fellow authors or professionals. Your readers will feel a greater connection to you, and you will feel a greater connection to your readers as you read, share, and respond to one another's tweets.

YouTube

YouTube (www.youtube.com) is a popular video-sharing platform that has grown into a major source of entertainment and news since it was first introduced in 2005. Some individuals known as "YouTubers" have built major followings by regularly posting video blogs, or "vlogs," to their own YouTube channels. YouTubers produce content that spans a wide range of topics, from make-up tutorials to cooking shows to comedy sketches. Viewers can subscribe to YouTubers' channels to keep tabs on the video content these vloggers put out. They can also rate, share, and comment on videos.

Some authors use YouTube to gain a following through vlogs. If you're a creative, charismatic individual with a quality camera and sharp video-editing skills, you may benefit from starting a YouTube channel. It doesn't necessarily have to be book- or writing-related, although both are viable ideas. If you've written a book on a certain topic, odds are you're an expert on it already. Is the topic interesting enough to attract viewers if you were to talk about it on camera? If you build an audience on YouTube, your faithful viewers will likely want to consume any content you put out—and that can include your books.

Crowdfunding Websites

Crowdfunding is the practice of raising funds online, often for some sort of entrepreneurial venture or creative project, by soliciting contributions from a large number of people. With the advent of social media and fundraising websites, crowdfunding has become a popular method of raising money on the Internet. Businesses, nonprofits, organizations, and individuals alike rely on crowdfunding to support all kinds of projects and business ideas. Some people have even begun using crowdfunding to cover financial obligations in more personal situations or emergencies, such as funerals or medical procedures.

There are thousands of crowdfunding websites on the web today, each with its own set of requirements and guidelines. Besides creating a compelling campaign page on whichever crowdfunding site you choose, you will also need to advertise it on as many social media platforms as you can. Post a link to your campaign on your personal social media pages, and encourage your friends and family to do the same. The most successful crowdfunding campaigns have been those that span across multiple social media platforms, landing on as many different profiles as possible.

The following crowdfunding websites are among the most popular examples of this type of service. Each one abides by its own set of rules, regulations, and price tiers. A few platforms are "all-or-nothing"—so if you don't meet your donation goal by a certain time, you will receive none of the funds you raised. Others are more flexible in terms of setting goals and time restraints. Some are selective, while others allow anyone to start a campaign for nearly anything.

GoFundMe

While anyone can start a GoFundMe (www.gofundme.com) campaign for almost any reason, it is most commonly used to raise money for charitable causes and advocacy, such as disaster funds, memorial services, and medical expenses.

GoFundMe has a simple user interface that makes the process easy for anyone who needs to raise money. There are no deadlines or goal requirements, and no penalties if you fall short of your donation goal. Even if you fail to reach your target amount, you will still be able to keep the donations you raised.

Indiegogo

Indiegogo (www.indiegogo.com) is a crowdfunding platform committed to raising support and funds for innovative products and exciting ideas from entrepreneurs, inventors, and other creative individuals. The types of projects on Indiegogo range from technology and innovation to creative works and community projects. Indiegogo campaigns typically offer each donor the option to choose a donation amount, with each amount being accompanied by one or more rewards. Rewards can be anything from a simple thank-you note to a T-shirt or some other free product upon the campaign's completion.

Indiegogo charges a 5-percent commission (plus credit card processing fees) on the funds you actually raise. While you have the option to go all-or-nothing or choose a more flexible plan, the stakes are high if you don't meet your goal. Giving out rewards promised to backers may prove difficult if you haven't raised enough money.

Kickstarter

Kickstarter (www.kickstarter.com) is one of the largest, most popular crowdfunding websites. Similar to Indiegogo and Patreon (see below), backers on Kickstarter receive rewards depending on the amount of money they have pledged. While having your project on Kickstarter means it will be visible to a large number of eyes, getting your project on Kickstarter is a highly competitive process. Not every campaign that is submitted for approval is accepted. In addition, each campaign lasts sixty days, which can be a short amount of time to raise money, depending on how popular your project is and the amount being raised.

Kickstarter uses the all-or-nothing model, in which you are paid only once your project has reached its donation goal. Pick your goal wisely—something attainable and realistic—since you will be expected to deliver all promised perks and actually complete your project if you reach your goal. If you fail to reach your goal, funds are returned to backers and you are not charged for the campaign.

Patreon

Patreon (www.patreon.com) is the most unique of the four crowdfunding websites listed here in that it works more like a subscription service than a one-time donation platform. People can support their favorite content creators, including musicians, podcasters, and cartoonists, by becoming "patrons" and pledging to donate a certain amount (at the patron's discretion) of funding each month.

If you have a blog, YouTube channel, or podcast, or you produce similar content that may be of interest to your readers, Patreon is a great way to gain support from your followers. The monthly income from Patreon would be helpful in allowing you to continue to write

Crowdfunding websites offer a way to fund entrepreneurial and creative enterprises—such as the writing and publicizing of your books. Just make sure that you understand a site's rules and regulations before making a commitment. Some platforms, for instance, have an "all-or-nothing policy," which means that if you don't meet your donation goal by a stated date, you will receive none of the funds you raised. Others impose no deadlines or goal requirements.

and create content. Keep in mind, however, that as patrons pay a small subscription fee every month in exchange for the content you put out, you will be expected to keep producing the new content they're paying for—and producing it can become time-consuming. If you don't have that many patrons, the time it takes to run a Patreon page and the pressure to keep coming up with content can seem unwarranted.

One strategy that may help you avoid this issue is to get involved with Patreon early in your writing process. If you space out the writing of your book—let's say to one chapter a month over twelve months—and provide a small excerpt each month to your Patreon subscribers, at the end of the year, you could have an entire book, and your subscribers, who received only excerpts, may be excited about buying the entire book. You might also dedicate a second year to publicity of your book by creating a monthly podcast related to your work.

The Importance of Reader Reviews

When I see a book with hundreds or even thousands of reader reviews on Amazon.com, I am really impressed. The sheer number makes me think the book has got to be amazing. I can guess what you're thinking. Hundreds of reader reviews? Thousands even? She's got to be kidding. But I am not. For example, *The Martian* by Andy Weir, which was originally self-published, has more than 30,000 reader reviews on Amazon.com. You may not be able to get that many reader reviews at this point in your publicity campaign, but you definitely want to shoot for at least twenty-five to fifty reader reviews of your book on Amazon.com or other book-friendly websites, such as Goodreads.com.

So, how do you get reader reviews on Amazon.com without being so blatant that it looks like you're trying to manipulate the public? It is very important to go after reader reviews in a way that is straightforward, so that if someone asked you about how your reader reviews came about, you would be very comfortable explaining it to them.

Of course, there are readers who will—independently and without any prodding from you or anyone else—feel compelled to write

The Power of Proactivity

Being proactive about possible media interviews really can work to your benefit—I know from experience. Yes, it takes a certain degree of effort, and a positive outcome is often a matter of timing or serendipity, but good things can happen when you try. For example, years ago, I wrote to a producer at ABC's *The View*. I briefly let the producer know I had just published a book entitled *Friendshifts*, which I hoped might fit in with their production plans. Fortunately, my letter of introduction coincided with the program's decision to devote almost an entire episode to friendship. And just like that, I had booked a national TV spot.

a reader review. Once your book becomes available, you may see several reviews pop up in various places. You shouldn't automatically expect them to appear, but you will be pleasantly surprised if they do. The key to promotion is to get the ball rolling, which you may accomplish by asking people you know through social media if they would like to read your new book. Offer each of them a complimentary copy, and let them know that you would be very grateful if they would post reader reviews after they have read it. It's as simple as that. No pressure. No manipulation. The people who receive complimentary copies should feel that they are free to voice their honest opinions, but if they actually take the time to write reviews, chances are they will be positive.

Be sure to avoid pressuring anyone to post a review. People are busy. It can take someone days, weeks, or even months to read your book and post a review. If you push too hard for a review, the reader may get annoyed and abandon your book completely. Give away as many free copies of your book as you wish, but keep a close eye on your inventory. In your enthusiasm, you may wind up giving away far more books than you should. If you can part with fifty or more copies of your book, then go ahead—you may get more reviews that way. If you need to watch your investment a little more carefully, though, you could concentrate on twenty or so people whose opinions you value and trust.

If you choose to provide readers with complimentary copies of your book with the goal of getting online reviews, be patient. It may take weeks or even months for some folks to read your book and write a review. If you pressure them to act more quickly, they may completely abandon your book.

> ## *Press Release Distribution Services*
>
> If you wish to use a press release service to publicize your book, you may find its reach worth its cost. A press release service can distribute your press release to hundreds or even thousands of media outlets, depending on which service package you choose. You may get numerous write-ups on your book as a result, whether regionally, nationally, or internationally. You may also get requests for interviews.
>
> Some press release services require you to provide them with a completed press release, while others will write one for you for a fee. Press release services cannot guarantee placement in any particular media outlet, so it is important that you carefully consider the amount you are willing to spend on a release that may not yield your desired outcome. Nevertheless, a press release service may lead to decent coverage, so make sure you have a solid distribution service in place to fulfill any incoming orders or requests for review copies. (For examples of press release services, see page 247.)

HIRING A PUBLICIST

Publicity is a time-consuming job that requires dogged persistence. If you don't have that kind of time or that kind of drive, consider hiring a professional publicist. An experienced publicist—who already has an up-to-date list of media contacts—may be worth the price.

There is a reason that most trade book publishers either have PR experts employed in-house or work with outside publicity firms. It is because publicity is a tough and time-consuming job, especially when done right. Many people who have written books find that they don't have the drive or dogged persistence necessary to promote their books. There's nothing wrong with this realization. If you do not wish to handle publicity yourself, you will simply need to hire someone to handle it for you, if you can afford to do so.

You can hire a freelance publicist or work with a part-time or full-time assistant who can pitch your book and manage your mailings. If you hire someone who does publicity full-time, she should have an extensive and up-to-date list of media contacts to which she can pitch your book for potential reviews or coverage. The advantage of hiring a publicist is that it is a more strategic approach than doing your own publicity and having to learn and improve upon the process with every step along the way.

Most credible publicity experts require a minimum time period of three months for any campaign they agree to handle. A good publicist will aim to book TV and radio segments for you from an established list of contacts, and will send out copies of your book for review to both traditional book review outlets and bloggers. Some publicists concentrate on specific kinds of media coverage. The nature of your book should help you and any potential publicist determine whether or not she is right for the job. Finally, you should request of any potential publicist at least three references, which you can contact to help you in your hiring decision.

Publishing Trends is a website (www.publishingtrends.com) that publishes an annual roundup of freelance book publicists. John Kremer, author of *1001 Ways to Market Your Book*, also has a list of book publicists on his website, bookmarket.com. (See page 240 of the Resources section.)

Lastly, if you have friends who have successfully promoted their self-published books using book publicists, ask them for referrals.

CONCLUSION

In this chapter, we have looked at the many steps involved in getting publicity for your book. You have learned how to get the best out of book reviews through the strategic use of quotations, how to create a relevant and timely publicity pitch, the necessary components of a press kit, and the pros and cons of doing your own publicity or hiring a publicist to handle it on your behalf.

The task of promoting your book can be a daunting one. Just remember that while there are more technological conveniences in our world than ever before, these expediencies allow for changes in the industry to occur at a rapid pace. The most effective means of book publicity today may not be the most proficient means of publicity next year or even next week. When it comes to promotion, it is just as important to be adaptable as it is to understand the tools currently at your disposal. The only thing you can truly control is the quality of your writing.

CHAPTER 12

SELLING YOUR FOREIGN RIGHTS

Without translation, I would be limited to the borders
of my own country. The translator is my most
important ally. He introduces me to the world.
—ITALO CALVINO, AUTHOR

This chapter concerns the business of foreign rights and provides insights into the process of getting your self-published book into the hands of readers who live in other countries and speak different languages. Of course, as with so many things in the publishing world, the path to a foreign rights deal for a self-published author is usually an uphill struggle. There is a well-established industry already in place to carry out this kind of work, and self-published authors are still considered uninvited guests to the party. Keep in mind that the traditional publishing industry is a somewhat sheltered group of folks who serve as arbiters of literary taste and content for much of Western civilization. You must therefore be nimble and nuanced when trying to work within the world of trade book publishing, whether at home or abroad.

Always be respectful of industry insiders and their expertise. These professionals have certainly earned the positions they hold, as their employment is contingent on their generating money consistently from well-negotiated foreign rights contracts. Remember, though, that you have something to offer as well, as evidenced by the continued popularity of self-publishing and the ways in which a determined "grass roots" approach may have helped you identify and fulfill a niche in the market. After all, the mainstream route is not always the one that generates the most attention or success. Nevertheless, to sell yourself as an exception to the established rules of publishing, you need to know what those rules are.

USING A DOMESTIC LITERARY AGENT

At this point in the publishing process, you may want to hire a literary agent in the United States to secure foreign rights contracts on your behalf. More often than not, though, literary agents keep their doors solidly closed to self-published authors. Instead, they work with writers who have enjoyed strong domestic sales through traditional trade publishers, to which agents may point as they try to convince foreign publishers that such successes can be replicated in other languages and countries. So, in addition to liking you and your book, a literary agent must be persuaded of your project's potential to make money.

Of course, agents make commissions from rights deals. These commissions are based on the gross (before taxes) advances authors receive, as shown in the following table:

AGENT COMMISSIONS		
Author Advance	**Domestic Rights Sales Commission (15%)**	**Foreign Rights Sales Commission (20%)**
$100,000	$15,000	$20,000
$75,000	$11,250	$15,000
$50,000	$7,500	$10,000
$25,000	$3,750	$5,000
$20,000	$3,000	$4,000
$15,000	$2,250	$3,000
$10,000	$1,500	$2,000
$5,000	$750	$1,000
$2,500	$375	$500
$1,000	$150	$200

Foreign Literary Agents and Rights Options

If you are able to convince a foreign literary agent of your book's potential, you will have to decide whether to grant him nonexclusive rights or exclusive rights to shop your title before you sign on with his agency. A nonexclusive rights option of four to five months might be your best option, as it would allow you to approach other agents and publishers during that period, but an exclusive rights option of at least three months will likely be required by the agency as an assurance that it will not be undercut by other parties who may be trying to sell your foreign rights. Be sure to establish in writing that an exclusive rights option is being granted.

It is important to note that it is rare for an unknown author's foreign rights to sell for more than a $20,000 advance. An advance of $1,000 to $2,500 for foreign rights is more likely. Needless to say, most US-based literary agents would not take on a self-published author whose foreign rights they would understandably value at only $200 to $500 per deal in commission. If an author could convince an agent of his ability to command sizeable advances on the sales of his domestic rights (for example, an advance of $50,000) and foreign rights (for example, an advance of $5,000 per contract), he might capture the interest of this agent, particularly if the agent truly likes the book. You may be able to accomplish this feat if you can show you have already cultivated a substantial audience for your work.

Literary agents want to meet authors who interact with their fans, and whose fans like to engage in discussions with one another about these authors and their works. Simply having Twitter followers is not enough (although having a really large number of Twitter followers is still impressive). If an author can point to a fan site dedicated to his work, such as a Facebook fan site on which

If you want to work with a domestic literary agent rather than selling your book's foreign language rights on your own, realize that if you can show strong domestic sales—and, therefore, the potential to make money in foreign sales—you will find it easier to attract an agent's interest.

thousands of people connect and interact, he may pique an agent's interest. So, before you approach a literary agent, try to establish an impressive online presence.

DOING IT YOURSELF

As you know by now, the DIY road is not an easy one to take. In fact, many in the book business would prefer if self-published authors simply gave up on the idea of securing foreign rights on their own. The industry continues to change, though, and you probably wouldn't be holding this book in your hands if you were already convinced it was a lost cause. I would like to believe that you are determined to find your way to a "yes" rather than a "no," so I will lay out an abbreviated version of the world of foreign rights and help you navigate your DIY journey.

Book Fairs

Attending an international book fair—such as Germany's Frankfurt Book Fair—can maximize your chance of securing foreign rights. To save money, consider attending as part of the Independent Book Publishers Association (IBPA) or the Combined Book Exhibit (CBE).

One way for you to maximize your odds of securing foreign rights deals is to attend international book fairs as an exhibitor. The Frankfurt Book Fair is the biggest book trade show in the world. It takes place in the month of October. The show is not cheap to attend, but you should be able to secure a small exhibitor's show booth for a few thousand dollars.

Since you will also more than likely need to ship your show materials to the fair ahead of time, which can be expensive, you may do well to consider attending the fair as part of the Independent Book Publishers Association (IBPA) or the Combined Book Exhibit (CBE)—both of which offer reasonable booth rental rates and will ship your materials to the trade show for a decent price. You should solidify your game plan approximately eight months to a year ahead of the date of the fair, as most trade shows (including the Frankfurt Book Fair) require confirmation of participation that far in advance.

The London Book Fair, which usually takes place in April, is not as big as the Frankfurt show, but it is a place where many deals are made (with emphasis placed on English-language deals between North American and UK book publishers), while the Bologna Children's Book Fair, which takes place in March or April, focuses on the children's and young adult market. The Beijing International Book Fair (BIBF), which is held in China at the end of August, has become one of the major international book fairs in recent years. Finally, BookExpoAmerica, commonly called BEA, which takes place at the end of May in New York City, is the largest book trade show in the United States. It includes a foreign rights section, where rights meetings may take place.

Securing a Foreign Rights Contract

First you will need a password-protected PDF of your book, which you can create using Adobe software. You will then be able to email it to the foreign publishers or foreign literary agents who have made their requests known in writing. (Be careful that you know exactly to whom you are sending your book. Make sure that the interested party is, in fact, affiliated with a real foreign book publisher that has a legitimate website. Even better, see if the foreign publisher has worked with other US publishers.) Once you are ready to send your book out, you will need to consider a few important matters.

When foreign publishers or foreign literary agents request an electronic copy of your book, send a password-protected PDF to prevent your book from being pirated and made available on the Internet without your permission.

Standard Foreign Rights Contract

Before pitching your foreign rights to publishers, get a look at a standard foreign rights contract—a boilerplate agreement. You will see a very good example later in this chapter. (See page 216.) It is indicative of what most foreign rights contracts look like and the terms they generally include.

Formats

A foreign rights contract should specify which formats are being granted to the foreign publisher and make sure each format has its own sliding-scale royalty rate. Traditional publishing formats are most often considered in the following order: hardcover, trade paperback/softcover, mass market/digest edition, and hardcover reprint (if the initial publication was first done in trade paperback format). Most foreign publishers will release trade paperback editions of books that were first presented in trade paperback format, or start with a hardcover edition if a self-publisher's version is in hardcover.

E-Book Rights

Over the years, e-book rights—also known as "electronic book download rights" or "digital verbatim rights"—have become a necessary part of a foreign rights contract. Aim to get 25 percent of net on each and every digital download of your work, and never agree to a rate that is less than 20 percent of net.

Advance and Royalty Rate

If a foreign publisher is interested in publishing your book and would like to know what you would consider a good offer on advance and royalty, try to get the publisher to make his own offer first. There is a nuanced way of achieving this goal. You could explain, for example, that you would prefer to defer to the publisher's notion of what a good offer would be in his market. You could also explain that it is the policy of your company—or the policy of your "business manager," if you wish to remain only the author in the negotiation—to be given contract terms upfront and then present a counteroffer, if necessary.

Be aware that a significant number of foreign rights deals in book publishing do not earn beyond their initial advances, which is why you should try to get the highest advance you can for your foreign rights. This money is very likely the only amount you will see for quite some time, or possibly at all. Your advance, of course, is meant to be offset by future royalties, and it could take years for your book's sales to generate enough income in royalty payments to surpass the amount you received as an advance.

It is important to keep track of your payment dates, especially if you find yourself fortunate enough to have secured multiple contracts. Keep an eye on when each advance is due, and know that a good contract should include the right to terminate the agreement if the publisher does not send payment of an advance within a certain number of days as of the contract date—typically, ninety days.

Whenever possible, try to ensure that a US dollar value is written into the contract. When it comes to your royalty rate, obviously try to get the best percentage possible, and always make it a percentage of net as opposed to retail. Doing so could lead to a greater return on sales, as there may be many different ways a foreign publisher could sell your book aside from strictly retail routes. Also, make sure you get what is called a "sliding scale" royalty—meaning that your percentage of earnings per copy rises according to the number of books sold by the publisher.

> Try to get the highest advance you can for your foreign rights. It may be years before the sale of your book produces enough income to surpass the amount you receive as an advance. In fact, many foreign rights deals never earn beyond the advance.

Subsidiary Rights

A foreign rights contract, like any other book contract, may include a *subsidiary rights* clause, which allows the publisher to produce different editions of your work—e.g., book club editions, large-print editions, illustrated editions, etc.—or sublicense it for adaptation to other media—e.g., film, television, etc. Be sure to specify that any revenue associated with subsidiary rights is to be split fifty-fifty between you and the foreign publisher. If possible, try for a little more of the pie by negotiating a sixty-forty split in your favor.

Duration of Contract

Limit the term of your contract with a foreign publisher to five years if possible—or to no more than seven years if more time is requested by the publisher. In addition, make sure your contract notes the period of time allowed the publisher to release your work in print. Twelve to eighteen months from the contract date (not the signature

When negotiating a foreign
rights contract, make sure
it stipulates that any legal
proceedings between you
and the foreign publisher
will be held in your home
state—or at least in your
own country. While this
may not seem important
now, if legal problems
surface at some point in the
future, you will not want to
travel to a foreign country
to resolve them.

date) is an acceptable length of time. Never let this period stretch beyond twenty-four months.

Territories

Limit the language rights granted in foreign rights contracts to particular countries, if possible. For example, if you are negotiating a Spanish-language contract, it may apply to Spain and certain Latin American countries. If possible, hold on to your US publishing rights for the Spanish language—and hold on to your rights in Mexico, as well. Your rights are commodities, so treat them that way.

Legal Issues

Request that any legal proceedings or instances of arbitration between you and the foreign publisher be held in your own home state, or at least in your own country.

Production Copies and Complimentary Copies

A foreign rights contract should specify the number of production copies of your book you will be required to send to the publisher, as well as the number of complimentary copies of the publisher's edition of your book you will receive. It is always best to keep your obligation to no more than two copies. (If your book is a hardcover with a page count of more than 300 pages, then limit your obligation to one copy.) As for your complimentary copies, most foreign publishers will agree to send you at least four and as many as ten. (You may want to stipulate that your complimentary copies be sent via airmail.)

Once you have a deal and have to send a foreign publisher translation copies by mail, always make sure that your package weighs no more than four pounds. If your package is over four pounds, it will cost considerably more to send overseas.

You may be able to avoid sending any physical copies of your book for translation purposes by instead providing the publisher with a password-protected PDF version. If your book has any illustrations

Translation

Quality of translation is extremely important—perhaps even more so for a work of fiction than for a work of nonfiction. Variances in style between different languages can affect the intention of your work of fiction in ways a foreign publisher may not notice or have the resources to correct. When it comes to nonfiction titles, however, any reputable foreign book publisher is going to want to produce a translation that makes sense in his own language. Otherwise, the book won't connect with its target audience, and sales will suffer.

If possible, add a "Translation Sample Chapter" clause to your rights agreement, which would specify that the publisher who translates your work must provide you with a sample chapter of your book in its respective language. If you do not speak this language, contact a local college or university and speak with a member of its languages department. There may be a student who could give you a line-by-line assessment of the translation for a fee.

The following text is an example of a standard translation clause that might be included in a foreign rights contract:

In the course of translation of the Work, any deviations made from the original manuscript in the English language must be noted and shown to the Author for written approval. Any such deviations of text must be shown to the Author in both the English language and the translated language in question as provided by the translator appointed by the Publisher. In order to ensure a level of accuracy that is deemed satisfactory by the Author, a sample chapter of the Publisher's translated version of the Work will be submitted to the Author in a mutually agreeable digital format. Upon receiving the translation, approval of said translation will not be unreasonably withheld by the Author. If a period of three months goes by from the date the Publisher sends the sample chapter to the Author and no approval and/or changes are forthcoming from the Author to the Publisher, the Publisher shall then be granted the right to move forward with the process of publishing the Work in the translated language.

Literary Scouts

While most foreign rights deals are negotiated through literary agents, in book publishing, there is also a player known as a *literary scout*. Literary scouts normally work on behalf of foreign publishers, not authors. If a scout is able to help secure the foreign rights to one of your books for an interested publisher overseas, any payments due the scout would come from the foreign publisher or that publisher's rights agent.

or artwork, you will have to send the publisher digital files of this material whether or not you also send physical copies.

Who Gets Paid and How

If you or a foreign publisher used a rights agent to help secure your foreign rights contract, this agent will take a commission on the deal (anywhere from 10 to 25 percent). As for distributions made to you, most foreign publishers prefer to send payments via wire transfer or international direct deposit as opposed to physical check, so you will need to have all your bank data and wire service instructions ready, including your bank's name and address, your account number, and your ABA bank routing number.

When it comes to your sending your financial information to a publisher, you can never be too careful. Instead of placing this sensitive information in the body of an email, save it in a DOC or PDF file, and encrypt the file with password protection if possible.

Foreign Taxes and Your Earnings

Once you have a finished contract in hand and are ready to sign it, be aware that the United States Internal Revenue Service (IRS) has a policy whereby you can achieve an exemption from double taxation on monies earned in other countries. To be granted this exemption, you must first go to the IRS website (www.irs.gov) and download

Form 8802. This form must be filled out and sent to the IRS in order for you to receive from the IRS what is called Form 6166, which stands as a double-taxation exemption document. There is also a "Penalties of Perjury" letter that you will be required to sign and send along with Form 8802.

Most foreign publishers do not want to make payments to authors via personal checks. Compile your bank data and wire instructions, and be prepared to email this information to the publisher in a password-protected DOC or PDF file.

The earliest you can postmark your fully filled-out and signed Form 8802 is December 1 of the year previous to the one in which you anticipate receipt of foreign payments. In other words, if you expect to make some money from foreign rights contracts in a certain year, then you should fill out and mail Form 8802 on December 1 of the year prior. Be sure to make copies of everything you send to the IRS when mailing your Form 8802 the first time.

Rights Auctions

If you have already secured a nonexclusive foreign rights option (see "Foreign Literary Agents and Rights Options" on page 207), either through an agent or directly with an interested publisher, keep in mind that you remain free and clear to send your book to as many other agents or publishers as you wish. In fact, as soon as you have received a nonexclusive foreign rights offer to publish your book in a particular language or territory, you may hold what is known as a *rights auction*. In a rights auction, you invite other publishers that might also consider publishing your book in this same language or territory to take part in a bidding war for the sole and exclusive right to publish your book.

Once you begin to receive offers for the rights to your book during the usual nonexclusive option period of four to five months, you may rely on the auction process to help you reach the very best offer possible. When you have the most lucrative rights offer within reach, you can negotiate the terms of an exclusive rights deal, which you may then sign. While self-published authors, who rarely have agency representation, do not often get a chance to hold a rights auction, there is no reason why you shouldn't try to hold one if an opportunity to do so arises.

FOREIGN RIGHTS CONTRACT TEMPLATE

The following contract may be used as a template for your foreign rights deal.

Foreign-Language Publishing Company
[Name of Your Company]

PUBLISHING RIGHTS AGREEMENT
[CITY, STATE]

Agreement made this **[DATE]**, between **[FOREIGN-LANGUAGE PUBLISHING COMPANY–the Publisher]** hereinafter referred to as the Publisher, and **[NAME/ADDRESS and/or your company's NAME/ADDRESS–the Proprietor]**, hereinafter referred to as the Proprietor, concerning the work entitled:

[YOUR BOOK'S TITLE]
by [NAME OF AUTHOR]

Hereinafter referred to as the Work.

Now, therefore, for and in consideration of their mutual promises and for other valuable consideration, receipt of which is hereby acknowledged, the parties hereto agree as follows:

1. Proprietor warrants that it is the sole Agent of the Work and of all rights granted to the Publisher under this Agreement and that the Book does not infringe upon any statutory or other copyright, or any right of others whatsoever. The Proprietor will hold the Publisher harmless against any loss or expense arising out of any breach or alleged breach of any of the foregoing warranties.

2. Proprietor hereby grants to the Publisher the sole and exclusive right for the term hereinafter stated to publish and sell a **[YOUR BOOK'S FORMAT – either Hardcover or Paperback]** edition of the Work in the **[FOREIGN LANGUAGE]** throughout the **[GEOGRAPHICAL TERRITORY or TERRITORIES]**.

3. The term of this license shall be for **[DURATION OF TIME – usually somewhere between five (5) and seven (7) years]** commencing on the date of publication of the Work by the Publisher and thereafter shall automatically continue until the Proprietor shall give to the Publisher ninety (90) days prior written notice of termination. Following the expiration of this Agreement, the Publisher may continue to sell or otherwise dispose of any stock on hand or any stock on which production has commenced as of the date of receipt of the notice of termination by the Proprietor.

4. Publisher agrees to publish the Work not later than **[PRODUCTION PERIOD – usually between twelve (12) and eighteen (18) months, though some publishers request a period of twenty-four (24) months to do their work]** from the date of this Agreement at the expense of the Publisher, and if

the Work is not published by that time, this Agreement will terminate automatically at that time, with all monies paid by the Publisher to be forfeited.

5. The Proprietor agrees to supply the Publisher with **[YOUR QUANTITY OF BOOKS – since you will most likely need to mail the Publisher your book, and since anything over four pounds and sent through the US Postal Service can be expensive, even more so if you use a delivery service like DHL or Federal Express, it is best for you if you can get the Publisher to agree to receiving only one (1) or two (2) copies]** of the Work for the purpose of production. The Publisher agrees to supply the Proprietor with **[THEIR QUANTITY OF BOOKS – it is usually customary for the Publisher to send the Proprietor ten (10) free copies of their edition, but it is usually no more than that]** within sixty (60) days of the publication of the Publisher's Edition.

6. The Publisher agrees to make the following payments:

a) a non-refundable advance payment against all royalties earned of **[ADVANCE AMOUNT – this amount depends on the prevailing patterns in any particular country's or territory's market]** dollars payable in US funds. The Publisher agrees to send the advance payment within **[PERIOD OF TIME – sixty (60) days would be great, ninety (90) days is standard]** days of the contract date. Should the Proprietor not receive the advance payment within this amount of time, then this Agreement shall become null and void.

b) a royalty rate of **[PERCENTAGE – always try for a sliding scale based on a steady increase of royalty earnings as more copies are sold over time]** percent (%) of the **[NET or RETAIL – RETAIL is usually preferred]** price on all copies sold.

c) on copies sold at remaindered prices, **[PERCENTAGE - this should be ten (10) percent (%), which is the usual trade standard]** of the amount actually received, unless such copies are sold at or below cost.

d) on payment for digital verbatim **["digital verbatim" is an equivalent term for "e-book rights," though the phrase "digital verbatim" is used in foreign rights contracts because it's a clearer indication of what the rights represent across various types of foreign languages]** rights, please see clauses 15–17 as written below.

7. All sums of money paid to the Proprietor under this Agreement shall be divided in the following manner: **[PERCENTAGE TO PROPRIETOR – this is usually ninety (90) percent (%), though the final figure can depend on what kind of local taxes may be pulled from earned monies in different countries. For example, various countries in the Far East have certain amounts taken from their earnings before they can issue paid earnings to parties in other countries. Reputable publishers or agents, however, will let you know what these amounts should be and often will want to spell out the exact amounts in the contract prior to signature]** ___ shall be paid in US funds directly to the Proprietor; **[PERCENTAGE TO AGENT – this depends on the agent and what is agreed upon, but it is normally between ten (10) percent (%) and fifteen (15) percent (%) of all Proprietor's earnings]** ___ shall be paid to the Proprietor's

agent: **[if there is an Agent on a rights deal, this is the place to provide the Agency's full name and mailing address]** is hereby authorized to collect and receive such monies as total commission for services rendered and to be rendered.

8. Statements and payments shall be made in accordance with the Publisher's usual practice but not less than once a year.

9. The Publisher shall keep accurate accounts and records (together with all supporting vouchers) in respect to its printing and sales of the Publisher's Edition and on all matters relevant to the calculation of royalties under this Agreement and shall if so required make such records, accounts and vouchers available to the Proprietor or its authorized representatives.

10. The Publisher agrees to print on the copyright page of each book the copyright notices as contained in the Proprietor's editions and any new copyright information as supplied by the Proprietor along with the phrase, "Reprinted by special arrangement with **[the name of your publishing house or whichever name designates to whom the Work belongs as per copyright, together with the city/state and country]** Copyright (c) **[this is where you list the publication date that appears on your book's copyright page, together with the exact name of the person/entity listed as holder of the copyright]**."

11. Should copyrighted materials contained in the Work not be controlled by the Author or Proprietor, it is then the responsibility of the Publisher to obtain copyright permission for these portions.

12. No extension of time or other indulgence which may be granted by the Proprietor to the Publisher shall constitute a waiver of the Proprietor's strict rights under this Agreement.

13. All rights not specifically mentioned herein remain the property of the Proprietor.

14. This Agreement shall not be assigned by the Publisher without the written consent of the Proprietor.

15. In addition to the aforementioned rights granted in this Agreement for the Work, the Proprietor grants the Publisher the following digital verbatim text only display and download rights:

a) The right to import or cause to be imported, to save or cause to be saved, as digital verbatim text content on secure electronic database platforms owned by the Publisher and/or by third parties on a paid-for customer basis, in which the Publisher retains full control over the display as well as customized accessibility defined by the Publisher, the **[this is where you place LANGUAGE for which this foreign rights contract is being created – since much of the three clauses listed here in the "Digital Verbatim" clauses can stand as a boilerplate template, it is a good idea for you to put into BOLD font any references to the LANGUAGE into which the Work is being published]** language translation of the Work, word by word as published in printed book form, and to make it publicly available to users through a customised request, for the purpose of reaching out to customers by publicizing, promoting and directing the public to the availability of the said Work in any published form under the terms of the above mentioned agreement.

b) In addition, the Publisher is granted the right to have such digital verbatim text content indexed and/or to have it annotated with keywords and other methods for researching, which enables a search of the full text and permits a user to search with keywords or excerpts the full digital verbatim text content.

c) The Publisher shall, for the purpose of clauses 15–17, have the right to add links with a sales function for any version of the Work in the **[FOREIGN LANGUAGE]** language available under the terms of this Agreement.

d) The Publisher shall ensure that the content visible to the user shall be limited to parts of the text only, the size of which to be determined by the Publisher, but in no way to exceed an aggregate ten (10) percent (%) of the Work. The extracts shall prominently display the title of the Work, the name of the Authors, all copyright and trademark notices and full purchasing information of the Publisher's edition(s) of the Work (including the name of the Publisher and the suggested retail price of the Work. It is understood that both the Proprietor and the Publisher share a common interest against abuse and undermining the sales of the Work under license.

e) The Publisher shall ensure that the digital verbatim text content shall be technically protected against manipulation and uncontrolled file-sharing. The Proprietor may at any time request the Publisher to have a security audit on the database platform. In the event that such security audit indicates serious security flaws, in that the displayed contents become easily accessed and copied and passed on to non-purchasing third parties on a commercial or non-commercial basis, the Publisher shall, upon discovery of such a flaw, be obliged to and/or the Proprietor shall have the right to request the display to cease immediately but no later than three working days from first notification, until satisfactory safety is demonstrably installed. While it is understood by both parties that there is no total security, illegal copying should be made very cumbersome and require exceptional technical skills.

f) Upon specific request, the Publisher shall provide the Proprietor's agents with copies of the full agreements including side letters they have entered with third party database platforms.

g) The Publisher shall be under obligation to pursue with commercially reasonable efforts any form of abuse and pirating of said work emanating from the rights granted in these clauses 15–17 within their legal means and possibilities. For this purpose, the Publisher will frequently police the security of digital verbatim text content on both third party and their own websites.

h) The Publisher shall indemnify the Proprietor against any claims arising from the publication as digital verbatim text content beyond what is agreed in this Agreement, as far as any/all **[FOREIGN LANGUAGE]** language territories are concerned.

i) It remains the Publisher's obligation to clear any permissions with third parties for this extended use of content not covered in this Agreement.

j) The Proprietor reserves the right, at its sole discretion, to terminate or modify the rights for promoting purposes granted pursuant this Section/Clause 15.

16. The Publisher shall have the right:

a) to sell the digital verbatim text content provided for in clause 15(a) through the internet (downloads), revenue generating displays (pay-per-view, dissemination for a fee) including, but not limited to rental, university, school and library use and/or downloads of the Work in its entirety, chapter by chapter or page by page or on physical media (whether by transmission of a copy electronically for reading by means of a computer and/or other electronic media or authorization to download content);

b) Except as hereinafter provided, with respect to copies of digital verbatim text content including electronic editions of the Work sold by or on behalf of the Publisher, the Publisher shall account for the revenue from sales as defined in clause 16 (a):

[E-BOOK ROYALTY PERCENTAGE – the most common and accepted percentage at this point in digital verbatim rights is twenty-five (25) percent (%), though you may be asked to agree instead to a twenty (20) percent (%) rate. You should try for twenty-five (25) percent (%), but go no lower than (20) percent (%)] percent (%) of the amounts received by the Publisher for each digital verbatim text content sold, [for the purposes of this paragraph, the basis of such amounts shall be no less than fifty (50) percent (%) of the full published recommended retail price for such sales of digital content] less any locally applicable taxes, which shall be settled separately by the Publisher at source. The Publisher is free to set different retail prices for such digital verbatim text content, as the prices for print editions of the same;

c) Clauses 15 (c), 15 (e), 15 (f), 15 (g), 15 (h), 15 (i) shall apply to this clause 16 as well.

17. It is mutually agreed by Publisher and Proprietor that:

a) There are no subsidiary rights included in these clauses 15–17. Any further rights, not provided for in these clauses 15–17, remain subject to separate negotiation;

b) Any revenue to be accounted for from the rights granted in these clauses 15–17 may be applied against advances stipulated as per clause 6 in this Agreement.

18. Without prejudice to any claim which the Proprietor may have against the Publisher for damages and/or otherwise, the Proprietor may forthwith by summary notice terminate this Agreement in any one or more of the following circumstances:

a) If the Publisher shall fail to make any payment on its due date as required by this Agreement or within seven days thereafter;

b) If the Publisher (being a company) shall go into liquidation (other than bona fide liquidation for the purpose of reconstruction the terms of which have been notified to the Proprietor prior to such liquidation) or shall suffer a Receiver to be appointed in respect of any part of its undertaking or (being an individual or partnership) such Publisher or any partner thereof shall become bankrupt;

c) If the Publisher shall commit any other breach of this Agreement which, in the case of a breach capable of remedy, it shall fail to remedy within thirty days of receiving written notice from the Proprietor or agent requiring it to do so;

d) If the Publisher shall allow the Publisher's Edition to remain out of print or off the market for more than six months;

e) If the Publisher shall sell any copies of the Publisher's Edition by way of remainder.

19. Advertisements may not be inserted or printed in any edition of the Work issued by the Publisher without the Proprietor's prior written consent.

20. The Publisher may not transfer or assign the translation rights to the Work as per this Agreement without the prior written consent of the Proprietor.

21. Any legal (or administrative) proceeding involving the Publisher and the Author relating to or brought in connection with this Agreement shall be governed by the laws of the State of **[STATE in which your company is located]**, and the parties hereto further agree that any such legal or administrative proceeding shall be adjudicated by the American Arbitration Association's [when identifying the location where any legal or administrative proceedings must be presided over concerning your book, always make sure to list the American Arbitration Association in your own home state as the selected place—this is important because you will save yourself much time and expense if some kind of legal action needs to take place, because you will already be fairly local to the said location] office in the State of **[STATE in which your company is located]**.

22. Any notice required to be given by either party under this Agreement shall be in writing and shall either be delivered by hand or by registered first class airmail to the other party at the address set out above or at any other address subsequently notified.

IN WITNESS WHEREOF, the parties hereto have executed this instrument as of the day and year first hereinabove written.

BY _____
    [FOREIGN-LANGUAGE PUBLISHING COMPANY]
Publisher

BY _____
    [NAME OF YOUR COMPANY]
Proprietor

BY _____
    [FOREIGN RIGHTS AGENT]
Agent

CONCLUSION

While it is absolutely true that securing foreign rights contracts can be made easier for you through literary agent representation, there is no reason why you cannot sell your foreign rights on your own now that you understand the details of the process. If you have taken the dream of self-publishing this far already, you can certainly get yourself a round-trip plane ticket to Germany and attend the Frankfurt Book Fair. You never know what you might achieve by taking such a chance.

If attending the Frankfurt Book Fair is simply not possible, consider adding your title to a co-op stand, which would display your book and possibly even pitch it. There are numerous co-op stands from which to choose, including those staffed by the Independent Book Publishers Association, *Foreword Reviews* magazine, and HBG Productions. (See Resources on page 231.) Foreign rights are a fascinating and important part of the industry and a potentially wonderful source of income for you as a self-publisher.

CONCLUSION

Self-publishing is a thriving industry. Authors, publishers, and readers are benefiting from all the self-publishing options available today. I hope you now have a comprehensive understanding of each of the three parts of self-publishing: writing your book, publishing your book, and marketing your book. Once you decide to take this route, every concern of a commercial or academic publisher—from typesetting and production to reviews and marketing—will become your concern as well.

As the number of self-publishers increases in the United States and around the world, it might seem harder than ever to get your work noticed; but as long as your book is worth reading, it is worth publishing. There is no guarantee it will be a bestseller—self-publishers have had runway hits, although these occurrences are extremely rare—but I have seen hard work pay off. If you follow the guidelines laid out in *How to Self-Publish Your Book* as you write, edit, design, produce, and promote your own book, you stand a good chance of finding an audience and seeing sales.

I have worked in the publishing industry for over forty years, whether as an employee at a publishing company, an author published by a major publisher, a self-publisher, or the owner of a publishing company. If I could give prospective self-publishers a final piece of advice, it would be this: Do what you can do well on your own, but don't be afraid to entrust tasks to other people. Just because you are a good writer does not mean you are a good editor. Just because you were able to complete your manuscript does not mean you have the time or talent to design your book's interior or cover. Focus on your strengths, and don't see yourself as a failure if you need to hire professional help or use a self-publishing service to see your project to fruition. Invest your time and energy into what you do best, and, if possible, find qualified freelancers or well-regarded companies to perform the remaining tasks. (Remember, of course, to be extremely skeptical of any self-publishing service that promises to make your book a bestseller for a fee. Such a promise is actually a warning sign that you should probably not use that service.)

Readers, in general, do not care about how a book was published or who published it. Whether they see the well-known Penguin Random House logo or a completely unfamiliar publishing company's image on the back cover of a book, as long as that book looks professional and compelling, readers will want to pick it up and read it.

My self-publishing journey began twenty-three years ago with *Friendshifts* and currently includes numerous other successful self-published titles in a wide variety of genres. Now that you know the necessary steps involved in the creation of a quality self-published book, you have every reason to believe in the promise of your own self-publishing endeavor.

LOSSARY

acknowledgments. A section in a book's *front matter* used by the author to give thanks to all the people involved in the book's creation.

advance. An amount of money paid to an author once a contract has been signed. This amount is then deducted from any future earnings.

advance praise. See *blurb.*

advance reading copy (ARC). A free copy of a book given out prior to its publication, usually for review or promotional purposes.

afterword. A section in the book's *back matter* that explains why a book was written or how it was developed.

appendices. Sections in the book's *back matter* that are used to add supplementary information or supporting data to a book. For instance, the *glossary, bibliography,* and *references* are considered appendices.

audience. A book's intended readership, specifically, the demographics for which a book has been designed.

audiobook. A recording of a text being read aloud.

author's credit line. A line that lists a specific

attribute of an author, such as "Best-selling author of *Friendshifts.*"

back matter. Also known as end matter, the part of a book designed to bring closure to the main text, offer additional clarification of subjects mentioned in the book, or suggest related works.

backlist. A publisher's titles that are more than six months old but still in print.

barcode. A code, typically in the form of numbers and parallel lines, that identifies a book when it is scanned by a machine. Usually, a book's barcode is printed on its back cover.

bibliography. A section of a book's *back matter* that lists the texts and other materials consulted by the author in the writing of the book.

BISAC Subject Headings List. A collection of categories created and maintained by the Book Industry Study Group (BISG), which enables publishers to classify their books for the benefit of bookstores and libraries.

blogger. A citizen journalist who writes articles, stories, or reviews online.

blurb. A brief promotional piece, often in the form of advance praise of the book. Blurbs may be placed on the front or back cover, printed on a page of advance praise in the *front matter* of the book, or used in marketing materials.

body matter. The chapters of a book, also known as body text.

body text. See *body matter*.

book columnist. A writer who covers the subject of books for a print or online media outlet such as a newspaper, magazine, or website.

book review editor. The person who manages the solicitation, acceptance, and review of books that are submitted to a publication.

book reviewer. A staff writer or freelancer who writes reviews of books for a publication.

brick-and-mortar bookstore. A traditional business with a physical location where you can buy books.

Cataloging-in-Publication (CIP) data. In publishing and library science, basic cataloging data prepared before publication by the Library of Congress. This data makes it easier for libraries to catalog a book.

complimentary copies. Copies of a book given at no charge.

conclusion. An ending section, placed after the last chapter of a book, that states the concluding ideas and concepts of the chapters.

contents page. A section in a book's *front matter* that lists the book's chapters and sections along with the page number on which each one begins.

copy editor. Also called a line editor, a person who revises a manuscript to ensure that it maintains stylistic consistency, correct spelling and grammar, and factual accuracy.

copyright page. A page that typically appears on the back of the *title page* and presents the copyright notice, including the year of the first publication of the book and the name of the copyright owner; printing history; legal notices; and cataloging information, such as the Library of Congress *Cataloging-in-Publication (CIP) data*. Other information that may appear on the copyright page includes contributors to the book, such as editors and designers; the publisher's name and address; the edition of the book; and bulk order information.

dedication page. A page in the book's *front matter* that is used to thank an individual or group of individuals for inspiration, support, or assistance.

developmental editor. An individual, sometimes called a substantive editor, who works with a writer to help develop the structure and content of a book.

digital review copy (DRC). An electronic version of an *advance reading copy* (ARC).

dingbat. A typographical symbol or shape (other than a letter) used to mark divisions in a text or as a decorative element.

disclaimer. An official statement absolving the publisher of any legal responsibility for the contents of a book.

distributor. A company that has an agreement with a publisher to sell its books to bookstores, libraries, or wholesalers, generally on an exclusive basis.

e-book. A book-length publication in digital form that can be downloaded from online retailers and read on handheld electronic devices.

electronic press kit (EPK). A digital version of a *press kit*.

end matter. See *back matter*.

epilogue. An optional section of a work of fiction that is often used to tie up loose ends regarding the fate of the book's characters.

fiction. Prose writing that describes imaginary people and events. Examples of *genres* within the fiction category include mystery and romance.

folio. The page number in a printed book.

font. A specific size, style, and weight of a *typeface*.

footer. The copy that runs within the space allotted for the bottom margin, usually providing the book's page number (or *folio*).

foreign rights. The *subsidiary rights* associated with the sale of a book in another language or territory beyond the original language, country, or territory in which the book was first published.

foreword. An introductory section of the book that has been written by someone other than the author of the work, usually to lend credibility to the book.

front matter. The opening sections of a book, also known as preliminaries or prematter, which include the *title page, copyright page,* and optional sections such as the *half-title page, acknowledgments, foreword, preface,* and *introduction*.

galleys. A rough advance version of a typeset book. Galleys have largely been replaced by *advance reading copies,* or ARCs.

genre. In publishing, a category of literary composition characterized by a particular form, content, or techniques. Both *fiction* and *nonfiction* categories have genres within them, such as biography (a genre of nonfiction) and romance (a genre of fiction).

glossary. A section of *back matter* that defines terms introduced in the main text which may be new or unfamiliar to readers.

half-title page. A page that features only the title of a book without including its subtitle, author's name, or publisher's name.

header. The copy that runs within the space allotted for the top margin. Also called a running head, the header can include the book title, chapter or section title, author's name, and/or page number (folio).

headshot. A photo of a person's head. A headshot of the book's author is usually included in a *press kit*.

index. An alphabetical list of important words, terms, concepts, and people mentioned in a book, and the corresponding pages on which they appear.

indexer. An individual who creates a book's *index*.

interline spacing. See *leading*.

International Standard Book Number (ISBN). A thirteen-digit number that acts as a unique identifier of a book for booksellers, libraries, book wholesalers, and book distributors. In the United States, ISBN numbers are available only through R.R. Bowker or a company authorized to sell ISBNs on R.R. Bowker's behalf.

introduction. A section that provides an overview of the topic of a book.

ISBN. See *International Standard Book Number.*

leading. The distance between lines of text. Pronounced "ledding," it is also called line spacing or interline spacing.

Library of Congress Control Number (LCCN). A serial-based number issued by the Library of Congress to a book in advance of publication. It has nothing to do with the contents of the book.

line editor. See *copy editor.*

line spacing. See *leading.*

list price. The manufacturer's suggested retail price.

literary scout. A book industry specialist who works on behalf of foreign publishers, seeking out and recommending titles that have the greatest potential for translation overseas.

logo. A graphic symbol or image used to identify a company, such as a publisher.

margin. The space between the main text of a page and the edge of the page.

marketplace. The means by which a book attempts to reach its audience. Most of the marketplace can be described as either *trade* or *non-trade.*

media kit. See *press kit.*

media release. A page-long description of a book, also called a press release, designed to win the attention of the media.

metadata. A book's specifications, which include a description of the book as well as its title, subtitle, author, *ISBN number*, retail price, number of pages, publication date, *genre*, publisher's contact information, and certain other information, as required by a *wholesaler, distributor,* or library.

narrator. The person who reads a book out loud in the recording of an *audiobook.*

nonfiction. Prose writing that is based on facts, real people, and real events. Examples of *genres* within the nonfiction category include biography, health, and history.

non-trade. Any bookseller not considered part of the *trade* marketplace. The non-trade marketplace includes book fairs, catalogs, corporate sales, gift shops, museum shops, and more.

orphan. In typesetting, a paragraph-opening line that appears by itself at the bottom of a page or column and is thus separated from the rest of the paragraph.

out of print. A term describing a book that is no longer available from a publisher.

PDF (portable document format). A computer file format that looks like a printed document and can be viewed, printed, and forwarded to other people.

perfect binding. A widely used paperback binding method that results in a flat, square *spine.* The flat edge allows for the book's title and other information to be printed on the *spine.*

pica. A unit of measurement used for type size and line length. One pica is equal to 12 points of type, and there are 6 picas to an inch.

pitch. A description of a book used to solicit promotional opportunities.

POD. See *print-on-demand (POD) book.*

preface. Written by the author, the section of the *front matter* that briefly outlines the story behind or inspiration for the writing of a book.

preliminaries. See *front matter*.

prematter. See *front matter*.

press kit. A package of promotional materials provided to members of the media to brief them on a new book. A press kit usually includes a *media release* (or press release), author biography and *headshot*, copies of book reviews and press coverage, and a list of suggested interview questions.

press release. See *media release*.

print run. The number of copies of a book printed at one time.

printer's key. Also called a number line, a line of sequential numbers used to indicate the edition of a book.

print-on-demand (POD) book. A book printed by a service that keeps an electronic version of that book on file to print and bind copies as needed.

prologue. A section of *front matter* that provides background for a work of *fiction*. It appears just before the first chapter.

proofreader. An individual who reviews the preliminary version of a typeset book for typographical errors (typos), page balance, and layout.

publicity. The spread of information about a product, such as a book, for advertising or promotional purposes.

quotation. A positive statement, often from a full book review, that offers the reader an understanding of what is in a book; or short quoted material that appears at the beginning of a chapter and is relevant to that chapter.

recto. A right-hand page of an open book.

references. A section of citations in the book's *back matter* that credit the sources used by the author in the writing of the book.

release date. The date that a book becomes available to the public.

resources. A list of businesses, associations, organizations, services, websites, manufacturers and distributors, and other sources that could be of help to a book's readers.

review quote. A significantly abridged version of a review used to focus on its positive points.

rights auction. An invitation to other publishers to bid on the foreign rights of a book during a nonexclusive rights option period.

royalty. An amount of money, usually expressed as a percentage of sales, that is paid to the author by the publisher of the book.

running head. See *header*.

sales seasons. The three seasons of the year—fall, spring, and summer—in which a publisher schedules new books for release.

sales sheet. A one-sheet presentation of a book's basic information, including its *metadata*, designed to sell the book to bookstore buyers and distributors.

sans-serif. A typeface that does not feature extended lines at the ends of its characters.

secondary title. See *subtitle*.

self-publishing. A publishing option in which

an author arranges and pays for every stage of the publishing process, from editing and typesetting to printing and binding, and often sets up a business to take care of the promotion, distribution, and sales of a book.

sell line. A single sentence, usually printed across the top of a book's front cover, that briefly describes the book and the benefits it offers.

serif. A typeface that features extended lines at the ends of its characters.

special sales. Sales of books in large quantities to companies that will not resell them to the trade marketplace. Special sales focus on non-trade outlets such as sports stores, museum gift shops, health food stores, etc.

specifications. See *metadata*.

spine. The portion of a book that covers the binding and usually faces outwards when a book is placed on a shelf. Generally, the spine bears the name of the author of the book, the title of the book, and the name or *logo* of the publisher.

style sheet. A document used by an author and/or editor during the writing process to ensure consistency of style—including the spelling and capitalization of certain terms—throughout a manuscript.

subsidiary rights. The right to publish a book in a different format based on the original material. Subsidiary rights can include book club editions; translation rights for foreign publishers; audio recording rights; dramatic rights for television, radio, theater, and movies; and more.

substantive editor. See *developmental editor*.

subtitle. A secondary title that clarifies the subject matter of a book.

talking points. Dynamic topics used to promote a book, usually as part of its *pitch*.

title page. Often the first page of the book, it should include the book's title and subtitle, the author's name, the name of the publishing company, and often, the city and state in which the book was published.

trade. The *marketplace* that consists of bookstores and libraries.

typeface. A family of characters that share a basic design. Some examples include Times Roman and Baskerville.

typesetter. A person who typesets text, turning a manuscript into a properly formatted book.

verso. A left-hand page of an open book.

wholesaler. A company that has an arrangement with a publisher to sell a publisher's books to bookstores and libraries on a nonexclusive basis.

widow. In typesetting, a paragraph-ending line that falls at the beginning of the following page or column and is thus separated from the rest of the paragraph.

ESOURCES

Whatever stage you are at in your self-publishing journey—whether you are just beginning to write a book, ready to produce your finished work, or looking for advice on how to market and sell your publication—there are many excellent resources available to help you. In addition to the various self-publishing services out there, there are a number of books, newsletters, publishing organizations, and professional groups designed to get you to your next step. While the following list is extensive, it is by no means complete, so do not hesitate to scout out resources on your own or with the help of your local reference librarian.

BOOKS

Ancowitz, Nancy. *Self-Promotion for Introverts: The Quiet Guide to Getting Ahead.* **New York: McGraw-Hill Education, 2010.**

Offering help to introverts so they too can get more exposure, Nancy Ancowitz' book includes chapters on speaking in public, expanding your network, and stopping negative self-talk.

Arana, Marie. *The Writing Life: Writers on How They Think and Work.* **New York: PublicAffairs, 2003.**

This book features stories from over fifty writers, each of whom provides insights into the craft of writing and the creative process.

Bunnin, Brad, and Peter Beren. *The Writer's Legal Companion.* **Third Edition. New York: Basic Books, 1998.**

This guide explains publishing law in a straightforward way, helping self-publishers gain a better understanding of matters such as copyright, taxes, subsidiary rights, and much more.

Burgett, Gordon. *Niche Publishing: Publish Profitably Every Time!* **Novato, CA: Communication Limited, 2008.**

This book is an updated version of Burgett's 1995 classic *Publishing to Niche Markets.* Offering an alternative to publishing as usual, it explains how to find a specific demand or audience and create a book that caters to it.

Chandler, Stephanie, and Karl W. Palachuk. *The Nonfiction Book Publishing Plan: The Professional Guide to Profitable Self-Publishing.* **Sacramento, CA: Authority Publishing, 2018.**

An informative guide geared to nonfiction self-publishers, this book covers the creation and sale of a book.

Crawford, Tad, with Stevie Fitzgerald and Michael Gross. *Business and Legal Forms for Authors and Self-Publishers.* **Fourth Edition. New York: Allworth Press, 2015.**

This book contains all the relevant contracts and forms you might require as a self-publisher, with step-by-step instructions on how to use them and advice on provisions you may wish to include.

Davis, Katie. *How to Write a Children's Book.* **Madison, CT: Institute for Writers LLC, 2016.**

Best-selling author and illustrator of books for children and teens, Katie Davis created this guide to teach prospective authors how to write children's books. She is also director of the Institute for Writers.

Deval, Jacqueline. *Publicize Your Book! An Insider's Guide to Getting Your Book the Attention It Deserves.* **New York: Perigee, 2008.**

Having created publicity and marketing campaigns for hundreds of authors, Jacqueline Deval offers expert advice on all the ways authors can publicize, market, and promote their books.

Dils, Tracey E. *You Can Write Children's Books.* **Cincinnati, OH: Writer's Digest Books, 1998.**

Written by an author and editor of children's books, this book provides guidance to aspiring children's writers on how to write, edit, and submit works for publication.

Friedman, Jane. *Publishing 101.* **MBA for Writers, 2014.**

Experienced editor and former publisher of *Writer's Digest* magazine, Jane Friedman covers all the basic publishing bases in this book, which includes a chapter on self-publishing.

Gardner, John. *The Art of Fiction.* **New York: Vintage, 1991.**

Written by professor and novelist John Gardner, this guidebook details the principles and techniques of good writing.

Gutkind, Lee. *Keep It Real*. New York: W. W. Norton & Company, 2009.

This book clarifies what to do and what not to do when writing creative nonfiction, providing advice on how to write with enthusiasm and passion while also holding fast to the truth of your subject.

Isenberg, Lynn. *Author Power*. Marina Del Rey, CA: Focus Media, Inc. Publishing, 2015.

Designed to help you generate income from your book even before you publish it, this book covers topics such as finding cross-promotional opportunities, creating revenue streams, and helping people discover your work.

Jacobs, Hayes B. *Writing and Selling Nonfiction*. Cincinnati, OH: Writer's Digest Books, 1981.

As its title suggests, this book is designed to teach the reader the ins and outs of writing and selling nonfiction works.

Jud, Brian. *How to Make Real Money Selling Books (Without Worrying About Returns)*. Garden City Park, NY: Square One Publishers, 2009.

This book gives advice on selling books through such non-trade markets as gift shops, book clubs, specialty stores, supermarkets, and airports, as well as through businesses, associations, academia, and even government agencies.

Karr, Mary. *The Art of Memoir*. New York: Harper Perennial, 2016.

Written by bestselling memoirist Mary Karr, this book details key aspects of successful memoir writing and reveals how many well-known memoir writers approach this literary form.

Kidder, Tracy and Richard Todd. *Good Prose: The Art of Nonfiction*. New York: Random House, 2013.

This book provides valuable insights into the nonfiction forms known as narrative, essay, and memoir. Written by longtime experts in the field of nonfiction, it is a guide for both beginners and professionals.

King, Stephen. *On Writing: A Memoir of the Craft*. 10 Year Anniversary Edition. New York: Scribner, 2010, 2000.

This critically acclaimed memoir by master storyteller Stephen King gives the reader glimpses into the author's life as well as his writing process.

Kremer, John. *1001 Ways to Market Your Books: Real World Edition*. Eighth Edition. Taos, New Mexico: Open Horizons, 2016.

In this book, John Kremer outlines the fundamentals of book marketing and outlines a plan that should inspire any budding author to self-publish.

Lamott, Anne. *Bird by Bird: Reflections on Writing and Life*. New York: Anchor, 1995.

Containing worthwhile advice on the writing process, this book is a beautifully written account of the author's writing journey.

Levine, Mark. *The Fine Print of Self-Publishing*. Sixth Edition. Minneapolis, MN: North Loop Books, 2016.

This book covers the basics of self-publishing, from production costs to marketing, and is a useful guide for writers who are considering publishing on their own.

Lopate, Phillip. *To Show and to Tell: The Craft of Literary Nonfiction*. New York: Free Press, 2013.

In this book, author Phillip Lopate reflects on his experiences as a successful writer and professor over the last forty years to create a guide to writing literary nonfiction.

Maass, Donald. *Writing the Breakout Novel: Inside Advice for Taking Your Fiction to the Next Level*. Cincinnati, OH: Writer's Digest Books, 2002.

In this book, literary agent Donald Maass describes writing techniques that can help your book stand out from the rest.

McCelland, Deke, and Amy Thomas Buscaglia. *Adobe InDesign for Dummies*. Foster City, CA: IDG Books Worldwide, Inc., 1999.

Covering both Mac and Windows versions of the program, this book teaches you how to use Adobe InDesign desktop publishing and type-setting software, which offers layout, text, and graphics tools to help you design your book on your own.

McPhee, John. *Draft No. 4: On the Writing Process*. New York: Farrar, Straus & Giroux, 2017.

Written by legendary author and teacher John McPhee, this book is a detailed guide to writing long-form nonfiction and includes expert advice on the gathering of facts, writing structure, and revision.

Poynter, Dan. *Self-Publishing Manual*. Sixteenth Edition. Goleta, CA: Para Publishing, 2007.

Self-publishing pioneer Dan Poynter's manual covers all aspects of the self-publishing process, from writing your book and starting your publishing company to producing your book and marketing it.

Penn, Joanna. *Successful Self-Publishing*. Third Edition. Bath, Somerset, England: Curl Up Press, 2018.

In this book, bestselling self-publisher Joanna Penn takes the reader through the process of self-publishing, describing the most effective way to publish and market your book.

Raab, Diana. *Writing for Bliss*. Ann Arbor, MI: Loving Healing Press, 2017.

A blogger and author of nine books, Raab uses this book to share her seven-step approach to writing a memoir.

Raven, Fiona, and Glenna Collett. *Book Design Made Simple*. Second Edition. Vancouver, Canada: 12 Pines Press, 2017.

Written by two book designer veterans, this book is a comprehensive guide to designing and type-setting your own book by using the leading book design software.

Rose, M.J., and Angela Adair-Hoy. *How to Publish and Promote Online*. New York: St. Martin's Griffin, 2001.

In their book, e-book pioneers Rose and Adair-Hoy cover everything from selling a book in both e-book and print formats to getting a book reviewed.

Royal, Brandon. *The Little Red Writing Book*. Cincinnati, OH: Writer's Digest Books, 2007.

This book offers instructive explanations of four important aspects of good writing: structure, style, readability, and grammar.

Stein, Sol. *Stein on Writing*. New York: St. Martin's Griffin, 2000.

By offering invaluable advice on how to write interesting prose, this book can be extremely useful to both new writers and seasoned professionals.

Strunk, William Jr., and E.B. White. *The Elements of Style*. Fourth Edition. Harlow, Essex: Pearson Education Limited, 2014.

This classic book about writing better is always worth reading, especially in today's era of texting and "Internet speak."

Wallin, Luke, and Eva Sage Gordon. *The Everything Guide to Writing Children's Books*. Avon, MA: Adams Media, 2011.

This guide aims to teach the reader how to write and promote a children's book successfully, providing advice on everything from storytelling to marketing.

Welty, Eudora. *On Writing*. New York; Modern Library, 2002.

In this book, one of the twentieth century's most renowned writers, Eudora Welty, offers her thoughts on what makes a story good and details the most important aspects of the craft of writing fiction.

Yager, Jan. *Effective Business and Nonfiction Writing*. Second Edition. Stamford, CT: Hannacroix Creek Books, 2001.

This guide is designed to help you hone your skills in nonfiction writing and master the techniques associated with writing successful business letters, memos, emails, proposals, reports, articles, and books.

Yager, Jan. *The Fast Track Guide to Speaking in Public*. Stamford, CT: Hannacroix Creek Books, 2013.

Based on the author's decades of experience in public speaking, this practical guide covers speech preparation as well as some of the challenges a public speaker might face and how to deal with them.

Yager, Jan. *Foreign Rights and Wrongs: Selling or Buying Digital Literary Rights Around the World*. Stamford, CT: Hannacroix Creek Books, 2018.

Based on more than a decade of research and several decades of practical experience, this book is a step-by-step guide to buying and selling foreign book rights.

Zinsser, William. *On Writing Well*. New York: Harper Collins, 2013.

In this book, writer, editor, and teacher William Zinsser teaches the fundamentals of nonfiction writing and shares his insights into the craft, making it a worthwhile resource for both new and experienced writers.

Zinsser, William. *Writing About Your Life*. New York: Marlow & Company, 2004.

This book is both a memoir and a guide to how to write a memoir. Zinsser shares moments of life while also pointing out the writing techniques he employs to do so effectively.

PRINT, E-BOOK, AND AUDIOBOOK SELF-PUBLISHING SERVICES

About Books (ABI)

Website: https://about-books.com

About Books is a company that designs and produces books for both self-publishers and traditional publishers.

ACX

Website: www.acx.com

Owned by Amazon, ACX is a marketplace where authors, literary agents, publishers, and other rights holders can connect with narrators, engineers, recording studios, and other professionals capable of producing a finished audiobook.

Amazon Kindle Direct Publishing (KDP)

Website: https://kdp.amazon.com

Offering e-book and print-on-demand services, Amazon Kindle Direct Publishing allows you to self-publish your work for free and distributes your e-book to Kindle stores worldwide within twenty-four to forty-eight hours.

Apple Books

Website: www.apple.com/apple-books

Formerly known as Apple iBooks, Apple's e-book reader application is now called Apple Books. Authors who wish to create e-books from their manuscripts through Apple may do so using its "Author" application, after which they may submit their e-books to Apple Books by following the proper steps.

Archway Publishing

Website: www.archwaypublishing.com

For writers seeking services in their self-publishing endeavors, Archway Publishing offers high-quality design, formatting, editorial, and marketing services, all of which are provided by a team of specialists at Author Solutions in association with Simon & Schuster.

Author Solutions

Website: www.authorsolutions.com

Author Solutions offers self-publishing services and works with a number of imprints, including AuthorHouse, iUniverse, Trafford, and Xlibris.

Author's Republic

Website: www.authorsrepublic.com

Author's Republic is an audiobook aggregate distributor, helping independent authors and small publishers sell their audiobooks through all major audiobook distributors.

Barnes & Noble Press

Website: https://press.barnesandnoble.com

Barnes & Noble's self-publishing service, known as Barnes & Noble Press, is an expansion of its former service, Nook Press, which offered only e-books. Barnes & Noble Press offers a print-on-demand service in addition to its e-book model.

Blackstone Publishing

Website: www.blackstonepublishing.com

Building upon its long history as a producer and distributor of audiobooks, Blackstone Publishing now seeks to publish groundbreaking books in both the fiction and nonfiction categories by talented writers in print, e-book, and audio formats.

Blurb

Website: www.blurb.com

This self-publishing creation and distribution platform specializes in photo books and illustrated books, especially those in color. In regard to trade books, Blurb offers two printing qualities: standard and economy. Self-publishers may opt to sell their books in hardcover, with or without a dust jacket, or in paperback, in a variety of trim sizes.

BookBaby

Website: www.bookbaby.com

This self-publishing platform enables you to create e-books as well as print books. BookBaby's business model differs from that of most other self-publishing services, in that it does not take a percentage of sales.

BookLocker

Website: www.booklocker.com

BookLocker offers several different self-publishing packages and features an online bookstore, where authors who publish through BookLocker may sell their books directly to customers.

Books on Tape

Website: www.booksontape.com

A subsidiary of Penguin Random House, Books on Tape's editorial staff accepts manuscripts and advance reading copies from agents, other publishing houses, and authors. It determines which titles it should make available as audiobooks to its customer base and then produces these audiobooks in its own studios.

Brilliance Audio

Website: www.brillianceaudio.com

Owned by Amazon, Brilliance Audio produces audiobooks in multiple formats, including compact disc, MP3-CD, and downloadable files, unlike Amazon's other audio-publisher ACX, which publishes only downloadable audiobooks.

Color House Graphics

Website: www.colorhousegraphics.com

This printer offers various short-run options, book cover design services, interior design and formatting services, and e-book conversion.

Draft2Digital

Website: www.draft2digital.com

Draft2Digital is an aggregator that partners with Amazon, Apple Books, Barnes & Noble, Kobo, Playster, Scribd, Tolino, 24Symbols, OverDrive, and bibliotheca. The company does not charge any fees for formatting or distributing your e-book. It simply keeps about 10 percent of the retail price. Draft2Digital allows its authors to set the prices of their books and even lets them give their books away for free.

Findaway

Website: https://findaway.com

Findaway is a digital content delivery service that circulates audiobooks, e-books, videos, and learning tools to libraries, schools, and military installations.

48 Hour Books

Website: www.48hrbooks.com

As its name suggests, this company offers self-publishers a two-day turnaround time on paperback book production, as well as a five-day turnaround time on hardcover and spiral-bound books.

Friesens Press

Website: www.friesens.com

Friesens Press provides publishers, self-publishers, institutions, businesses, and schools with quality in-house services at its state-of-the-art production facility.

Google Play Books

Website: https://play.google.com/books/publish

To sell books through Google's e-book service, known as Google Play Books, you have to join the Google Books Partner Program. If you are interested in joining the program, Google asks that you make a request to do so through its online interest form.

IngramSpark

Website: www.ingramspark.com

With facilities located around the world, Ingram-Spark boasts the ability to get your book to retailers, warehouses, libraries, distributors, and individual readers quickly and reliably through its print-on-demand service.

Kobo Writing Life

Website: www.kobo.com

Kobo publishes its e-books in the EPUB format, and it can convert a book into this format as long as it is a DOC, DOCX, ODT, or MOBI file. Kobo also provides an online preview service to authors, which allows them to see how their books will appear to customers before they go live.

Lightning Source

Website: www.lightningsource.com

Lightning Source is a self-publishing platform owned by US wholesaler Ingram. It allows self-publishers to print quality books on demand in a variety of formats, bindings, and trim sizes. It boasts advanced print technology that allows the text and graphics in their books to appear comparable to those found in traditionally printed books.

Outskirts Press

Website: www.outskirtspress.com

Outskirts Press is a self-publishing service that prints paperback and hardcover books on demand. It is a full-service self-publishing company that charges flat rates to authors in exchange for wholesale printing, order fulfillment, and distribution to major vendors, with authors keeping 100 percent of the rights to their books and any earnings.

OverDrive

Website: www.overdrive.com

OverDrive is a digital distributor of e-books, audiobooks, music, and video titles, especially to schools and libraries worldwide. It is owned by Rakuten, the parent company of Kobo.

PublishDrive

Website: www.publishdrive.com

PublishDrive is free to join but takes a cut of 10 percent of your e-book's list price on each sale. It distributes e-books to over four hundred online retailers, including Amazon, Apple, Google, Kobo, and Barnes & Noble, and numerous digital libraries all over the world. It also features a free e-book converter that is available to everyone.

Scribus

Website: www.scribus.net

Scribus offers free typesetting software that is similar to InDesign. It cannot, however, open or save typesetting files created by other design programs.

Smashwords

Website: www.smashwords.com

Smashwords allows authors to upload their manuscripts to its website, through which the company will convert them into a number of file formats that may be sold through multiple online e-book retailers and read on different devices. As a distributor, the company will take a percentage (typically 15 percent) of net sales.

Spoken Realms

Website: www.spokenrealms.com

Spoken Realms offers to connect authors with its "featured voices," which refer to narrators who are already part of Spoken Realm's production system. After an author contacts a featured voice directly, the two parties then work out a production arrangement, whether a royalty-sharing deal, flat-fee deal, or some combination of the two.

Tantor Media

Website: https://tantor.com

Tantor Media produces unabridged fiction and nonfiction audiobooks as both physical discs and downloads. It works with 150 of the industry's best narrators, taking care to match the right voice to each of its books. It also offers print and e-book versions of its titles.

Thomson-Shore

Website: https://thomsonshore.com

Thomson-Shore offers a number of print-on-demand models. Using its "Publisher-Driven Order Fulfillment" model, self-publishers receive orders through their own websites and collect payments themselves. Using its "Direct-to-Consumer POD" model, self-publishers use links to direct their shoppers to the pages on Thomson-Shore's online store, through which their books may be ordered.

DO-IT-YOURSELF WEBSITE BUILDERS

Duda

Website: www.duda.co

While Duda's monthly rates may be slightly pricier than its competition, it boasts features that other website builders may not, such as the ability to create multilingual websites and send visitors customized offers. Duda also allows a free thirty-day trial.

Jimdo

Website: www.jimdo.com

Using artificial intelligence, Jimdo's service promises to help you build your website in just three minutes. It offers a free subscription plan as well as paid monthly plans, which include additional features.

Squarespace

Website: www.squarespace.com

Squarespace is a website-building platform that offers pre-built websites to suit its customers' needs. Users start with a fourteen-day free trial, after which they are charged a monthly fee based on choice of product.

Weebly

Website: www.weebly.com

Weebly is a web-hosting service that is geared towards the online shopping experience. Basic websites are free of charge, while monthly fee-based options range from $5 to $25 a month. Weebly also features an app store, which contains a variety of apps that users can add to their websites to enhance functionality.

Wix

Website: www.wix.com

Wix allows users to create professional-looking websites for free without the need to code anything themselves. It offers fee-based services as well, but these are not required for the creation of a fully functioning website.

PRINT AND E-BOOK REVIEWS AND PROMOTION

Booklist

Website: www.booklistonline.com

Booklist is a prepublication review journal that offers critical reviews of books and audiovisual materials for all ages. It is a respected resource for librarians, booksellers, and educators.

Bookmarket

Website: www.bookmarket.com

This website is run by book marketing expert John Kremer, author of *1001 Ways to Market Your Books*. It provides resources on writing, publishing, and marketing print books, e-books, and other informational products, and offers a newsletter with helpful tips and advice for authors.

Choice

Website: www.choice360.org

Choice magazine publishes 500 reviews of academic nonfiction titles each month, in addition to editorials, features, and bibliographic essays.

Clarion Reviews

Website: www.forewordreviews.com/reviews/clarion

Clarion Reviews is a pay-for-review service offered by *Foreword Reviews,* a magazine devoted to the independent publishing industry. It promises authors comprehensive critiques and evaluations written by qualified professionals.

The Creative Penn

Website: www.thecreativepenn.com

Written by best-selling author Joanna Penn, The Creative Penn offers information and inspiration on writing, self-publishing, book marketing, and how to make a living with your writing through articles, podcast episodes, videos, books, and courses.

Edelweiss +

Website: www.abovethetreeline.com

Edelweiss+ is a comprehensive digital cataloging service that allows publishers and authors to share digital review copies with librarians, educators, and booksellers.

Foreword Reviews

Website: www.forewordreviews.com

Foreword Reviews reviews and promotes books from independent publishers, self-publishers, and university presses, and may be found in print and online. Its reviews are licensed to Baker & Taylor, Ingram, and Bowker, allowing librarians and booksellers to discover their books easily. It has created the Foreword INDIES Book of the Year Awards to honor independent books in numerous genres each year.

Help a Reporter Out (HARO)

Website: www.helpareporter.com

Distributed three times a day, Help a Reporter Out is a free e-newsletter of available publicity opportunities. Each e-newsletter contains numerous queries from journalists, radio or TV producers or interviewers, and book authors.

The Hot Sheet

Website: https://hotsheetpub.com

The Hot Sheet is a biweekly publishing industry newsletter started by book publishing executive Jane Friedman. Annual subscriptions may be purchased for a fee, and potential subscribers are offered a free trial.

The Indie View

Website: www.theindieview.com

This website provides a list of individuals who review independently published books. To appear on the list, reviewers must actively post reviews, review e-books, not charge any fees for reviews, not be affiliated with any publisher, have submission guidelines in place for submissions, and place a link to The Indie View on their websites.

IndieReader

Website: www.indiereader.com

Created by Amy Edelman, IndieReader is a pay-for-review service for self-published authors and independent publishers. It also presents the IndieReader Discovery Awards to fiction and nonfiction writers every year.

Kirkus Indie

Website: www.kirkusreviews.com

Kirkus Indie is a pay-for-review program created by *Kirkus Reviews*. Independent authors can submit their works to *Kirkus Indie* for review and the opportunity to have their reviews published on the *Kirkus* website.

Kirkus Reviews

Website: www.kirkusreviews.com

Kirkus Reviews is a biweekly American book review magazine and a respected source of critical, comprehensive book reviews.

Library Journal

Website: www.libraryjournal.com

Library Journal reports on news in the library world, particularly public libraries, and features book reviews and articles about all aspects of the profession.

Midwest Book Review

Website: www.midwestbookreview.com

This organization, which is devoted to promoting literacy, libraries, and small presses, features monthly book reviews with an emphasis on independently published titles on its website. These reviews are aimed at public and academic libraries as well as booksellers.

NetGalley

Website: www.netgalley.com

NetGalley enables self-publishers to send digital ARCs to reviewers at a fraction of the cost of sending out physical copies. Reviewers may request, read, and recommend books and then submit feedback directly to authors and publishers.

PitchRate

Website: http://pitchrate.presskit247.com

PitchRate is a free daily e-newsletter of available media opportunities.

Publishers Weekly

Website: www.publishersweekly.com

Publishers Weekly is a print and online magazine

that covers all aspects of the book publishing industry, including sales, marketing, author interviews, and book reviews. It also offers a free daily e-newsletter known as PW Daily.

Publishing Perspectives

Website: https://publishingperspectives.com

Publishing Perspectives is an online business magazine that covers the global book industry. It also offers a free daily e-newsletter about the international publishing scene.

School Library Journal

Website: www.slj.com

School Library Journal is a subscription magazine that specializes in children's, teen, and young adult literature, as well as professional development titles for educators and school and children's librarians. It also provides book reviews and articles.

Self-Publishing Review

Website: www.selfpublishingreview.com

Self-Publishing Review functions as both an online book review periodical and a pay-to-review service for self-published authors hoping to gain exposure for their books.

Writer's Digest

Website: www.writersdigest.com

Writer's Digest magazine is designed to help authors improve their writing and publishing skills. Its website contains worthwhile information and resources for the writing community. The magazine features a number of writing competitions, including the Self-Published Book Awards.

AUDIOBOOK REVIEWS AND PROMOTION

AudaVoxx

Website: https://audavoxx.com

AudaVoxx subscribers receive a newsletter every Thursday morning, which features hand-picked, top-rated audiobooks in six genre categories. It highlights a mixture of new and old as well as traditional and independent audiobooks.

Audiobook Boom!

Website: https://audiobookboom.com

Audiobook Boom! subscribers can opt to receive free audiobooks from Audible, Downpour, and CDBaby, which they may review within thirty days.

Audiobook Jukebox

Website: www.audiobookjukebox.com

This website hosts links to audiobook reviews from all over the Internet and allows audiobook reviewers to add links to their reviews to its site.

Audiobook Reviewer

Website: https://audiobookreviewer.com

Audiobook Reviewer currently reviews only specific genres of fiction, including sci-fi, horror, game-lit, mystery, and thriller.

AudioBookRadio

Website: http://audiobookradio.net

AudioBookRadio.net is a free Internet radio station that broadcasts a varied and compelling range of spoken word content.

The Audiobookworm

Website: https://theaudiobookworm.com

The Audiobookworm offers audiobook reviews and promotional services.

AudioFile

Website: www.audiofilemagazine.com

AudioFile is a magazine dedicated to audiobooks. It reviews and recommends listening experiences, interesting performances, and audiobooks that are worth your listening time.

AudioGals

Website: www.audiogals.net

AudioGals is a labor of love for a small and dedicated group of volunteer reviewers. Its goal is to provide honest reviews of romance audiobooks and promote the genre.

GROUPS AND ORGANIZATIONS

Alliance of Independent Authors (ALLi)

Website: www.allianceindependentauthors.org

The Alliance of Independent Authors is a nonprofit professional association for self-published authors. It offers different levels of membership according to need.

American Society of Journalists and Authors (ASJA)

Website: http://ASJA.org

Founded in 1948, this professional organization of nonfiction writers consists of freelance writers of magazine articles, trade books, and other forms of nonfiction writing. Its website features job postings for freelance writers as a benefit of membership.

Association of Ghostwriters (AOG)

Website: http://associationofghostwriters.org

The Association of Ghostwriters is a professional organization for ghostwriters of books, articles, speeches, blogs, and social media content. Members enjoy a wide range of benefits designed to help them improve their craft and find profitable projects.

Association of Publishers for Special Sales (APSS)

Website: http://community.bookapss.org

The Association of Publishers for Special Sales offers educational materials and marketing opportunities to self-publishers who want to explore sales opportunities other than traditional bookstores and libraries, also known as special sales.

Audio Publishers Association (APA)

Website: www.audiopub.org

The Audio Publishers Association is a membership organization of audiobook publishers and narrators that promotes their business interests. It gives annual awards to the best audiobooks of the year and hosts educational webinars and networking events for those in the audiobook field.

Author Marketing Experts (AME)

Website: www.amarketingexpert.com

Started by author Penny Sansevieri, Author Marketing Experts offers book promotion services to both traditionally published and independent authors. It uses personalized marketing strategies to promote their books successfully and create effective publicity campaigns.

Authors Guild

Website: www.authorsguild.com

Offering legal and web services to writers, this association boasts thousands of authors as members. Self-publishers are invited to apply for membership, with their books being assessed on a case-by-case basis.

Book Editing Associates

Website: www.book-editing.com

Thanks to its selective screening process, this network is able to connect writers with qualified editors, proofreaders, and other publishing professionals who are available for hire.

Book Industry Study Group (BISG)

Website: https://bisg.org

The Book Industry Study Group is composed of trade, education, professional, and scholarly publishers, as well as distributors, wholesalers, retailers, manufacturers, service providers, and libraries. It provides BISAC subject codes for books and maintains best practices within the book industry.

Book Marketing Works

Website: www.bookmarketingworks.com

Created by Brian Jud, Book Marketing Works provides publishers with the leads, guidance, and continuing assistance they need to increase their revenues and profits in special sales markets.

Books in Print

Website: www.booksinprint.com

Maintained by R.R. Bowker LLC, Books in Print is a bibliographic database with information on over 20 million titles. It is a valuable resource for potential buyers, including retailers, consumers, and libraries around the world.

BookWorks

Website: www.bookworks.com

BookWorks is an international organization of self-publishing authors and the professionals who serve them. Providing insider knowledge and guidance, it helps its members prepare, publish, and promote their books.

Bowker

Website: www.bowker.com

Bowker is the world's leading provider of bibliographic information and the official ISBN agency of the United States. It offers a number of resources to help authors promote and sell their books.

Editorial Freelancers Association (EFA)

Website: www.the-efa.org

The EFA is made up of editors, writers, indexers, typesetters, proofreaders, researchers, desktop publishers, translators, and other skilled freelancers. Its directory and job listing service offer clients access to these publishing professionals.

Fiverr

Website: www.fiverr.com

Fiverr is an online marketplace for freelance book publishing professionals of all sorts, from editors and designers to typesetters and marketers. Fees for services start as low as five dollars but can reach into the hundreds or thousands.

Independent Book Publishers Association (IBPA)

Website: www.ibpa-online.org

Membership in the IBPA offers independent publishing companies and self-publishers the opportunity to network and succeed in the process of publishing. The IBPA Benjamin Franklin Awards, which honor independent publishers, have become a popular way to promote independent titles.

Independent Editors Group (IEG)

Website: www.independenteditorsgroup.com

The Independent Editors Group is made up of professional freelance editors in New York City who have held senior editorial positions in major publishing houses and are available for hire.

Independent Publisher Book Awards

Website: www.ippyawards.com

The Independent Publisher Book Awards are an awards program open to independent authors and publishers worldwide who produce books intended for an English-speaking audience.

Library of Congress

Website: www.copyright.gov/registration

When it comes to copyright, there are legal benefits to registering your book with the Library of Congress. For more information, visit the web address provided.

National Book Awards

Website: www.nationalbook.org

These American literary prizes are administered by the National Book Foundation and currently honor the best fiction, nonfiction, poetry, translated literature, and young people's literature published each year. Self-published books are eligible, provided that the author also publishes titles by other authors. Books published through self-publishing services, however, are ineligible.

National Writers Union (NWU)

Website: https://nwu.org

With chapters in cities throughout the United States, the NWU is the only union that represents freelance writers working in all formats, genres, and mediums. Its services include author advocacy and legal assistance.

New York Book Editors

Website: https://nybookeditors.com

Consisting of editors with a wealth of experience from New York's major publishing houses, New York Book Editors is an organization that connects authors with well-regarded editors in the industry.

Nonfiction Authors Association

Website: https://nonfictionauthorsassociation.com

The Nonfiction Authors Association provides useful information and resources to authors of nonfiction books. It offers different levels of membership, the basic version of which is free of charge.

Proofreading Pal

Website: http://proofreadingpal.com

Proofreading Pal is a professional proofreading service that uses two proofreaders for every project. Its staff includes experienced proofreaders, many of whom have their master's degrees or are pursuing their PhDs.

Publishing Trends

Website: www.publishingtrends.com

Publishing Trends provides up-to-date information on the publishing world, including new markets, digital publishing, deals, events, retailing, technology, and distribution. It also features an annual list of freelance book publicists.

Pulitzer Prizes

Website: www.pulitzer.org

The Pulitzer Prize is an award for achievements in newspaper, magazine and online journalism, literature, and musical composition in the United States. Self-published books may be nominated as long as they meet the basic criteria for consideration.

Reedsy

Website: https://reedsy.com

Reedsy is a network of publishing professionals, including designers, typesetters, editors, and marketers. Authors can look for the services they need on this website to complete their projects and publish them successfully.

Small Publishers, Artists & Writers Network (SPAWN)

Website: http://spawn.org

The Small Publishers, Artists & Writers Network provides information, resources, and opportunities to authors, freelance writers, artists, and publishing companies. Its members form a supportive networking environment.

Society of Children's Book Writers and Illustrators (SCBWI)

Website: www.scbwi.org

The Society of Children's Book Writers and Illustrators is one of the largest organizations of writers and illustrators. Its membership includes individuals who write or illustrate works for children and young adults.

Women's National Book Association (WNBA)

Website: www.wnba-books.org

The Women's National Book Association is an organization of women and men who work with and value books. It was created to inform women about matters relevant to themselves and the book world so they can inform and help each other.

SOCIAL MEDIA AND CROWDFUNDING WEBSITES

Amazon Author Page

Website: https://authorcentral.amazon.com/gp/help

Amazon Author Pages give readers a chance to learn more information about their favorite authors and find (and buy) other books written by them. An author can create an Author Page by signing up for an Author Central account.

Facebook

Website: www.facebook.com

Facebook is a highly popular social media platform that connects friends and family members using a simple interface. It is an excellent marketing tool for companies, brands, public figures, or anybody who has something about which they'd like to spread the word.

GoFundMe

Website: www.gofundme.com

GoFundMe has a simple user interface that makes the process easy for anyone who wishes to raise money through crowdfunding. There are no deadlines or goal requirements, and no penalties if you fall short of your donation goal.

Goodreads

Website: www.goodreads.com

Goodreads is a great way to expose your work directly to the book-loving community. If a book isn't listed on the Goodreads website, anybody—not just the author—may add it to the database and start the reviewing and rating process.

Indiegogo

Website: www.indiegogo.com

Indiegogo is a crowdfunding platform committed to raising support and funds for innovative products and exciting ideas from entrepreneurs, inventors, and other creative individuals.

Instagram

Website: www.instagram.com

Instagram is a popular photo- and video-sharing service. People share photos of their friends, family, pets, travels, and just about anything else on their Instagram profiles. Users can follow the accounts whose posts they want to see in their newsfeeds. Many businesses, celebrities, and public figures use Instagram to promote themselves and build their brands.

Kickstarter

Website: www.kickstarter.com

Similar to backers on Indiegogo and Patreon, backers on Kickstarter receive rewards depending on the amount of money they have pledged. Having a project on Kickstarter means it will be visible to a large number of eyes, but getting a project on Kickstarter is a highly competitive process.

Patreon

Website: www.patreon.com

Patreon works more like a subscription service than a one-time donation platform. People can support their favorite content creators, including musicians, authors, podcasters, and cartoonists, by becoming "patrons" and pledging to donate a certain amount (at the patron's discretion) of funding to them each month.

Pinterest

Website: www.pinterest.com

Pinterest is an image-sharing and cataloging site. Its users create "pinboards," each of which is a collection of images related to a single topic. Many businesses use Pinterest to promote their companies, with pinboards that display their products in a sort of "virtual storefront."

Twitter

Website: www.twitter.com

Twitter (www.twitter.com) is a social networking service designed for sharing short status updates and messages known as "tweets." It is a quick, easy way for users to share and spread their thoughts and ideas.

YouTube

Website: www.youtube.com

YouTube is a popular video-sharing platform. Users can build followings by regularly posting video blogs, or "vlogs," to their own YouTube channels.

PRESS RELEASE DISTRIBUTION SERVICES

Business Wire

Website: www.businesswire.com

Business Wire distributes press releases to news media, databases, bloggers, social networks, and other sources of potential publicity. Membership is required to send a press release and is free of charge.

eReleases

Website: www.ereleases.com

eReleases provides an array of press release options according to fee. The company also offers a press release writing service to its customers.

Newswire

Website: www.newswire.com

Newswire offers a number of distribution plans to meet the needs of a wide variety of publicity campaigns. Customers may opt for a single press release or a monthly subscription service.

PR Newswire

Website: www.prnewswire.com

Owned by public relations company Cision, PR Newswire is a press release distributor that requires paid membership to use its services and charges additional fees to send press releases. It also offers editorials services and detailed reporting.

PRWeb

Website: www.prweb.com

Owned by the same parent company as PR Newswire, PRWeb focuses on online press release distribution. It offers a variety of service packages to suit different budgets.

WHOLESALERS AND DISTRIBUTORS

Baker & Taylor (Wholesaler)

Website: www.baker-taylor.com

Baker & Taylor is one of the largest distributors of books, video, and music products to libraries, institutions, and retailers in the country. It is also a leader in digital media delivery.

Brodart (Wholesaler)

Website: www.brodart.com

Brodart provides libraries with shelf-ready books, electronic ordering systems, furniture, and supplies.

Consortium Book Sales & Distribution (Exclusive Distributor)

Website: www.cbsd.com

Consortium is a full-service North American distributor. It distributes books to the trade, academic, library, wholesale, and specialist markets, and works with independent publishers that have published a required minimum number of titles.

Emery-Pratt (Wholesaler)

Website: https://emery-pratt.com

Emery-Pratt provides books to academic, public, and hospital libraries.

Follett Corporation (Wholesaler)

Website: www.follett.com

The parent company of Baker & Taylor, Follett distributes books, entertainment products, digital content, and multimedia to libraries, schools, and retailers.

Ingram (Wholesaler and Distributor)

Website: www.ingramcontent.com

Ingram is a fully integrated distribution service for print and digital books. In order to be distributed through Ingram, a self-publisher must use IngramSpark or Lightning Source self-publishing services.

Independent Publishers Group (IPG) (Exclusive Distributor)

Website: www.ipgbook.com

The first book distribution company designed to represent titles from independent publishers to the book trade in the United States, IPG offers access to a variety of sales channels, including gift, specialty, wholesale, and digital markets.

Midpoint Trade Books (Exclusive Distributor)

Website: www.midpointtrade.com

Founded by a group of industry professionals, Midpoint Trade Books is a full-service book sales and distribution company that represents independent book publishers.

Midwest Library Service (Wholesaler)

Website: www.midwestls.com

Midwest Library Service supplies academic and scholarly books to libraries.

National Book Network (Exclusive Distributor)

Website: http://nbnbooks.com

National Book Network is an independent sales, marketing, and distribution company serving North American and overseas independent publishers of nonfiction, fiction, and children's titles.

New Leaf Distributing Company (Wholesaler and Distributor)

Website: https://newleafdist.com

New Leaf Distributing Company is the world's largest wholesale distributor of books related to spirituality and metaphysics, natural alternative wellness, and conscious living.

Nutri-Books & Products (Wholesaler)

Website: www.nutribooks.com

Nutri-Books & Products is a wholesaler of health books, cookbooks, and lifestyle products to retailers that focus on health and wellness.

Publishers Group West (PGW) (Exclusive Distributor)

Website: www.pgw.com

Dedicated to independent publishing for over forty years, PGW offers full-service print and digital distribution to independent publishers of all sizes.

FOREIGN RIGHTS AND BOOK FAIRS

Babelcube

Website: www.babelcube.com

Babelcube enables authors to audition translators and have their books translated on a royalty-sharing basis with their translators. The company then gets a percentage for distributing these translations.

The Combined Book Exhibit (CBE)

Website: www.combinedbook.com

The Combined Book Exhibit offers to showcase your book at any of the book fairs it attends worldwide, which include the London Book Fair, Frankfurt Book Fair, and Beijing International Book Fair. If you have an e-book, CBE can display it on large monitors at these book fairs.

Foreword Reviews

www.forewordreviews.com

Foreword Reviews offers authors the chance to have their books on display at different trade shows, including the China Children's Book Fair, American Library Association Midwinter Meeting, Beijing International Book Fair, Frankfurt Book Fair, and Bologna Book Fair.

Hannacroix Creek Books, Inc.

Website: www.hannacroixcreekbooks.com

Hannacroix Creek Books, Inc. has organized co-op stands at the Frankfurt Book Fair, London Book Fair, Book World Prague, and New York Rights Fair. To be notified about future co-op stand opportunities, contact the company through its website.

HBG Productions

Website: www.hbgproductions.com

HBG Productions aims to bring authors to the world through its co-op exhibit at the Frankfurt Book Fair.

Independent Book Publishers Association (IBPA)

Website: www.ibpa-online.org

The IBPA has a co-op stand at the Frankfurt Book Fair and resells booth space in its aisle to those who would like to have their own stands. IBPA executives attend the fair and meet with potential buyers—foreign agents and publishers—as well as create a catalog that is emailed to a network of several hundred global contacts.

IPR License

Website: https://iprlicense.com

IPR License provides an online portal that allows rights holders to complete domestic and international licensing deals.

Jenkins Group, Inc.

Website: www.globalbookshows.com

Jenkins Group, Inc. sells space at most major book fairs for individual titles to be displayed. It also offers editorial and ghostwriting services to book authors.

Publishing Perspectives

Website: https://publishingperspectives.com

Publishing Perspectives is a project of the Frankfurt Book Fair New York Inc. and offers a daily newsletter that features articles on foreign rights and rights-related events in New York City.

Pubmatch.com

Website: www.pubmatch.com

Pubmatch is a partnership between *Publishers Weekly* and the Combined Book Exhibit. An automated rights selling system, it enables authors to make titles available for rights transactions.

ABOUT THE AUTHOR

Dr. Jan Yager received her BA in fine arts from Hofstra University, her MA in criminal justice from Goddard College, and her PhD in sociology from CUNY Graduate Center. She has taught at the University of Connecticut, The New School, and Penn State, and is currently an adjunct assistant professor in the Department of Sociology at John Jay College of Criminal Justice, CUNY.

Over the course of her extensive career in publishing, which has included stints at Macmillan and Grove Press, Dr. Yager has been an editor, director of subsidiary and foreign rights, book publicist, permissions editor, acquisitions editor, event planner, media trainer, consultant, book coach, and award-winning writer of such books as *Foreign Rights and Wrongs*, *When Friendship Hurts*, and *How to Finish Everything You Start*. Her books have been published by Simon & Schuster, Doubleday, Scribner, Prentice-Hall, and Penguin Random House. She has self-published thirty of her titles through the publishing company she founded, Hannacroix Creek Books, Inc. Her books have been translated into thirty-three languages.

Dr. Yager has also appeared on many nationally broadcast television shows, including *The Oprah Winfrey Show*, *Today*, *Good Morning America*, *CBS This Morning*, and *The View*.

For more information, visit hannacroixcreekbooks.com or www.drjanyager.com. If you are interested in booking Dr. Yager for a speaking engagement or workshop on self-publishing or other aspects of the book business, contact your favorite lecture bureau or email Dr. Yager directly at jyager@aol.com.

ℐNDEX

How to Publish Your Nonfiction Book

Second Edition

A Complete Guide to Making
the Right Publisher Say Yes

Rudy Shur

So, you have a great idea for a nonfiction book, but you don't know a thing about getting it published. Where do you start? What should you send? Are some book publishers better than others? So many questions—but where do you find the answers? The fact is that most budding writers are in the dark when it comes to

the publishing world—as are many published authors. *How to Publish Your Nonfiction Book* was written to provide you with an insider's knowledge of how publishing companies operate. Now, in response to a rapidly changing industry, author Rudy Shur has revised and updated this complete guide to making the right publisher say yes to your nonfiction book.

This edition of *How to Publish Your Nonfiction Book* starts off by helping you define your book's category, audience, and marketplace so that you know exactly where your book "fits in." Following this, you are guided in choosing the best publishing companies for your book and in writing a winning submission package. Then the Square One System tells you exactly how to submit your package so that you optimize success while minimizing your time, cost, and effort. Also included is a special section on contracts that will turn legalese into plain English, allowing you to be a savvy player in the publishing game. Most importantly, this book will help you avoid the most common errors that so often prevent writers from reaching their goal.

Dreaming of seeing your book in print is easy. Getting it published can take some work. With *How to Publish Your Nonfiction Book* in hand, you have a proven system of getting your book from the desk drawer to the bookstore.

$18.95 US • 256 pages • 7.5 x 9-inch paperback • ISBN 978-0-7570-0430-8

How to Publish Your Children's Book

Second Edition

A Complete Guide to Making the Right Publisher Say Yes

Liza N. Burby

It is the place where wizards live, forests are enchanted, and things are often not what they seem. It is also the home of editors, agents, marketers, and art directors. It is the world of children's book publishing. Until the first edition of this book was released, it was also one of the most confusing places for hopeful writers to navigate. Now, in response to a rapidly changing industry, award-winning writer Liza N. Burby has revised and updated this complete guide to making the right children's book publisher say yes to your book for children or young adults.

This edition of *How to Publish Your Children's Book* begins by helping you define your book's category, audience, and marketplace so that you know exactly where your book "fits in." You are then taught how to choose the best publishing companies for your book proposal, as well as coached in how to write a winning submission package. Then the Square One System tells you exactly how to submit your package so that you optimize your chance of success while minimizing your time, cost, and effort. Also included is a special section on contracts that will turn legalese into plain English, allowing you to be a savvy player in the publishing game. Most important, this book will help you avoid the most common errors that so often prevent writers from reaching their goal.

Whether you're just thinking about writing a YA or children's book, or are already a published author, you're sure to find *How to Publish Your Children's Book* a solid reference guide you can use time and time again.

$19.95 US • 320 pages • 7.5 x 9-inch paperback • ISBN 978-0-7570-0409-4

For more information on our books, visit our website at www.squareonepublishers.com